CONTENTS

CONTENTS

THE END OF
THE WELFARE STATE?

Throughout the world, politicians from all the main parties are cutting back on
state welfare provision, encouraging people to use the private sector instead and
developing increasingly stringent techniques for the surveillance of the poor.
Almost all experts agree that we are likely to see further constraints on state
welfare in the 21st Century.

The book gathers together the findings from up-to-date attitude surveys in
Europe East and West, the US and Australasia. It shows that, contrary to the
claims of many experts and policy-makers, the welfare state is still highly popular
with the citizens of most countries. This evidence will add to controversy in an area
of fundamental importance to public policy and to current social science debate.

Stefan Svallfors is lecturer of sociology, Umeå University, Sweden.
Peter Taylor-Gooby is professor of social policy at the University of Kent.

ROUTLEDGE/ESA STUDIES IN
EUROPEAN SOCIETY
Edited by Thomas P. Boje
Umeå University, Sweden

EUROPEAN SOCIETIES
Fusion or fission?
Edited by Thomas Boje, Bart van Steenbergen and Sylvia Walby

THE MYTH OF GENERATIONAL CONFLICT
The family and state in ageing societies
Edited by Sara Arber and Claudine Attias-Donfut

THE END OF THE WELFARE STATE?
Responses to state retrenchment
Edited by Stefan Svallfors and Peter Taylor-Gooby

THE END OF THE WELFARE STATE?

Responses to state retrenchment

*Edited by Stefan Svallfors
and Peter Taylor-Gooby*

London and New York

First published 1999
by Routledge
2 Park Square, Milton Park, Abingdon, Oxon, OX14 4RN

Simultaneously published in the USA and Canada
by Routledge
270 Madison Ave, New York NY 10016

Routledge is an imprint of the Taylor & Francis Group

Transferred to Digital Printing 2007

© 1999 edited by Stefan Svallfors and Peter Taylor-Gooby

Typeset in Garamond by
BOOK NOW Ltd

British Library Cataloguing in Publication Data
A catalogue record for this book is available
from the British Library

Library of Congress Cataloging-in-Publication Data
The end of the welfare state? : responses to state retrenchment /
edited by Peter Taylor-Gooby and Stefan Svallfors.
    p.   cm.   (Routledge/E.S.A. studies in European society : 3)
Includes bibliographical references and index.
ISBN 0-415-20771-1 (hardcover)
1. Public welfare—Public opinion.   2. Welfare state—Public
opinion.   I. Taylor-Gooby, Peter.   II. Svallfors, Stefan.
III. Series. Pacific Asia Programme.   IV. Title.
HV51.E53 1999
361.6'5—dc21   98–51386
                                                                 CIP

ISBN10: 0-415-20771-1 (hbk)
ISBN10: 0-415-46326-2 (pbk)

ISBN13: 978-0-415-20771-3 (hbk)
ISBN13: 978-0-415-46326-3 (pbk)

Publisher's Note
The publisher has gone to great lengths to ensure the quality of
this reprint but points out that some imperfections in the
original may be apparent

FIGURES

TABLES

CONTRIBUTORS

Jørgen Goul Andersen is Professor of Political Sociology in the Centre for Comparative Welfare State Studies at the Aalborg University, Aalborg, Denmark.

Helena Blomberg is Professor of Social Policy in the Swedish School of Social Science at the University of Helsinki, Finland.

Jonas Edlund is a Research Assistant in the Department of Sociology, Umeå University, Umeå, Sweden.

Zsuzsa Ferge is Professor of Sociology at Eötvös Loránd University, Budapest, Hungary.

Pauli Forma is Senior Researcher at the Local Government Pensions Institution of Finland, Helsinki.

Olli E. Kangas is Professor of Social Policy in the Department of Social Policy, University of Turku, Finland.

Christian Kroll is a Researcher in the Department of Social Policy at Åbo Akademi University, Gezeliusgatan, Finland.

George Matheson is Senior Research Officer in the Social Policy Research Centre at the University of New South Wales, Sydney, Australia.

Stefan Svallfors is Senior Lecturer in the Department of Sociology at Umeå University, Sweden.

Peter Taylor-Gooby is Professor of Social Policy at the University of Kent, UK.

Michael Wearing is Senior Lecturer in the School of Social Work at the University of New South Wales, Sydney, Australia.

Krzysztof Zagórski is a Director at CBOS (Public Opinion Research Center), Warsaw, Poland.

1

'HOLLOWING OUT' VERSUS THE NEW INTERVENTIONISM

Public attitudes and welfare futures

Peter Taylor-Gooby

The traditional interventionist–Keynesian European form of state is no longer in crisis. Most commentators have abandoned any hope of a return to the comfortable security of post-war expansionism. Now the welfare state is undergoing 'restructuring', 'transformation' or 'transition'. The key question is whether a butterfly or a slug will emerge from the metamorphosis.

This volume examines current developments in values on the basis of recent survey research. The focus is primarily, but not exclusively, on the traditional heartland of state welfare – the Scandinavian countries – with comparative evidence from other developed welfare states, a study of a former socialist country in transition and reflections on the role of government in the civilising process in the context of the onward march of liberal markets. The material presented here allows us to take a considered look at the welfare-capitalist state in its most developed North European form and to chart the way in which recent pressures on the capacity of governments to intervene in the economy and to deliver services (and current fears about their future capacity to do so) are influencing values and attitudes in the field of welfare state citizenship.

The most interesting point to emerge from the studies here presented is the stability of public attitudes. Despite the pressures and changes in the economic and political climates, people's values are more remarkable for continuity rather than change. However, the persistence of a particular ideology under altered circumstances does mean that some aspects of traditional value patterns which received little attention in the golden age of the welfare state now show more clearly.

In this chapter we will describe some of the pressures on traditional welfare states of recent years and then discuss briefly the arguments of ensuing chapters in the light of these pressures. Challenges have emerged from four directions – economic, political, social and technological change. In some cases the challenges can be seen as simply exacerbating existing problems. For example, technological changes account for a very considerable proportion of the unemployment among less skilled people that is currently identified as a major issue (OECD 1994: 33–4). Changes in population structure lead to a situation in which the cost of providing pensions, health and social care for older people – already the most expensive aspect of public provision – will continue to increase rapidly during the next half-century (Commission of the EU 1996: 42).

The point about the current challenges, however, is that it is no longer possible to meet these needs by continuing in the traditional way. Governments simply cannot pursue further economic regulation or increase spending on services as they did during the post-war boom. The openness of international trade (sometimes referred to as 'economic globalisation') makes it difficult for any national government to intervene in the labour market in a way that might reduce the competitiveness of its workforce, so that the provision of benefits has always to be justified in terms a contribution to productivity, flexibility or innovation. This constrains the way in which governments can tackle income inequalities or job security. Changes in the acceptability of tax increases to the key players in the international financial markets which exert substantial influence on currency stability make it difficult to finance redistributive benefits through higher taxes. Similarly, shifts in the pattern of gender roles in domestic work and in formal employment undermine the traditional assumption underlying social care policy – that unwaged women kin will meet the need through the family. It is the awareness that current changes are bringing the era of 'business as usual' for the welfare state to an end that marks out the present as transition and generates intense debate about how the state can respond to these challenges. The sense of transformation is heightened by the claim that the forces driving the development of the traditional welfare state – pre-eminently the struggles across the class divisions of capitalist market economies to secure greater protection from the play of market forces that Esping-Andersen famously terms 'decommodification' (1990: 3) – are of declining importance. Social class differences in political attitudes, it is suggested, have been substituted by other factors that lead to a fundamentally different pattern of state involvement in welfare.

We will review the pressures on the state in more detail and then move on to consider what the research reported in subsequent chapters reveals about where these transformatory pressures are leading.

Transformatory pressures on the state

The pressures for change can be considered from two directions – changes in the context in which governments operate, and the response of governments to those changes as they pursue new directions in policy-making.

The context of policy-making

The main changes in the context of policy-making as a governmental process are four: economic globalisation; demographic shifts; high unemployment and subemployment; and for most of the countries under consideration the growing importance of the EU and of the Maastricht Treaty constraints on government borrowing.

Globalisation refers to the increased openness of international markets, both in goods and capital, as a result of improvements in communications, the entry of former Eastern and Central European socialist nations into world trade and the commitment of the major governments to liberalisation after the Uruguay accord in the early 1990s. However, the bulk of trade for the major nations is internal – exports or imports account for about 8 per cent of the national output of the US and of Japan, and a similar proportion for the EU as a whole, when trade between EU member states is ignored (Gough 1997: 88). Some commentators have argued that the most important feature of globalisation is the development of trading blocs (the EU, the Americas, South-East Asia) rather than true international-isation (Hirst and Thompson 1996).

The openness of markets exerts a powerful effect on the industrialised nations. Developed countries are subject to an increasing amount of competition from overseas in many areas of industry. The newly-industrialised countries of Asia are taking an increasing proportion of the expanded activity in developing markets such as Africa or the rest of Asia where western countries were once dominant. Since three-quarters of the world's population live in Asia this is a serious long-term threat to the dominant position of older industrialised nations in world markets. There are strong pressures to ensure that policy assists the competit-iveness of national industry because the possibility of penetration by industries overseas exists, even if that possibility is not put into practice, and because devel-oped countries are failing to establish a leading position in the new export markets.

A second aspect to globalisation refers to the operation of capital markets. The amount of currency available for international investment has expanded rapidly since the oil-price rises of the 1970s concentrated large sums of petro-dollars in the hands of a small number of players in financial markets. The confidence of international speculators in national economic management can be expressed in trade in the national currency which can constrain national fiscal policies. In practice, this often operates to constrain state spending. Mitterand's experiment in Keynesian interventionist expansionism in the early 1980s was brought to an end by pressure on the Franc from investors who mistrusted those policies and were unwilling to hold the currency. The British and Italian governments were forced to leave the European monetary system and effectively to devalue by speculation in 1992. The Swedish currency came under heavy pressure very soon after and a crisis package of cost-cutting measures was agreed by the government and the Social Democrat opposition. The net effect of the two aspects of globalisation is that governments can no longer claim to remain sovereign in their own houses.

Demographic changes result from two factors. First, the ratio of elderly people compared to those of working age has risen sharply in recent years, and stands to increase dramatically in the first half of the next century. Second, participation in the labour force by those of working age has fallen and appears likely to continue to fall. This is particularly true of two age-groups – those aged under 25 are more likely to be in education and training than in the past, and those over 50 are more likely to retire early.

In 1995, around 15 per cent of the population of the EU was aged 65 or over, equivalent to about 23 per cent of the population of working age. By 2005, the number of those aged 65 and over will be equivalent to 26 per cent of the working age population, by 2015, 30 per cent, by 2025, 36 per cent (Commission of the EU 1996: 43–4). The situation varies between countries. By 2025, the number of pensioners will be equivalent to 40 per cent of the working age population in Italy, and over 36 per cent in Belgium, Germany, France and Sweden. Only in Portugal will it be less than 30 per cent and in Ireland and Luxembourg less than 32 per cent (Commission of the EU 1996: Graph 6). The result of these changes is pressure on provision for older people, especially pensions and health and social care. This pressure differs in different countries, but is likely to grow more severe in the future.

Unemployment has risen rapidly throughout the EU and remains at an average level roughly twice that of the US and four times that in Japan (Gough 1997: 81). There are strong variations between the rates in different European countries, in the length of unemployment and in the availability of benefits, so that the proportion of the unemployed who are in receipt of benefit varies from about 10 per cent in Greece and Italy to nearly 90 per cent in Belgium and Denmark (Commission of the EU 1996: Graph 34). These levels of unemployment pose serious problems for the governments of European countries which vary according to the structure of their labour markets and benefit systems. These problems are compounded by the fact that other government policies, especially in taxation and in social insurance systems, provide a disincentive for employers to expand employment.

The Maastricht Treaty requirements for membership of the single European Currency include a central government deficit no greater than 3 per cent of GDP and public debt at a level below 60 per cent of GDP. These conditions, which will almost certainly form part of a continuing 'Stability Pact', impose restraints on welfare spending, since government borrowing is curtailed in a context where politicians are reluctant to raise taxes to pay for high levels of public expenditure.

All these factors contribute to a policy environment in which the freedom of action available to governments is restricted. Governments can respond to these restrictions in various ways.

Responses to the pressures on government

One school of thought argues that the social changes associated with globalisation and the restructuring of the industrial system will sweep away the whole Beveridge/Bismarck welfare settlement, with its emphasis on state economic intervention to provide employment and state benefit provision to maintain incomes and levels of consumption:

> Crudely . . . if Fordism is represented by a homology between mass production, mass consumption, modernist cultural forms and the mass provision of welfare, then post-Fordism is characterised by an emerging coalition between flexible production, differentiated and segmented consumption patterns, post-modernist cultural forms and a restructured welfare state.
>
> (Burrows and Loader 1994: 1)

The traditional welfare state pursued full employment, redistributive welfare and mass consumption in a social system where industry regimented the workforce into social classes and the nuclear family neatly divided the population into breadwinners serviced by home-makers who provide domestic services. Economic globalisation and technical change have rendered this structure increasingly inappropriate to capital accumulation. In a more diverse society the welfare state must pursue the interests of national capital, primarily by ensuring a flexible and competitive labour force. Some writers stress the role of benefit cuts, union-busting and deregulation in this (Burrows and Loader, 1994: 6–7).

The current transformation is seen as a 'hollowing-out' process, whereby the state loses much of its autonomy and its control over national economic and social life. Its powers are displaced 'upward, downward and outward, to international or pan-regional agencies or international bodies, to regional layers of government or economic institutions or to global market forces' (see Jessop 1994: 24–5). However, it is by no means clear that the liberal approach to competitiveness is the only possible one. In a careful analysis of the contribution of welfare strategies to competitiveness in Europe, Gough concludes that there is no simple link between welfare spending and competitiveness. The relationship is contingent – it all depends on how particular social programmes mesh with the needs and opportunities of particular welfare state regimes: 'different welfare regimes exhibit different configurations of effects on performance and structural competitiveness' (Gough 1996: 228).

Thus, liberal economies such as the US have competitive strengths which result from low wages but face problems in guaranteeing good quality education and training and improving the skills base. Conversely, corporatist regimes are successful in producing and protecting a high-quality labour force, but pay the costs of a growing underclass and high social, and therefore labour, costs. Social democracies on the Scandinavian model may be highly effective in ensuring both skilled and well-motivated labour and social solidarity, but face very high taxation (threatening social solidarity) and non-wage costs (threatening competitiveness). If this approach is correct, retrenchment and the retreat of the state are not the only possible responses to globalisation. Governments, under appropriate circumstances, can pursue strategies which reassert national sovereignty and allow them to act as command centres for policies which aid national capital in its competitive struggles – a 'New Interventionism'. Such policies include interventions designed to improve the quality and motivation of the workforce, in terms of training and education, the regulation of industry and support of research and development, the coordination of efforts in new markets or in innovation and the promotion of social cohesion, which will reduce the costs of social control and help workers accept and accommodate greater flexibility in the labour market. From this perspective, the traditional European model of the democratic welfare capitalist state still has a future, and the forces which sustained it are still influential.

None the less, policy debate about the future of welfare often focuses on restructuring and retrenchment. For example:

> The high level of non-wage labour costs [in the EU] is prejudicial to employment, exerting a dissuasive influence.
>
> (Commission of the EU 1994: 154)

> Economic and social policy are inextricably linked: they are two sides of the same coin. . . . A new sort of welfare state is required to match an investment-led industrial strategy.
>
> (Commission of the EU 1994: 12)

> Programmes introduced during the post-war era of rapid economic growth, and sustained with increasing difficulty during the 1980s are now seen as insufficiently responsive to the realities of the 1990s.
>
> (OECD 1994a: 7)

In an influential contribution to the debate, Pierson discusses the problems and pitfalls which face governments seeking to cut social programmes 'in an era which viewed retrenchment not as a necessary evil but as a necessary good' (1995: 1). He argues that transformation comes about not so much through dramatic and contested policy shifts as through the incremental effect of relatively minor changes which alter the 'rules of the game' and the pattern of social interests. Such shifts can be hard to reverse and offer the potential to lead on to further changes. Retrenchment is high on the policy agenda across Europe, for example in the Juppé Plan of 1995/6 in France, the German 1995–6 *Sparpaket*, the attempts to cut spending on pensions and health care in Germany in 1996, the Spanish pension and benefit cuts of 1989, and the commitment of the 1997 Labour government in the UK to zero growth in public spending. In some cases, governments have been forced to moderate the cuts, particularly where these have involved job losses or changes to conditions of service in the public sector, but retrenchment rather than expansion has remained the dominant policy theme. The key question is whether the ideological climate of retrenchment leads to the hollowing out of the state and the adoption of a strategy that leads to minimalism on the part of government, or to a new welfare settlement that retains the main features of interventionism.

Public opinion and state restructuring

The new policy environment of the 1990s has led to pressures for retrenchment and restructuring in the state. Some theoretical perspectives imply a diminution or hollowing out of the state, while others suggest that governments may retain considerable authority, although pursuing a rather different policy orientation. How do these shifts relate to popular values? The question arises of whether the end of the era of confident expansionism is marked by a corresponding shift in popular values. Alternatively, values associated with support for interventionism may facilitate the shift to a new interventionism, designed to support competitiveness. The remaining chapters of the book contain evidence from attitude studies in countries representing all the main welfare regimes identified in recent debates and with an emphasis on the most highly developed welfare states of Scandinavia. To these we now turn.

The first two chapters consider reactions to welfare state retrenchment in two Scandinavian countries – Denmark and Sweden – focusing particularly on the impact of changes in social structure on welfare state support. Jørgen Goul Andersen starts out from the theory that social inequalities, especially in access to stable employment, will undermine the social solidarity on which the welfare state rests (see for example, Dahrendorf 1994; Hutton 1996). He points out that Denmark, like other Scandinavian countries, does not provide a clear example of the social divisions between welfare state 'insiders' and 'outsiders' that Esping-Andersen identifies in the social insurance-based regimes of countries such as Germany. The large state sector and high rates of female employment mean that the group of core 'private sector insiders' who might be expected to identify with liberal anti-state policies and be less favourable to welfare spending for weaker groups in the labour market is small. However, there are some indications of growing welfare state scepticism since the mid-1990s, founded more on concerns about the impact of welfare spending on economic competitiveness rather than a declining solidarity with unemployed people. Whether this will prove to be a temporary phenomenon is at present unclear.

Stefan Svallfors pursues a rather different aspect of the polarisation thesis that has been developed by writers like Wilensky – that high welfare spending which is seen to be directed at working and lower working class groups will alienate the support of the middle class for the welfare state (Wilensky 1975). The leading commentators have argued repeatedly that it was the incorporation of middle class support that sustained the Scandinavian model of welfare capitalism so successfully (Korpi 1983; Esping-Andersen 1985). Like Goul Andersen, Svallfors finds little evidence of polarisation. However, there are splits within the middle class. The higher echelons among non-manuals display decreasing support for the welfare state, while lower and middle level non-manuals display increasing support.

These two chapters indicate that the many of the concerns that had been expressed about the impact of demands for higher spending on the Scandinavian welfare state have been misplaced. However, there are shifts in allegiance, and these are associated with concerns about the impact of welfare on competitiveness (the first aspect of the globalisation argument reviewed above) and with the interests of particular sub-groups in the population.

The next two chapters consider the relationship between the opinions of the general public and of particular elite groups. The research focuses on Finland, which has experienced considerable pressure on welfare spending during the early 1990s resulting from the economic adjustments that followed the collapse of the Soviet Union, and the consequent loss of trade and leap in unemployment. Here the main research questions concern whether there has been a divergence between public opinion and elite opinion during this period of constraint and, more generally, whether it is the opinion of the citizenry or of the elite that is the best guide to policy developments.

Helena Blomberg and Christian Kroll analyse the relationship between public attitudes on the one hand and the attitudes of senior officials and chief executives of the municipalities responsible for providing services on the other between 1992 and 1996. There is a considerable gap between the attitudes of the two groups. The citizens oppose cuts and in fact want service improvements, while the elites are willing to go on making cuts, although their attitudes do soften somewhat over time. The main reason for the difference seems to be a difference in understanding of the realities that face social provision. The elites see the cuts as necessary.

Pauli Forma's chapter considers broader questions of support for welfare and defines elites as groups as politicians, business-men, civil servants, editors and researchers. In general there are substantial differences in attitudes on particular issues. However, there is strong support for the welfare state in principle among the elites as well as the population at large. The only exception is the group of business leaders who are less likely to endorse universal government provision.

These two chapters present a contrasting picture. There is a gap in attitudes between mass and elite in relation to concrete issues of municipal provision based on a different understanding of the exigencies of the policy environment, and a more complex and supportive picture at the general level of policy values. It may be that the national elites reflect public opinion because many members (particularly in the Finnish variant of democratic welfare capitalism), for example, as MPs seeking to be elected, newspaper editors and so on, tend to be sensitive to that opinion, while municipal administrators and chief officers are confronted with responsibility for ensuring that a feasible policy is pursued, whatever people happen to want.

The next three chapters adopt a cross-national comparative methodology and consider issues of redistribution, inequality and desert – the justification for state welfare. The comparative frameworks, which include Scandinavian (Finland, Norway, Sweden), market liberal (the UK and the US), Bismarkian (Germany), labourist (Australia) and, in one case, former socialist (Poland) countries, permit the main regime types which have been identified in the debates surrounding Esping-Andersen's seminal work to be discussed.

Jonas Edlund's study of attitudes to progressive taxation in all three countries takes place in the context of attempts to restrain total tax revenues and to reduce the tax rates affecting high-income people. He shows that there is a substantial similarity in attitudes between core Scandinavian (Sweden) and liberal (the UK, the US) nations in attitudes. A large majority in each country endorses the principle of progressive taxation and expresses dissatisfaction that the tax rates on high earners are too low, whereas those on low earners are too high. In other words, public opinion is opposed to the recent reforms. However, there are some differences between countries in the social structure of attitudes to taxation. In Sweden, differences in tax attitudes are most significantly structured by social class, while in Britain – and particularly in the US – the pattern of attitudes is more fragmented. The evidence of class divisions in dissent from regressive tax reforms shows an interesting contrast with the evidence presented by Goul Andersen (for Denmark) and Svallfors (for Sweden) of Scandinavian overall class solidarity in favour of redistributive welfare provision, although Svallfors does indicate that cleavages within the traditional middle class groups are emerging.

George Matheson and Michael Wearing explore the relationship between work status and pro-welfare state values in Australia, West Germany, Norway and the US. Their interest is in whether those groups who are supported outside direct participation in the labour market (in Esping-Andersen's language, whose labour power is 'decommodified') are more inclined to support redistributive state provision. The survey data they use (from the International Social Survey Programme) is particularly useful for this research, since it includes groups which tend to be dependent on state benefits (unemployed people), groups whose benefit dependency varies in the different countries and who may also have access to private or occupational benefits (pensioners), those whose dependency on the state is subject to complex patterns of variation (students), and those whose state dependency is, in most countries, limited (home-makers). The structure of attitudes is complex. In general the support for state welfare emerges most strongly in the Scandinavian and Bismarkian nations, as other studies indicate. Those groups who have the highest use of state benefits (pensioners and unemployed people) tend to be most supportive of these benefits. These findings indicate that simplistic class models of welfare support have a limited explanatory power in relation to attitudes to welfare in modern societies with complex and cross-cutting patterns of dependency.

The study by Pauli Forma and Olli Kangas contrasts attitudes to state pensions in Australia, Finland and Poland. The findings show that, in all these countries, universal basic state pensions are more popular than selective ones, although there is greater support for selectivism in Australia and less in Finland, reflecting current patterns of provision. In all the countries there is also overwhelming majority support for earnings-related provision. As to mechanisms for ensuring that these pensions are provided, Poles tend to favour statutory government pensions, while Australians and Finns are inclined to prefer compulsory superannuation schemes organised through private insurance companies. Class divisions show more clearly in relation to preferences for how pensions should be organised than in attitudes to the principle of providing a basic guarantee of security.

The three comparative chapters show in general a high level of support for the traditional welfare state model of universal benefits financed through tax and contributions. The traditions of different countries, and in particular their different levels of commitment to state welfare, clearly exert an influence. None the less, there are indications that attitudes may be shifting. Tax attitudes are becoming increasingly fragmented in liberal regimes, implying that the increased complexity of modern economic systems may now be reflected in interests and in social values. Factor such as 'decommodification' are also mediated by national traditions. Social class membership still exerts an influence on preferences for particular pension systems.

Krzysztof Zagórski considers the relationship between egalitarian attitudes and support for economic and political transition in Poland using panel data from 1994 to 1997. The study shows that the perception of social conflicts is an important influence on egalitarian attitudes. Since egalitarianism strongly influences attitudes toward liberal economic reforms and towards transformation in general, the perception of conflicts exerts strong indirect and some direct effects on these attitudes as well. However, it is not so much the intensity of perceived difference in interests as whether the differences are seen as admitting of a positive-sum outcome, in which both sides can be gainers, which relates to support for a transition to a more liberal capitalist model. Ideas about the economic prospects of the country as a whole are more important in influencing attitudes than ideas about the individual's own circumstances. Thus, it appears to be judgements on the nature of the society towards which Poland is moving in serving the interests of its members that are dominant in attitudes to state transition.

The final chapter, by Zsuzsa Ferge, moves away from the reliance of earlier chapters on the analysis of attitude survey data to take a considered look at the implications of state transformation in both East and West. The theoretical frameworks considered earlier indicate that the western model of interventionism in both social and economic spheres is under severe pressure from the increased intensity of international competition and from social changes within countries. In the East, the collapse of the soviet-inspired command economies leads to a retreat of government authority in the face of market forces. Drawing on the work of Elias (1939) and others on the civilising process, Ferge argues that the development of a humane European culture over the past three centuries could only have taken place under the protection of the evolving democratic system of government. It was this system which provided the security for the development of a civilisation in which individual freedom was reconciled with social interdependence through the development of a collective 'super-ego' in sophisticated systems of self-control. The current transformation carries with it the dangers of 'de-civilisation' as rapid social change erodes this system of social regulation. It may be possible to see the first stages of this social disintegration in the emergence of mafias in East and Central Europe, the process of social exclusion amid plenty, and the segregation of better-off groups defended from an underclass by private security guards.

Conclusion

The material contained in the following chapters traces shifts in attitudes in the context of the processes of state transformation taking place in Western and

Eastern Europe. In general, public opinion is broadly supportive of more or less traditional patterns of state interventionism, despite the emphasis on market liberalism and on retrenchment in public policy-making. Some concern about the sustainability of state welfare appears to be emerging even in those nations where it had previously been most secure, for example in the link between uncertainty about Danish economic success and the endorsement of state welfare (Chapter 2) or in the divergence between the enthusiasm of administrative elites for cost-cutting and mass support for higher spending in Finland (Chapter 4). There is also some indication that the cleavages that are emerging within previously clear-cut class structures are leading to an erosion of social solidarity on welfare issues. However, these are relatively minor influences on a pattern of support for interventionism. Other work shows that, even where the enthusiasm for the market is greatest, there is strong support for state welfare. The major SOCO study, carried out in five former soviet countries in 1995 showed that the new political and economic freedoms were generally welcomed, but that there is a pervasive feeling in all the countries that basic securities (of guaranteed welfare provisions) are being undermined (Ferge *et al.* 1996: 5).

These attitudes imply that policies which respond to economic globalisation and the demographic and social changes likely to increase costs through retrenchment and a hollowing out of the state will encounter substantial opposition. The survey evidence shows that the traditional divisions and concerns which drove the development of the modern welfare state still make a major contribution to the way people think about welfare. Some change in patterns of interventionism may be inevitable, especially in those countries whose policies produce high labour costs and severe labour market rigidities without corresponding benefits in productivity or labour quality. However, the future may be one of a reordering of the state's activities into a 'new interventionism' rather than the simple retreat that much discussion assumes. Political values support the view that the European social model of state interventionism in the interests of social protection and of redistribution to those in need has life in it yet.

References

Burrow, R. and Loader, B. (1994) (eds) *Towards a Post-Fordist Welfare State?* London: Routledge.

Commission of the EU (1994) *White Paper on European Social Policy*, Com (94) 333.

Commission of the EU (1996) *Social Protection in Europe: 1995* (Luxembourg).

Dahrendorf, R. (1994) 'The Changing Quality of Citizenship', in B. Van Steenbergen (ed.), *The Condition of Citizenship*, London: Sage.

Elias, N. (1939) *The Civilising Process*, Oxford: Blackwell.

Esping-Andersen, G. (1995) *Welfare States in Transition*, London: Sage.

Esping-Andersen, G. (1990) *The Three Worlds of Welfare Capitalism*, Cambridge: Polity Press.

Esping-Andersen, G. (1985) *Politics against Markets: the Social Democratic Road to Power*, Princeton: Princeton University Press.

Ferge, Z., Sik, E., Robert, P. and Albert, F. (1996) *Social Costs of Transition: International Report*, Vienna: Institute for Human Sciences.

Gough, I. (1996) 'Social welfare and competitiveness', *New Political Economy*, Vol. 1, pp. 209–24.

Gough, I. (1997) 'Social Aspects of the European Model and its Economic Consequences' in W. Beck, L. Van der Maesen and A. Walker (eds) *The Social Quality of Europe*, Amsterdam: Kluwer.

Hirst, P. and Thompson, G. (1996) *Globalisation in Question: The International and the Possibilities of Governance*, Cambridge: Polity Press.

Hutton, W. (1996) *The State We're In* (revised edition), London: Vintage.

Jessop, B. (1994) 'The transition to post-Fordism and the Schumpeterian welfare state', in R. Burrows and B. Loader (eds) *Towards a Post-Fordist Welfare State?* London: Routledge.

Korpi, W. (1983) *The Democratic Class Struggle*, London: Routledge and Kegan Paul.

OECD (1994a) *New Orientations for Social Policy*, Paris: OECD.

OECD (1994) *The Jobs Study*, Paris: OECD.

Pierson, P. (1994) *Dismantling the Welfare State?* Cambridge: Cambridge University Press.

Wilensky, H. (1975) *The Welfare State and Equality*, Berkeley: University of California Press.

2

CHANGING LABOUR MARKETS, NEW SOCIAL DIVISIONS AND WELFARE STATE SUPPORT

Denmark in the 1990s

Jørgen Goul Andersen

It is generally acknowledged that chronic unemployment and the emergence of a low-skilled 'surplus population' constitutes one of the major challenges to contemporary welfare states. It constitutes a social change that may undermine citizenship for significant parts of the population, i.e. it may involve what has variously been labelled 'New poverty' (Room 1990), 'social exclusion' (Room 1995), the emergence of an 'underclass', or a 'two-thirds society' (Dahrendorf 1988, 1994). Alongside with ageing populations, it may also undermine the economic foundations of the welfare state. However, little has been done to examine empirically whether it also undermines the legitimacy of the welfare state by generating new political divisions between the employed majority and those who are at the fringe of the labour market, or entirely outside of it.

The question of polarisation is not a matter of active social protest among the unemployed. In line with classical findings, the unemployed and other groups outside the labour market are generally found to be 'politically harmless' (Schlozman and Verba 1979; Bild and Hoff 1988; Visser and Wijnhoven 1990; Goul Andersen 1991; Svensson and Togeby 1991; Bjørklund 1992). Rather, the question is whether the solidarity of the employed majority can be maintained. Thus, it is often claimed that labour market marginalisation leads to a decline of solidarity among the employed which will undermine the legitimacy of the welfare state (Christoffersen 1995). Our main purpose here is to examine this hypothesis.

However, the legitimacy of the welfare state may not only be related to the notion of social change, new conflicts and solidarity. It may also be linked to perceptions of economic feasibility. If solidarity is maintained, there still remains a common concern for the economic consequences of the increasing 'burden of support' for those outside the labour market. Our second purpose is to examine whether this may challenge the legitimacy of the welfare state.

Such questions must be posed against the background of the policies pursued in different countries. As pointed out by Esping-Andersen (1996: 10–20), different welfare regimes have employed different strategies to handle the problem of the low-skilled 'surplus population'. The archetypal liberal response is to deregulate labour markets and accept increasing inequalities in order to expand low-paid, low-productive employment in private services.[1] The response in Social Democratic Scandinavian welfare states has until recently been expansion of public sector employment plus active labour market policies, increasingly with emphasis on the last mentioned. And the typical Continental European response, Esping-Andersen contends was, at least until recently, to reduce labour supply, not least by means of early retirement.

However, Denmark constitutes a rather extreme case in combining both the last-mentioned techniques and avoiding entirely the first mentioned (Goul Andersen 1996). As shown in Table 2.1, Denmark is among the few countries that did not experience increasing inequality during the 1980s. The proportion of the population falling below the (relative) poverty level is unusually low, and the proportion of poor among households where head of household is unemployed, is even lower (3 per cent, c.f. Commission 1995; Dalgaard *et al.* 1996).

Because of the maintenance of high *de facto* minimum wages (there is no legal regulation), and in line with the suggestions of Esping-Andersen, Denmark had the lowest expansion of employment in the private service sector among all OECD countries from 1980 to 1991, and the second lowest proportion of the

Table 2.1 Indices of inequality in the 1980s. Inequality in disposable incomes (gini coefficients), annual change in gini coefficients in the 1980s, and inequality in primary income distribution (wage inequality index).

Country	Gini disp.incom[1] (around 1986/7)	Change per year[2] (1980s)	Wage difference index[3]	
			1980	1990
Denmark	0.21	−0.003	2.14	2.15
Sweden	0.22	0.004	2.00	2.08
Finland	0.21	−0.005	n.a.	n.a.
Germany	0.25	0.001	2.67	2.52
France	0.29	0.001	3.08	3.02
Netherlands	0.27	0.003	n.a.	n.a.
UK	0.31	0.008	2.53	3.21
USA	0.34	0.002	4.80	5.55

Source
1 Ministry of Finance (1995: 275), based on OECD (1993a). Income distribution in OECD countries, based on data from the Luxembourg income study (LIS).
2 Ministry of Finance (1995: 276), based on Rowntree report 1995.
3 Calculated from Ministry of Finance (1995: 277) whose data are based on OECD (1993b) Employment Outlook. Entries in the table are ratios between the incomes of the 'high' and 'low' income groups.
n.a. = not available.

employed working in private services among the rich countries (see Table 2.2). The other side of the coin is a very large public service sector.

This means that it becomes inescapable to consider three major groups: Publicly supported, public employees, and the privately employed (or privately supported). Alongside with the above-mentioned scenario of a 'two-thirds society', we also have to consider the possibility of a 'one-third society', i.e. a political polarisation between the majority of public employees and publicly supported who receive their income from the state, and the privately employed/privately supported.

Following a rational choice line of reasoning, there is reason to expect negative welfare sentiments among the last mentioned. However, this does not necessarily imply any welfare backlash at the aggregate level because of the sheer numbers of those who receive their income from the state. From a rational choice perspective, one might even be concerned with the maintenance of democracy in such a system. But the question is to which degree welfare attitudes are determined by such narrow self-interests (Lewin 1991; Udehn 1996). We have suggested earlier (Goul Andersen 1993) that generally shared values as well as values related to way of life/life experience such as gender, generation, and class are more important than self-interests in the narrow sense.[2]

In the following section, we describe the social structure according to labour market position or position vis-à-vis the public sector. Section three describes the overall trend in welfare legitimacy and discusses the dimensions of welfare attitudes to be applied here. Section four examines the question of decline of solidarity and new conflicts (including party choice and indicators of political trust) from a perspective of crude economic categories, whereas section five refines the concepts and the hypotheses to conform better with sociological

Table 2.2. Private service employment in selected countries. Proportion of labour force in private service sector, and increase in proportion, 1980–91. Percentages.

Country	Proportion of labour force in private services	Increase in proportion in private services, 1980–91
Denmark	36.6	1.3
Sweden	36.4	3.8
Norway	41.9	2.8
Germany	42.0	6.4
Italy	45.9	9.9
UK	50.3	11.1
Netherlands	55.2	n.a.
USA	58.1	7.2
Unweighted average 14 OECD countries with full information	44.7	5.9

Source: Own calculations from OECD (1993a) *National Accounts.*

reasoning. Finally, section six briefly comments on the most recent trends in welfare attitudes in Denmark and examines the suggestion that concern for the economy is a more likely source of declining legitimacy than is declining solidarity, at least in a society where institutional preconditions for polarisation are limited. Unless otherwise indicated, the data source in the following is the Danish 1994 election survey, a nation-wide, representative sample of 2021 cases, conducted in October/November 1994 (Borre and Goul Andersen 1997).[3]

Social structure according to labour market position

Table 2.3 pictures the social structure from the perspective of position vis-à-vis the public sector. It emerges that almost two-thirds of the adult Danish population receive their main income from the state. Some 21 per cent are public employees, and 45 per cent are (temporary or permanent) publicly supported

Table 2.3. Categories of public employees, welfare recipients and state non-dependants

		Percentage of adult population in survey[†]
State non-dependents, total		33.7
Employees		25.3
Manual workers	12.2	
Nonmanuals	12.3	
Not classified	0.8	
Self-employed, assisting spouse		7.1
Housewives		1.4
Public employees, total		21.1
Manual workers	4.4	
Nonmanuals	16.4	
Not classified	0.3	
Publicly supported/welfare recipients, total		45.2
Students, pupils (largely supported by the state)		7.4
Unemployed (unemployment benefits or social assistance)*		7.7
Parental, maternity, educational or sabbatical leave		2.8
Disabled/early retirement pensioners		5.1
Early retirement or transitional allowance		4.2
Old-age pensioners, state pensioners		17.4
Others		0.6

Source: Election Survey 1994. N = 2021.

Notes

† The sample is not perfectly representative. State non-dependents, early retirement pensioners and to some degree old-age pensioners are somewhat under-represented. But the deviations are relatively small.

* Including unemployed on parental leave.

(if we include students who receive very generous support from the state independently of parents' income from the age of 20).[4]

If identities and perceptions of self-interests follow these lines, this would put a strong pressure on the solidarity of the employed in the private sector. Below, we examine both the difference in attitudes between the gainfully employed and welfare recipients, and the difference between those who rely on income from the state vs. the rest of the population, those who are employed in the private sector and a few housewives (who comprise only 1½ per cent of the adult population).

Welfare state legitimacy in Denmark, 1969–94

Relevant dimensions

Welfare state attitudes are multidimensional, and there has been little accumulation of consensus about how to identify the relevant dimensions. The dimensions produced by factor analyses tend to be affected by question format. However, elaborating on Rothstein's (1994) distinction between substantial and procedural justice, one may perhaps distinguish between three levels (which may also be identified in e.g. Svallfors 1989, 1996): (1) The level of *basic values or preferences*; (2) the level of more *'practical' attitudes towards the implementation of welfare policies*; and (3) attitudes to *specific issues or expenditure items*. At the level of 'practical' attitudes we encounter at least four aspects which are discernible in factor analysis on Danish data: Attitudes to abuse, to efficiency/privatisation, to paternalism/responsiveness, and to economic feasibility. For our purpose here, abuse and economic feasibility are the relevant dimensions at this level. At the level of specific expenditure items, some three or four dimensions have been identified, among which we have selected attitudes to (the level of) unemployment benefits and social assistance. Finally, at the level of basic values and preferences, we have developed an index on general preferences for welfare (see below).

From a rational choice perspective, we should expect an alliance between public employees and publicly supported on the general preference index, but not on the three others. Apart from welfare attitudes, we have also examined political trust and party choice. As far as political trust is concerned, the classical expectation is that labour market marginalisation is related to low political trust. However, the opposite is also imaginable if the privately employed become frustrated over high taxes to pay for the majority who receive their income from the state.

Trends in welfare legitimacy

We have only three indicators that cover most of the period since 1969–71 when the first Danish election surveys were conducted (earlier indicators from various sources are meagre and not comparable with later surveys). These three indicators include: General support for the welfare state, attitudes to abuse, and perceptions that 'politicians are too lavish'. Although the last-mentioned item is two-dimensional (measuring both attitudes to welfare and political distrust), the three items roughly follow parallel trends, as described in Figure 2.1.

We observe a 'welfare backlash' in 1973–74 when Mogens Glistrup's anti-tax Progress Party entered the Danish parliament with 15.9 per cent of the votes cast,[5] but support gradually recovered. It peaked in the mid-1980s and consolidated at a somewhat lower level in the 1990s – nearly the same level as in the 1960s. From other sources it may be inferred that the level of welfare state support in Denmark is probably roughly equivalent to what is found in other Scandinavian countries (Pettersen 1995; Taylor-Gooby 1995; Borre and Goul Andersen 1997: ch. 8).

However, the relatively stable aggregate figures do not exclude the possibility that a polarisation may be taking place beneath the surface. In the 1994 election survey, we are able to develop somewhat improved measures.

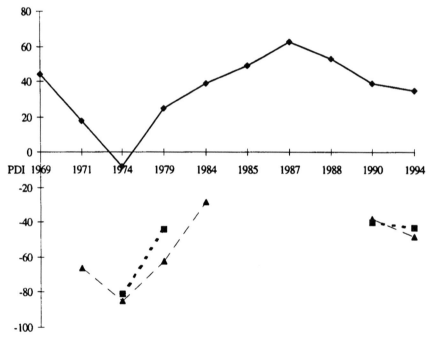

———◆— Maintain social reforms . . . (see note, Table 2.4)

▪ ▪◼ ▪ Too many people receive welfare support without really being in need of it

— ▲— · Politicians are too lavish with the taxpayers' money

Figure 2.1 Development of welfare state attitudes in Denmark, 1969–94. PDIs in favour of welfare state.

18

Dimensions of welfare state support

Basic preferences for welfare are measured by an additive index composed of three items (see Table 2.4).[6] The first one is the item referred to above which indicated a broad popular support as 63 per cent of the adult population answered that social reforms should be maintained at least at the present level,

Table 2.4 Welfare state attitudes, 1994. Percentages and PDIs (percentage difference indices)

	Agree	Disagree	Indiffer-ent/don't know	Total	PDI (in favour of welfare state)
1. Social reforms have gone too far	28	63	9	100	+35
2. Prefer bourgeois balance welfare and tax	40	25	35	100	+15
3. Prefer tax relief before improved public service	47	44	9	100	−3
Index 1: General welfare support (1+2+3)					+16
4a. Too many people receive welfare support without really being in need of it[1]	63	20	17	100	−43
4b. Far too many people abuse social systems[1]	79	15	6	100	−64
5. Many unemployed don't really want a job	52	39	9	100	−13
Index 2: Abuse (4+5)					−33
6. In the long run, we cannot afford to maintain the welfare state we have known	50	36	14	100	−14
7. Income transfers are getting beyond control	58	20	22	100	−38
Index 3: Can Afford Welfare (6+7)					−27
8. Unemployment benefits (level)	12	69	12	7	0
9. Social assistance (level)	22	54	11	13	−11
Index 4: Unemployment expenditure (8+9)					−06

Reliability coefficients (Cronbach's alpha): Index 1: 0.52; index 2: 0.44; index 3: 0.42; index 4: 0.68. Dimensionality is confirmed by factor analysis but reliability is poor on index 2 and index 3.
1 Split-half; used as one single question for index construction (see footnote 8).

Wordings:
1   'First a question about government spending on social programs.
     A says: We have gone too far with social reforms in this country. People should to a larger extent manage without social welfare and public contributions.
     B says: The social reforms already adopted in our country should be maintained, at least at the present level.
     – Do you agree mostly with A or with B?'
2   'Who do you think are the best to solve the (following) problems . . . – The present government with its Social Democratic leadership, or a bourgeois government? . . .
     To ensure a proper balance between tax burden and social security?'
3   'If it becomes possible in the long run to lower taxation, what would you prefer: . . .
     A: Tax relief or B: Improved public services?'
8–9 'Now I'd like to ask about your view on public expenditure for various purposes. For each purpose, please tell me if you think the public sector spends too much money, an appropriate amount, or too little for this purpose.'

whereas only 28 per cent believed that reforms had gone too far. It may be more accurate to ask explicitly about preferences between welfare and taxes, however, and in order to avoid possible asymmetries and fiscal illusions when each spending item is considered separately, we have used two general questions rather than questioning on individual spending areas. The first question forms part of a battery where respondents were asked which government alternative they preferred to solve a number of problems. On the item 'ensure a proper balance between tax burden and social security', 40 per cent answered that they preferred the present (Social Democratic) government, whereas only 25 per cent preferred a bourgeois government, the rest being indifferent or in doubt. Next, voters were asked whether they would prefer lower taxes (47 per cent) or improved public services (44 per cent) if it became possible to lower taxes in the future. For most of the analyses below, the three questions are combined into a simple additive index.

Our questions on abuse are easy to answer affirmatively but nevertheless indicate that people may be very critical towards abuse in spite of general support for the welfare state. As suspicion of abuse furthermore tends to penetrate the working class and other low-status groups who normally support the welfare state, abuse may be the Achilles heel of welfare state legitimacy (Svallfors 1989; Hviid Nielsen 1994). However, the time series above shows that suspicions of abuse were much more widespread in the mid-1970s; thus it does not seem that abuse is considered a pertinent problem in the 1990s.[7,8]

Despite strong attempts by governments to campaign on tax relief, voters have not been very responsive; for instance in the 1990 election, 54 per cent of the voters answered that taxes was the most important issue in the election campaign in the media but only 9 per cent themselves regarded taxes as the most important problem (Bille, Nielsen and Sauerberg 1992: 89). Voters seem much more responsive to the argument that the welfare state is threatened by increasing burdens of income transfers. Some 58 per cent agreed that 'transfer incomes are getting beyond control', and 50 per cent agreed that 'if we take a long view, it becomes impossible to maintain the welfare state as we know it today'. These questions are also combined into an additive index.[9]

Although most Danish voters believe that it is an unconditional government responsibility to provide for decent unemployment benefits, there may be different opinions as to appropriate standards. In 1994, an absolute majority believed that present standards are just appropriate. At this point, however, attitudes have changed up and down, responding to policy changes. For instance, by 1979, before downward adjustments in the 1980s, a majority believed that unemployment benefits were too generous.

Social divisions: crude economic categories

We begin by examining the polarisation hypothesis on the basis of the crude economic categories as suggested by rational choice theory and, more generally, by narrow economic reasoning. As dependent variables, we have not only included general preferences for welfare but also party choice (socialist voting and voting for 'extreme parties',[10] as voting for extreme parties may be a expression of feeling of powerlessness and distrust. From Table 2.5 it emerges that there are no significant aggregate differences between the employed and the publicly supported, neither in terms of attitudes to welfare, nor in percentages voting for 'extreme' parties, or for socialist parties. Sector position is important, but what counts is the question of public vs. private employment, not employment vs. living on income transfers. This also means that we do encounter significant differences between privately employed and those who receive their income from the state when public employees and those publicly supported are collapsed. However, this is not legitimate as they do not by any means constitute a group. Correspondingly, public employees distinguish when

Table 2.5 Basic welfare state attitudes and party choice, by labour market position, 1994

	General welfare support		Per cent 'extreme'		Per cent 'extreme left'		Per cent 'extreme right'		Per cent socialist		(n)
	Index	eta	per cent	eta	per cent	eta	per cent	eta	per cent	eta	
1. Non-dependents[1]	0.02		14		6		7		35		677
2. Public employees	0.33		23		19		2		56		423
3. Publicly supported	0.18	0.18‡	18	0.09‡	9	0.16‡	8	0.09‡	47	0.16‡	905
Employed (1+2)	0.14		18		11		5		43		1100
Publicly supported (3)	0.18	0.04	18	0.00	9	0.03	8	0.05*	47	0.04	905
Private income (1)	0.02		14		6		7		35		677
Public income (2+3)	0.23	0.16‡	20	0.07†	13	0.10†	6	0.03	50	0.14‡	1328
Publicly supported:											
Students	0.20		19		15		2		37		149
Unemployed	0.35		27		18		6		64		154
Parental and other leave	0.48		18		15		3		55		56
Disabled	0.29		19		10		10		60		103
Early retirement allowance	0.12		16		6		11		49		82
Old age pensioner	0.03	0.24‡	14	0.13*	3	0.21‡	11	0.13*	39	0.21‡	347
Privately employed[1]											
Unskilled worker	0.19		22		7		14		49		125
Skilled worker	0.25		16		8		7		53		121
Lower non-manual	0.08		14		9		5		38		168
Higher non-manual	−0.21		4		2		2		17		82
Self-employed[2]	−0.30		15		4		11		13		139
Housewives	0.32	0.34‡	6	0.16*	0	0.12	6	0.15*	46	0.33‡	25
Public employees:											
Manual worker	0.43		27		19		7		61		88
Lower non-manual	0.33		21		17		2		57		257
Higher non-manual	0.18	0.13	30	0.11	28	0.12	0	0.15*	47	0.11	73

Notes
Last four columns weighted by party choice 1994.
1 Including housewives (and a few apprentices not presented in the table).
2 Including wives working in husband's firm.
* significance < 0.05   † significance < 0.01   ‡ significance < 0.001

21

it comes to socialist as well as voting for 'extreme' parties – left wing parties have a stronghold here – but the remaining differences are negligible.

With the exception of public employees, it is the intra-class variations that are most important, not the inter-class variations. Thus, there are highly significant class differences in welfare attitudes and party choice among privately employed, as there are significant differences between various categories of publicly supported. The important divisions cut across formal relationships to the public sector: Workers, public employees and some publicly supported groups are the most positive towards the welfare state; self-employed, higher non-manual employees in the private sector and old-age pensioners are the most negative.

In short, publicly supported is a formal umbrella category, not a group in any sociological sense. The polarisation hypothesis receives no data support at all as long as we apply the crude economic categories. In particular, three sub-groups diverge: Students, old-age pensioners and people on early retirement allowance. At best, the hypotheses need specification. The deviations may appear odd from an economic point of view, but they are self-evident from a sociological point of view. Old-age pensioners, people on early retirement allowance and students are not publicly supported for any social reasons, but only as a stage in the life-cycle.[11] Receiving public support as a life cycle phenomenon cannot be expected to generate common outlooks or common identities in any broader sense.

From a political–sociological point of view, only those who are publicly supported for social reasons are relevant. This group includes the unemployed, the disabled aged less than 60 years, and persons on various leave arrangements.[12] Taken together, however, the politically relevant groups of publicly supported comprise only some 15 per cent of the adult population.

Labour market position and welfare state attitudes among the 18–59-year-old population

To test the polarisation hypothesis properly, we have to move beyond the crude economic categories. In the first place, we must exclude students and persons aged more than 60 years. Next, we must take account of the fact that people live in families. Actually, this is one of the strongest arguments against narrow economic reasoning as well as against exaggerated claims that a two-thirds society is emerging, not least in a country where housewives have virtually disappeared. Even though there are more single persons among the unemployed, and even though there is a weak association between unemployment of husband and wife, the majority of the unemployed have a working spouse. Besides, people have children or parents that may experience unemployment. This means that the distinction between those who are 'integrated' and those who are 'marginalised' or 'excluded' is highly blurred.

This sets limits for prospects of polarisation, but it does not exclude the possibility of political conflict along these lines. There may be an accumulation of dissatisfaction with taxes and welfare among a minority of the privately employed, and a minority of politically aggressive people excluded from the labour market could emerge at the other pole. To test this reformulated polarisation hypothesis, we have tried to identify a 'core insider' group among the privately employed by sorting out those who have had any personal or family contacts with the social security system within the past two years.[13] These contacts include:

1   Unemployment experience: Respondent, spouse, parents or children have been unemployed for more than one month within the last two years.
2   Leave experience: Respondent or spouse has been on parental, educational or sabbatical leave (maternity leave is not counted as leave experience).[14]

The distribution of 18–59 year olds (excluding students and a handful of state pensioners) according to these criteria is presented in Table 2.6. According to the survey estimates, we are left with only some 20 per cent of all adults (28 per cent of the above-mentioned group of 18–59 year olds) who are 'core insiders' in the private sector. Publicly supported aged less than 60 years comprise some 14 per cent (21 per cent of age group). If we do not find any polarisation between these two minority groups *and* negative welfare state attitudes among the 'core insiders', it gives little meaning to speculate about polarisation and breakdown of solidarity.

Table 2.6. Distribution of 18–59 year olds (excluding students)[1], according to labour market position, 1994. (A) As percentage of age group, and (B) As percentage of adult population[2]

	Percentage of age group[1]	Percentage of adult population
1. Core insiders: Privately employed[3] without any unemployment or leave experience in family	28	19
2. Privately employed[3] with some unemployment or leave experience in family	20	13
3. Public employees	31	21
4. Publicly supported	21	14
Total	100	67
(*n*)	1331	2021

Notes
1 Apart from students, a few state pensioners have been left out from the calculations. This holds also for the percentage basis of the first column in the table.
2 Publicly supported defined as above. Unemployment experience includes respondent, spouse, children or parents having been unemployed for at least one month within the last two years. Leave experience includes respondent or spouse having been on parental, educational or sabbatical leave (but not maternity leave) within the last two years.
3 Including housewives

How much polarisation in attitudes?

The hypotheses that follow from the polarisation hypotheses are easy to specify. On general welfare support, we should expect a sharp division between public employees and publicly supported on the one hand, and core insiders on the other. On the dimensions of abuse and level of benefits for the unemployed, we should rather expect a division between core insiders and public employees on the one hand, and publicly supported on the other. On all dimensions, people with some unemployment/leave experience should fall in between. Finally, the polarisation hypothesis does not only imply that there is an association; it also implies that 'core insiders' should hold quite negative attitudes to the welfare state.

Our results are ambiguous. General welfare support largely confirms the predicted association as we find a highly significant difference between public employees and publicly supported on the one hand and 'core insiders' on the other. However, on the abuse dimension, the most uncritical group is public employees rather than publicly supported. Even though it is reasonable to expect a certain spill-over from general welfare support – even on issues that do not affect the interests of public employees – this finding contradicts our expectations. On the remaining dimensions, public employees are in an intermediary position but come rather close to the publicly supported. Besides, the effects of social class is equally strong or stronger than the effect of labour market position. Still, significant differences do remain between 'core insiders' on the one hand, and public employees/publicly supported on the other, and these differences remain significant even when we control for party choice; as shown in Table 2.7, socialist party choice is quite strongly related to labour market position (eta = 0.24).

When it comes to political trust and 'extreme' party choice, predictions from the polarisation hypothesis are less clear: Both directions of associations are, in principle, imaginable. Our data, however, confirm the classical association with political trust: Unemployed and people with unemployment experience are more distrustful of politicians. Extreme vote is also a bit higher among publicly supported, but not more than among public employees.[15]

Before we proceed, it is necessary to ask whether the described associations may be inflated by spurious effects, as labour market position is related to a number of other variables. However, controls for education, gender and age only have negligible impact (gender effects are mediated by labour market position and social class rather than the opposite way around; see Table 2.8). Unfortunately, we are not able to make perfect controls for the most important control problem: Former class and sector position for the publicly supported. Former class position for the early retired is not available from the data set, and previous sector for the publicly supported is not measured at all. However, if we leave out the early retired as well as public employees, we may perform a test by assuming that all the unemployed are formerly employed in the private sector; this may lead to a small over-estimation of the causal effects of unemployment.

Table 2.7 Welfare attitudes among 18–59 year olds, by labour market position, 1994. Index values and PDIs (percentage points)

	Privately employed		Public employees	Publicly supported	Population average	Effect of labour market position eta	Effect of social class[1] eta
	Core insiders	Some unemploy-ment/leave experience					
General welfare support	–02	15	34	38	16	0.26‡	0.34‡
Abuse	–30	–13	03	–05	–27	0.20‡	0.18†
Can afford welfare	–35	–24	–22	–09	–33	0.13‡	0.17†
Unemployment expenditure	–14	–06	03	14	–06	0.21†	0.20‡
Political trust [2]	16	–05	18	–11	08	0.13‡	0.11
Extreme vote	15	13	23	24	18	0.12‡	0.16†
Socialist vote	31	46	57	61	45	0.24‡	0.33‡
(n)	376	271	417	267	2021		

Notes
1 Among privately employed.
2 'How much trust do you have in Danish politicians in general?' (great + some) – (not much + very little).
Indices and significance levels: see Table 2.5.

Table 2.8 Effect of labour market position, class and gender upon welfare attitudes among 18–59 year olds who are privately employed or unemployed, 1994. MCA analysis; Eta- and beta-coefficients

	eta coefficients			beta coefficients			R^2 (per cent)
	Labour market position	Class	Gender	Labour market position	Class	Gender	
General welfare support	0.25	0.31	0.11	0.18‡	0.26‡	0.05	13.3
Abuse	0.15	0.16	0.06	0.15†	0.14†	0.00	4.4
Can afford welfare	0.13	0.16	0.01	0.11†	0.14†	0.03	3.3
Unemployment expenditure	0.23	0.21	0.02	0.20‡	0.17‡	0.04	8.3
Political trust (PDI)	0.13	0.13	0.08	0.10†	0.12†	0.07	3.2

Indices and significance: see Table 2.5.

Our labour market position variable then becomes a simple inclusion/exclusion variable. The results are presented in Table 2.8. It emerges that a minor part of the effect of unemployment is a spurious effect of social class (and that part of the class effect is mediated by differences in risk of unemployment). But both the effects of class and labour market position are only marginally affected. Thus, we feel safe in concluding that the political effects of labour market position are genuine, even though there is a small spurious component.

However, as illustrated by the moderate absolute level of distrust among the unemployed, an association between labour market position and attitudes is not tantamount to any polarisation. On general welfare support and on concern for the economic consequences, we find stronger associations with social class; on attitudes to abuse and to unemployment expenditures, the effects of class and labour market position are about equally strong.

Even though a majority among the 'core insiders' in the private sector would prefer tax relief rather than improved welfare services in the future (PDI = 30), an equally large majority (PDI = 26) declare that social reforms should be maintained at least at the present level. By the same token, in all four groups, 60 per cent or more think that the present level of unemployment benefits is 'just appropriate'; only in one instance do we find more than one-quarter demanding lower levels: 26 per cent of the 'core insiders' want lower social security benefits. Furthermore, as shown in Table 2.8, even on the questions of levels of benefits which relate very strongly to the immediate interests of the unemployed, class effects are almost as strong as effects of labour market position.

In short, the 18–59 year olds who benefit from the welfare system are very positive towards maintaining the welfare system. But to a large extent, they are joined by those who pay the bill, and there is certainly no sign of increasing political distrust among this group. The effects above reflect differences in interests, but they do not justify the use of such labels as 'polarisation' or 'erosion of solidarity'.

Emerging trends among the young?

As a final step we may examine if a polarisation is taking place among the younger generations. In Denmark, young people have moved significantly to the right, in party choice as in attitudes. This holds in particular for ideals of (increasing) equality (Svensson and Togeby 1991; Gundelach and Riis 1992), but also for some welfare state attitudes (Borre and Goul Andersen 1997: ch. 8). Does this reflect an emerging trend towards a decline of solidarity and increasing polarisation among the young generations?

The evidence presented in Table 2.9 is mixed. We find little or no generation difference in attitudes or in associations as far as general support, attitudes to abuse and concern for the economic future of the welfare state are concerned. However, when it comes to attitudes towards the level of unemployment benefits, the difference is quite pronounced, as attitudes seem more polarised among the young, i.e. much more negative among young 'core insiders'.

This does not mean that young 'core insiders' feel politically alienated; on the contrary, we find a high level of political distrust among the publicly supported and among those who are affected by unemployment in this age group, i.e.

Table 2.9 Welfare attitudes by age and labour market position, 1994. Index values and PDIs (percentage points)

		Privately employed		Public employees	Publicly supported	Effect of labour market position eta	Effect of social class eta
		Core insiders	Some unemployment/leave experience				
General welfare support	18–34 years	–02	20	31	36	0.25[†]	0.25[*]
	35–59 years	–02	10	35	39	0.27[†]	0.36[†]
Abuse	18–34 years	–36	–11	–04	–10	0.21[†]	0.21
	35–59 years	–27	–15	05	–01	0.20[†]	0.14
Can afford welfare	18–34 years	–32	–23	–21	–05	0.14[*]	0.17
	35–59 years	–37	–24	–22	–12	0.12[†]	0.19[*]
Benefits to unemployed	18–34 years	–27	–08	–03	12	0.28[†]	0.22
	35–59 years	–06	–03	05	15	0.17[†]	0.26[†]
Political trust (PDI)	18–34 years	19	–11	11	–25	0.18[†]	0.13
	35–59 years	14	01	20	–02	0.09	0.19
Extreme vote	18–34 years	9	17	21	28	0.17[†]	0.26[*]
	35–59 years	18	10	24	21	0.12[†]	0.16[*]
Socialist vote	18–34 years	22	39	50	56	0.26[†]	0.22[*]
	35–59 years	35	53	59	64	0.23[†]	0.40[†]
(n)	18–34 years	140	134	108	109		
	35–59 years	236	137	309	158		

Notes
1 Among privately employed.
Indices and significance: See Table 5.

political trust is also more polarised. To a certain extent, this seems to hold even for extreme voting, but not for socialist voting; there is a movement to the right among the younger generation that affects all groups, regardless of labour market position. On all dimensions except attitudes to abuse and extreme vote, class effects are smaller among the young than among the 35–59 year olds. At least on some dimensions, this pattern could conform with an idea that labour market position is increasingly important whereas class is becoming less important. But there are, of course, a large number of alternative interpretations.

Conclusions

When we move to sociologically relevant categories, we at the same time abandon the notion of a polarisation between the employed majority and a minority of marginalised or excluded from the labour market. Rather, we face a polarity between a minority of 'core insiders' in the private sector at the one pole, and a minority of publicly supported at the other. Even together, these two groups comprise only one-third of the adult population.

Clearly, this polarity is politically important, in some respects equally important as social class (although some of the effect hinges upon the sector difference between public and private employees). There is no doubt that the effects are largely non-spurious (they may to some extent be mediated by party choice, but party choice may also be an effect of welfare attitudes): Class differences explain only a small part of the effects. We even found indications that the polarity is becoming stronger on political trust and attitudes to benefit levels to the unemployed, although the age difference here may also have life-cycle interpretations (as young have lower wages, benefit levels may appear more generous). Still, increasing polarisation among the young is not a general phenomenon that pertains to all aspects of welfare attitudes.

Clearly, then, labour market position is a quite important interest factor. But the notion of employed majority as opposed to marginalised/excluded minority does not make much sense – and the crude economic notion of employed vs. publicly supported (as applied to the entire population) does not make sense at all. Most importantly, there are no signs in our data of a decline in welfare legitimacy, nor of waning solidarity among the employed. Finally, the polarity between core insiders and publicly supported (among the 18–59 year olds) does not seem important in understanding or predicting aggregate welfare legitimacy.[16] At this point we have to turn to other explanations, not least economic problems and political discourse. We finalise this chapter with some recent findings concerning this problem.

Since the welfare backlash in the early 1970s, welfare state support in Denmark has survived severe economic crises as well as sometimes quite aggressive (but verbal rather than institutional) attacks on the welfare state during more than ten years of bourgeois political rule (1982–93). In fact, during the years of economic prosperity in the mid-1980s, welfare support reached the highest levels ever measured. To some degree, this may follow from our measurement instruments which typically ask whether people want more or less welfare; when a bourgeois government imposes strong controls upon public expenditure, it is perhaps only natural that people tend to answer that they want 'more', whereas the demand for more welfare declines when Social Democrats are in office and much more generous with money for the expansion of welfare.

However, it has nevertheless come as a bit of a surprise that, according to some opinion polls, people have become more sceptical about welfare during the period of economic prosperity since 1994. Thus, according to our main historical indicator, PDIs in favour of maintaining welfare reforms at least at the present level suddenly declined from +35 in 1994 to +10 in 1996 – the second lowest level ever recorded.[17] It turned out that the preferences for tax relief vs. improved public services had not changed (or rather, it had tipped a bit in favour of improved services, see Goul Andersen 1997: 158).

It appears that the main reason is to be found in an increasing concern for the problems of financing the welfare state in the future. As shown in Table 2.10, the distribution of answers on the two items that constituted our index of economic concern above have changed quite dramatically: In particular, the proportions that 'fully agree' have increased greatly, and the proportions answering 'don't know' have declined sharply, indicating that a process of cognitive mobilisation has taken place. It furthermore transpires that the association between attitudes towards these items and attitudes towards the item that welfare reforms have gone too far has been strengthened from 1994 to 1996. But the remarkable point is that we find no signs whatsoever of an increasing social polarisation from 1994 to 1996; as a proxy for labour market position, we have used a distinction between people living on transfer income and the employed: if a polarisation had taken place, this would also be observable on these crude economic categories. But if anything, the opposite seems rather to have happened (see Table 2.11)

To some extent these data reflect short-term fluctuations as the debate over increasing transfer expenditures probably peaked in 1996. However, the fear of future costs of ageing populations will contribute to keep the issue on the political agenda. Besides, political incentives among political forces that are critical towards the welfare state contribute to keep this issue a 'hot' one. Thus, in the absence of (intended or perhaps unintended) institutional change which could change identities and orientations (Svallfors 1996, ch. 10), it is probably in such economic problems of the welfare state, and in their political articulation, that we should seek possible sources of declining legitimacy – even among the publicly supported – much less so in new social divisions and political conflicts between the employed and the unemployed.

Table 2.10 Voters' perceptions of economic problems of the welfare state, 1994 and 1996. Percentages and PDIs

	Year	Fully agree	Partly agree	Partly dis-agree	Fully dis-agree	Don't know	PDI: disagree minus agree
Income transfers are getting beyond control	1994	29	29	12	8	22	–38
	1996	54	20	7	11	8	–56
In the long run, we cannot afford to maintain the welfare state we have known	1994	21	29	20	16	14	–14
	1996	41	18	11	23	7	–25

Source: Ugebrevet Mandag Morgen and AC Nielsen AIM. Survey conducted in cooperation with Jørgen Goul Andersen, August, 1996. Nation-wide, representative telephone survey of *c.*1000 respondents.

Table 2.11 Perceptions of economic problems of the welfare state, 1994 and 1996, by labour market position. PDIs in Percentage points

		1994	1996	*change*
Transfers beyond control (–)	Work income	–43	–58	–15
	Transfer income	–33	–53	–20
	Difference	+10	+5	
Cannot afford welfare (–)	Work income	–12	–18	–6
	Transfer income	–22	–36	–14
	Difference	–10	–18	
Social reforms gone too far (–)	Work income	+38	+12	–26
	Transfer income	+33	+10	–23
	Difference	–5	–2	

Note
Students and housewives not included.
Source: As Table 2.10.

Notes

1 Until recently, many economists were attracted by the liberal market solution which at least had the quality of improving employment opportunities. More recently, scepticism has increased as upward income mobility, according to some sources, is much lower than expected (OECD, 1997).
2 Social class is both a value factor and an interest factor, but the predictions are different: When class is considered an interest factor, the main dividing line is between the middle class and the working class. When class is considered a way of life-factor, the main dividing line should be between ordinary wage earners on the one hand, and self-employed and managers on the other.
3 The research group behind The Danish Election Programme has conducted surveys of all parliamentary elections since 1971. A minor survey including some of the items to be applied in subsequent later time series was conducted for the first time in 1969.
4 The survey-based figures are not exact measures but good approximations. We do not know the 'true' figures, as social and labour market statistics are still not perfectly commensurable. Standard survey weighting does not affect the figures but it does seem that early retirement pensioners (previously 'disablement pensioners') and privately employed are somewhat under-represented, whereas most of the remaining categories, in particular public employees, are slightly over-represented in the survey.
5 Since the mid-1980s, the party has survived more as an anti-immigration party; in 1995 the party was split into two parties with roughly equivalent programmes.
6 Technically, all indices in the following are constructed by recoding the component variables into three categories: –1, 0 and +1. Next, the sum of values is divided by the number of items. This means that an index value is interpretable as a sort of 'average percentage difference index'. Respondents with 'don't know' answers on one half or more of the questions in the index are treated as missing, otherwise recoded as neutral on the component items. The dimensionality implied by the construction of indexes is confirmed by factor analysis, but reliability is not always satisfactory.

7 This is also confirmed by surveys conducted for the news media (see Goul Andersen 1995: 43–5).
8 The 1994 election survey used a split-haft procedure where alternative formulations of a few questions, including one of the two items on abuse, were applied in the first and second interview rounds, respectively (each consisting of some 1000 randomly selected respondents). However, for the purpose of index construction, we have treated the answers as if they were obtained from one single question.
9 Both the index on abuse and the index on economic sustainability of welfare have low reliability; however, as the individual items reveal roughly the same patterns as the two indexes, we have applied the indexes anyway as a space-saving device, rather than reporting on a large number of individual items showing the same. It could be added, that a more reliable measure of abuse, applied in 1990, revealed the same social patterns (see Hvid Nielsen 1994).
10 'Extreme' parties include two left wing parties: Unity List and Socialist People's Party; the right-wing populist Progress Party, and candidates outside the party lists. 'Extreme' parties should not be conflated with 'extremist' parties; it is a relative concept that signals a distance to the more influential parties close to the political centre.
11 The formal pension age in Denmark is 67 years and previously, persons on early retirement allowance were often referred to as a marginalised or excluded group. But this has little connection with reality. New value priorities in favour of self-actualisation and leisure activity means that more and more people want to exploit the opportunities of early exit, and the *de facto* pension age in Denmark is approaching 60 years.
12 This does not include people on maternity leave but parental, educational and sabbatical leave which was introduced in 1992–3. Sabbatical leave is now abolished, and economic compensation for parental leave is significantly reduced.
13 It is also possible to sort out a 'core outsider' group at the other pole, but as it does not have any significant impact on the results, we have abstained from complicating the categories.
14 This involves a small (but negligible) deviance as compared to my own previous operationalisations on the same data.
15 The publicly supported include both long-term and short-term unemployed (as well as early retired). However, a distinction between short-term and long-term unemployed reveals no significant differences; at best, there may be a certain (but statistically insignificant) difference in attitudes to benefits to the unemployed.
16 Strictly speaking, welfare legitimacy has other aspects to it than political attitudes. But this is less relevant in the context here.
17 According to a survey conducted by A. C. Nielsen AIM, August 1996 (for a fuller description, see Goul Andersen 1997).

References

Bild, Tage and Hoff, Jens (1988) *Party System and State Dependents*, Arbejdspapir: Institut for Statskundskab, Københavns Universitet.

Bille, Lars, Nielsen, Hans Jørgen and Sauerberg, Steen (1992) *De uregerlige vælgere*, Copenhagen: Columbus.

Bjørklund, T. (1992) 'Unemployment and Party Choice in Norway', *Scandinavian Political Studies*, vol. 15, pp. 329–52.

Borre, Ole and Goul Andersen, Jørgen (1997) *Voting and Political Attitudes in Denmark*, Aarhus: Aarhus University Press.

Christoffersen, Henrik (1995) 'Når velfærdsstaten bliver til transfereringssamfundet', pp. 102–16 in *Effektivisering av välfärdsstaten. Rapport från ett seminar 16–17 mars 1995, Reykjavik, Island.* TemaNord 1995: 578. Copenhagen: Nordisk Ministerråd.

Commission (1995) *Employment in Europe, 1994.* European Commission (Danish ed., 1995).

Dahrendorf, Ralph (1988) *The Modern Social Conflict*, London: Weidenfeld & Nicolson.

Dahrendorf, Ralph (1994) 'The Changing Quality of Citizenship', pp. 10–19 in Bart van Steenbergen (ed.), *The Condition of Citizenship*, London: Sage.

Dalgaard, Esben, Ingerslev, Olaf, Ploug, Niels and Rold Andersen, Bent (1996) *Velfærdsstatens fremtid*, Copenhagen: Handelshøjskolens Forlag.

Esping-Andersen, Gösta (1990) *The Three Worlds of Welfare Capitalism*, Princeton: Princeton University Press.

Esping-Andersen, Gösta (1996) 'After the Golden Age? Welfare State Dilemmas in a Global Economy', pp. 1–31 in G. Esping-Andersen (ed.), *Welfare States in Transition*, London: Sage.

Goul Andersen, Jørgen (1991) *Class Theory in Transition*, Aarhus: Department of Political Science, Aarhus University.

Goul Andersen, Jørgen (1993) 'Sources of Welfare State Support in Denmark: Self-Interest or Way of Life?' pp. 25–48 in E. J. Hansen, S. Ringen, H. Uustitalo and R. Erikson (eds) *Welfare Trends in the Scandinavian Countries*, New York: M. E. Sharpe.

Goul Andersen, Jørgen (1996) 'Marginalisation, Citizenship and the Economy: The Capacity of the Universalist Welfare State in Denmark', pp. 155–202 in Erik Oddvar Eriksen and Jørn Loftager (eds) *The Rationality of the Welfare State*, Oslo: Scandinavian University Press.

Goul Andersen, Jørgen (1997) 'Krisebevidsthed og velfærdsholdninger i en højkonjunktur', pp. 151–70 in Gert Graversen (ed.) *Et arbejdsliv*, Festskrift tilegenet Professor dr.Phil Eggert Petersen. Aarhus. Dept. of Psychology, University of Aarhus.

Gundelach, Peter and Riis, Ole (1992) *Danskernes værdier*, Copenhagen: Forlaget Sociologi.

Hviid Nielsen, Torben (1994) 'Velfærdsstatens attituder: Ambivalens og dilemmaer', pp. 57–92 in Johannes Andersen and Lars Torpe (eds) *Demokrati og politisk kultur. Rids af et demokratisck medborgerskab*, Herning: Systime.

Lewin, Leif (1991) *Self-Interest and Public Interest in Western Politics*, Oxford: Oxford University Press.

Ministry of Finance (1995) *Finansredegørelse 1995*, Copenhagen: Finansministeriet.

OECD (1993a) *National Accounts*, Paris: OECD.

OECD (1993b) *Employment Outlook.* July 1993, Paris: OECD.

OECD (1997) *Employment Outlook.* July 1997, Paris: OECD.

Pettersen, Per Arnt (1995) 'The Welfare State: The Security Dimension', pp. 198–233 in Ole Borre and Elinor Scarbrough (eds) *The Scope of Government*, Oxford: Oxford University Press.

Room, Graham (ed.) (1990) *New Poverty in the European Community*, Cambridge: Cambridge University Press.

Room, Graham (ed.) (1995) *Beyond the Threshold: The Measurement and Analysis of Social Exclusion*, Bristol: Policy Press.

Rothstein, Bo (1994) *Vad bör staten göra?* Stockholm: SNS Förlag.

Schlozman, Kay Lehman and Verba, Sidney (1979) *Injury to Insult. Unemployment, Class, and Political Response*, Cambridge, MA: Harvard University Press.

Svallfors, Stefan (1989) *Vem älskar välfärdsstaten? Attityder, organiserede intresser och svensk välfärdspolitik*, Lund: Arkiv.

Svallfors, Stefan (1996) *Välfärdsstatens moraliska ekonomi. Välfärdsopinionen i 90-talets Sverige*, Umeå: Boréa Bokförlag.

Svensson, Palle and Togeby, Lise (1991) *Højrebølge?* Århus: Forlaget Politica.

Taylor-Gooby, Peter (1995) 'Who wants the welfare state? Support for state welfare in European countries', pp. 11–51 in Stefan Svallfors (ed.) *In the Eye of the Beholder*, Umeå: Impello Säljsupport/The Bank of Sweden Tercentenary Foundation.

Udehn, Lars (1996) *The Limits of Public Choice*, London: Routledge.

Visser, W. and Wijnhoven, R. (1990) 'Politics Do Matter, but Does Unemployment? Party Strategies, Ideological Discourse and Enduring Mass Unemployment', *European Journal of Political Research*, vol. 18, pp. 71–96.

3

THE MIDDLE CLASS AND
WELFARE STATE RETRENCHMENT

Attitudes to Swedish
welfare policies

Stefan Svallfors

> During this campaign, I heard a great deal of talk about the
> 'middle classes'. Can you find out who they are and what they
> want, and we will see if we can give it to them.
> Harold Macmillan, 1959[1]

The middle class appears as less mysterious nowadays than it did to the British
Prime minister in the 1950s. However, one thing that both Macmillan and
contemporary observers would agree upon is that adjusting to the middle class
is essential for political success. The industrial working class, once the core of
political movements for change and portrayed by many social scientists as the
prime political subject, is declining in size and strength. Instead, various forms
of non-manual occupations, from routine office workers to higher professional
and managerial strata, have grown both in numbers and in political importance.

Of particular importance is the relationship between the middle class and the
welfare state. As shown by Baldwin (1990), the middle class has often been
instrumental in promoting welfare state development during the twentieth
century. Not only workers and their organisations but also various groups
within the middle class have, at different times in different countries, acted to
extend state support. The politics of an established welfare state may be even
more dependent on the middle class.

The question of how the middle class will act in safe-guarding its interests in
respect of welfare policies has elicited quite different responses. According to
Wilensky (1975), the 'middle mass' (lower middle class and upper working
class) will mainly act as a reactionary force in relation to welfare state growth.
As they become more prosperous, their interest in the welfare state will decline.
Resistance against taxation and less than generous attitudes towards the
marginalised, who are dependent on the welfare state for their livelihood, are
likely responses from the 'middle mass'.

34

Others have argued the exact opposite. King (1987) maintains that the middle class has a considerable stake in the welfare state, and that they will defend it to an extent which will make failures out of the conservative attempts to 'roll back' the welfare state. Notions of social rights have been woven into the social fabric of contemporary capitalism, and are accepted not only by workers, but also by broad sections of the middle classes. Large parts of the middle class also have interests to defend, as welfare state employees or as welfare consumers, particularly in 'institutional models' such as the Scandinavian one.

In this chapter, the reactions from the middle class in Sweden to economic crisis and welfare state retrenchment in the 1990s will be studied, using attitude survey data. The Swedish case is especially interesting in this respect, since the design of welfare policies had as one of its explicit aims to win the support of the middle class. As Svensson (1994) shows, considerations about how to win the support of non-manual groups were central in the social democratic design of core social insurances in the 1950s (see also Korpi 1980, 1983; Esping-Andersen 1985). On the whole, these attempts were also successful. The welfare state has enjoyed support not only from workers, but to a great extent also from large groups of non-manual employees (Svallfors 1989, 1996).

The welfare state in Sweden has gone through a period of retrenchment in the 1990s (Stephens 1996). The rapid rise in unemployment in the early 1990s, combined with a major crisis in the bank system, created a sky-rocketing budget deficit, which peaked in 1994. The incoming social democratic government in 1994 put a fast reduction of the budget deficit high on its agenda. This was implemented through a combination of tax increases and cutbacks in the welfare state. Income replacement levels have been reduced to 75 per cent in the major social insurances, at the same time as eligibility has become more restricted. Health care, care for the elderly, child care and education have gone through major savings, which have decreased the number of employees considerably; arguably, this also has led to a decline in the quality of services. Child care allowances and housing allowances have also been lowered and/or more restricted.

The main reason for middle-class support for the Swedish welfare state in the past has been the fact that the income replacement levels and the service quality have been high. There have been few incentives for broad sections of the non-manual employees to opt out of the welfare state. But how will members of the middle class react to welfare state retrenchment, when replacement levels are lowered and the quality of services decline? Will they come to the defence of welfare policies, or will they opt for private solutions?

Esping-Andersen maintains that the future of the Swedish welfare state 'depends on middle-class support, which, in turn, requires expanding and improving the quality and quantity of services' (Esping-Andersen 1990: 223). In this perspective, the prospects for the Swedish welfare state may look bleak indeed.

As Pierson (1994, 1996) emphasises, however, periods of retrenchment

35

cannot be analysed with the same assumptions as periods of welfare state formation and extension. The institutions that have been formed as a result of welfare state expansion will affect both actors' interests and their possibilities for successful strategies. As emphasised in the burgeoning literature within institutional theory, institutions affect not only rational actions and strategies, they help constitute the very interests that actors pursue (Thelen and Steinmo 1992; Rothstein 1995). Pierson (1996) also suggests both that public support for the welfare state extends considerably beyond the working class, and that such support may become even stronger in periods of welfare state retrenchment. In these respects, it should be highly interesting to see whether middle-class support for the welfare state declines or increases in a period of welfare state retrenchment in an encompassing welfare state such as the Swedish one.

In the following, we will take our departure in three possible scenarios. The first is that middle-class support for the welfare state decreases, and decreases more than is the case in the working class, so that we find a polarisation between the working class and the middle class in their support for welfare policies. The second is that middle-class support increases relative to the working class, so that we find class convergence in views about welfare policies. The third is that we find a split within the middle class, so that some sections become more similar to the working class, while other sections become more different.

Data and aggregated trends

The data on which the analysis builds comes from Swedish national surveys conducted in 1986, 1992 and 1996.[2] The purpose of the surveys was to pose questions dealing with a broad range of welfare policy issues, instead of just using a few single indicators of attitudes to the welfare state. In this way, it was sought to bring out the complexity and possible ambivalence and contradictions in attitudes instead of relying on a simplified notion of 'for or against the welfare state' (Svallfors 1989, 1996). The present analysis rests on a sub-set of all these questions, a number of rather specific questions dealing with the service delivery aspects of welfare policies, the preferred way of financing various welfare policies, and issues of suspected abuse of welfare benefits and services. The questions thus relate less to levels of spending, and more to preferred ways of organising and financing the welfare state.

In Tables 3.1–3.4, aggregated levels for the various questions are displayed. As shown in Table 3.1, support for the public sector was best suited to handle services increased even more in the welfare state crisis of the 1990s, from an already high level in 1992.[3] This applies especially to health care and child care. Support for the public sector increased even more in the welfare state crisis.

In Tables 3.2 and 3.3, we find great stability in Swedes' views about how to finance services and benefits. It is only when it comes to child care that we find any substantive support for increasing private financing.

36

Table 3.1 Attitudes to service delivery. Answers to the question 'Who do you in general consider best suited to deliver the following services' 1986, 1992 and 1996

	State or local authorities			Private enterprises			Family and relatives			Other[a]		
	1986	1992	1996	1986	1992	1996	1986	1992	1996	1986	1992	1996
Education (b)	84.8 (90.5)	81.5 (86.9)	87.3 (87.4)	7.6	11.2	10.0	0.6	0.4	0.2	6.6 (1.2)	6.3 (1.4)	2.5 (2.4)
Health services (b)	83.3 (90.7)	77.5 (85.3)	92.8 (93.0)	8.8	14.2	6.8	0.0	0.0	0.0	7.9 (0.5)	8.5 (0.7)	0.3 (0.1)
Child care (b)	48.6 (54.7)	48.4 (57.4)	63.6 (63.7)	10.0	20.4	18.5	29.4	11.2	10.6	12.0 (5.9)	20.0 (11.0)	7.4 (7.3)
Care for elderly (b)	75.5 (81.0)	75.9 (83.1)	83.8 (84.0)	5.2	9.9	9.6	10.6	4.6	3.7	8.7 (3.1)	9.6 (2.4)	2.9 (2.7)
Social work (b)	87.8 (91.4)	85.5 (88.8)	91.8 (92.0)	2.0	4.4	3.4	1.8	2.1	1.6	8.4 (4.7)	8.0 (4.8)	3.2 (3.0)

(n = 1986, c. 960; 1992, c. 1410; 1996, c. 1270)

(a) Cooperatives, Trade unions, Charity organizations, Various combinations of answers.
(b) All combinations of answers which include 'State or local authorities' are included in that category.

Table 3.2 Attitudes to financing welfare policies. Answers to the question 'How do you think the following services should be financed?' 1986, 1992 and 1996

Per cent answering 'Primarily through taxes and employer contributions'*	1986	1992	1996
Education	79.0	74.6	76.9
Health services	89.9	90.3	91.5
Child care	63.3	63.4	62.2
Care for the elderly	—	91.9	88.8
(*n*)	(c. 970)	(c. 1490)	(c. 1340)

* The alternative was 'To a larger extent through special fees from those who use the services'.

Table 3.3 Attitudes to financing of social insurance 1986, 1992 and 1996

Per cent answering 'Should primarily be paid through taxes and employer contributions, which are kept at their present level'*	1992	1996
Sickness insurance	78.4	79.1
Unemployment insurance	70.9	69.6
Pensions	77.4	75.3
(*n*)	(c. 1420)	(c. 1250)

* The alternative was 'To a larger extent through individual insurance contributions, at the same time as taxes and employer contributions are lowered'.

Table 3.4 Attitudes to abuse of welfare policies. Answers to the question 'How usual do you think it is that social benefits and services are used by people who don't really need them?' 1986 and 1992

Per cent that 'fully agree' with certain propositions	1986	1992	1996
Many of those using health services are not all that ill	13.9	17.2	8.8
Many of those receiving unemployment benefits could get a job if they only wanted to	42.2	28.8	23.7
Many of those receiving social assistance are not really poor	29.4	28.8	14.9
Many of those receiving housing allowances should move to smaller and cheaper dwellings	23.8	28.8	24.7
Many of those who report themselves ill are not really ill	27.1	27.9	12.4
(*n*)	(c. 980)	(c. 1500)	(c. 1340)

In Table 3.4, we find that suspicions of abuse decreased considerably in the welfare crisis. Smaller shares believed in 1996 that those who use health services are not really ill, that those who receive social assistance are not poor, or that those who report themselves ill are not really ill.

In the following, we will concentrate our comparison of group differences to what happened in the period 1992–6. Previous analyses have shown that the period 1986 to 1992 was characterised by large stability in group differences (Svallfors 1995, 1996). But will such stability remain also in the 1990s, when changes in actual policies and programmes have been much greater?

In order to do this comparison, three additive indices were constructed. The 'Service index' consists of the items from Table 3.1, recoded into 1 ('state and local authorities' and 0 (all others) and summed. The index can then vary between 0 and 5. The 'Finance index' consists of all the items from Tables 3.2 and 3.3, recoded into 1 (financing through taxes and employer contributions) and 0 (increased user fees and private insurance contributions) and summed. The index can then vary between 0 and 7. The 'Suspicion index' consists of all the items from table 3.4, recoded into 0 ('fully agree'), 1 ('partly agree' and 'partly disagree') and 2 ('fully disagree') and summed. The index can then vary between 0 and 10. The indices have then been rescaled into a 0–1 range, to allow comparisons between indices. The way the indices are constructed means that higher values always indicate more support for welfare policies, something which makes interpretations easier. The indices all have satisfactory reliability (Cronbach's Alpha varies from 0.71 to 0.80 for the indices).

Class differences 1992–6

In order to study class differences in attitudes, and in particular those found in different parts of the middle class, we need to present what is here understood as 'class'. The class concept used here draws on the categorisation created by John Goldthorpe and his associates, and used in a multitude of studies of social mobility and class voting (for a recent exposition, see Erikson and Goldthorpe 1992: 35–47). In this conceptualisation, classes are distinguished through the employment relations, in terms of different positions in labour markets and production units, which they entail.

The middle class, thus conceptualised, consists of several distinct categories. One is, of course, the self-employed and the small employers who typically are neither employed nor living mainly from the work of employees. A second group comprises the higher- and middle-level non-manuals (the 'service class' in Goldthorpe's terms); groups with delegated authority and/or specialised knowledge and expertise within the work organisation. Such groups are typically bound to the employer in a 'service relationship', that is, a long-term commitment and relations of trust vis-à-vis the employer. Lastly, the lower-level – or 'routine' – non-manuals consist of employees who have neither a 'service relationship' towards the employer nor a pure working-class character. In this sense, they occupy an intermediate position between workers and the 'service class'.

In order to study the development of attitudes in the middle class, we will use a rather fine-grained categorisation. The categorisation is based on the Swedish

Socio-economic classification (SEI), which to a large degree resembles the Gold-thorpe class schema. We will distinguish between lower non-manuals, middle non-manuals, higher non-manuals and 'elite' occupations, and compare these to workers on the one hand, and to the self-employed on the other.[4] The index values in these groups will be plotted in 'abacus plots', in order to compare both across categories, between indices and between years.[5]

As shown in Figure 3.1, support for state and local authorities in handling services increased in every class, except for the elite group. The elite group was in 1996 the least supportive of the public sector, while in 1992 they were more positive towards it than the self-employed and the higher non-manuals. Support for the public sector increased most among middle and higher non-manuals (the elite group excepted), so that in 1996 differences between manuals and non-manuals were very small.

When it comes to views about the financing of welfare policies, Figure 3.2

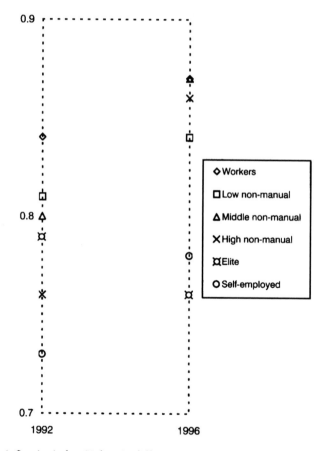

Figure 3.1 Service index. Values in different groups.

40

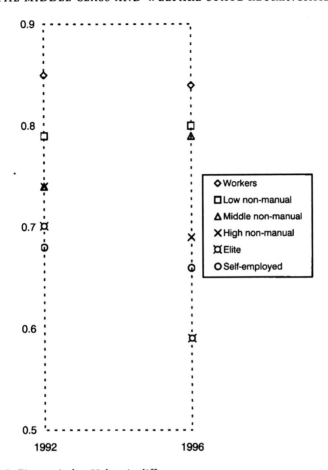

Figure 3.2 Finance index. Values in different groups.

shows a slightly different pattern. While support for collective financing is rather stable among workers and lower non-manuals, it *increased* among middle non-manuals, and *decreased* among the self-employed and higher non-manuals and, in particular, in the elite group. We find here a clear case of a split within the middle class.

Suspicions of abuse, as displayed in Figure 3.3, are patterned in a different way. In 1992, we find that middle and higher non-manuals, the elite group included, were *least* suspicious of abuse. Differences between workers and non-manual groups were slight, only the self-employed are more suspicious than others. This pattern changed in 1996. All groups became less suspicious, with the exception of the elite group, which stayed stable. Suspicions decreased most among the middle and lower non-manuals, and less among the higher non-manuals, so that in 1996 we find very small attitudinal differences between workers and the non-manual groups (the elite group excepted).

41

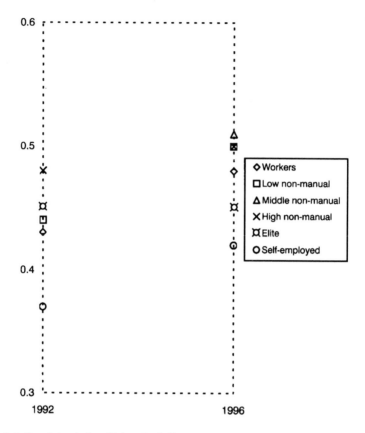

Figure 3.3 Suspicion index. Values in different groups.

If we compare the indices, we find that there is more dispersion between classes on the issues of financing welfare policies than where service delivery or suspicions of abuse are at stake. This is hardly surprising, since financing is more clearly related to the various risks and resources distributed through the labour market than the other aspects are.

In sum, we find little support for any polarisation between the working class and the middle class when it comes to attitudes towards the welfare state. Instead, we find that broad sections among the non-manual groups became more similar to workers in their support for welfare policies. A clear exception was found in the elite group, where changes were contrary to what was found among lower and middle level non-manuals. The higher non-manuals, apart from the elite group, changed their attitudes in a less consistent way, increasing their support for the public sector in handling services, but decreasing their support for collective financing.

42

Splits within the middle class: gender, sector and level

In discussing splits within the middle class we may distinguish between vertical and horizontal divisions. Vertical divisions are those found between higher- and lower-level non-manuals; horizontal are those we find within the same layer between non-manual employees with different other characteristics.[6] Two such dividing lines are between men and women and between private and public sector employees. As emphasised by Esping-Andersen (1990: 227), the likelihood of a gender/sector-based conflict is quite high in Sweden due to the exceptionally segmented labour market, with a public sector predominantly populated by female employees.

Some authors have argued that splits along gender and sector lines are more pronounced among the non-manual groups than among workers. While working conditions and workplace experiences do not differ particularly between men and women or between public and private sector employees among the workers, things are different among non-manual groups (Goul Andersen 1985: 102–3; Wright and Cho 1992). Empirical research seems also to confirm this, since attitudinal differences across gender and sector cleavages have repeatedly been shown to be greater among non-manuals than among workers (Ahrne and Leiulfsrud 1984; Wright and Cho 1992; Blomberg *et al.* 1996).

These findings were confirmed also in this analysis. Differences among workers between public and private sector employees, and between men and women, were indeed minor on all the three attitudinal indices which were constructed. Among the non-manuals, however, sector and gender differences were clear, as displayed in Figures 3.4–3.6.

The figures compare attitudes among private and public sector employees and among men and women in three groups of non-manuals. The elite group has been included with the other higher non-manuals, since it contains too few cases for its subdivision.[7] The two columns on the left-hand side of each diagram display differences between public and private sector employees, while the two columns on the right-hand side of each diagram display differences between men and women. For example, the circles in the diagrams indicate index values among higher-level employees in the private sector in the two columns to the left in each diagram, while they indicate index values among male higher-level employees in the two columns to the right.

As shown in Figure 3.4, attitudes among the non-manuals were clearly more structured by sector and gender than by level. All the public sector and women categories were more supportive of state and local authorities than the most positive private or male group. This fact changed little from 1992 to 1996, since support for public handling of services increased in all groups. It should be noted that in 1996, the groups that supported state service delivery most were higher non-manuals in the public sector and female higher non-manuals.

As shown in Figure 3.5, attitudes towards financing welfare was more clearly structured by level in 1996. Private sector and male higher-level non-manuals

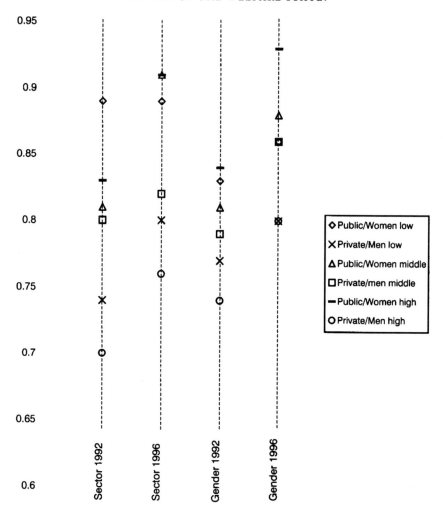

Figure 3.4 Service index. Values in different groups.

are the groups which were clearly most sceptical about collective financing. It is interesting to note that public sector and female middle-level non-manuals became considerably more supportive of collective financing during the welfare crisis, while their private sector and male colleagues hardly changed their views at all. We also find that higher-level non-manuals, regardless of their gender or sector location, became more sceptical about collective financing from 1992 to 1996.

Moving to Figure 3.6, we find a considerable convergence between groups. Public sector and female higher-level employees are consistently the least suspicious groups. Since their views hardly changed at all from 1992 to 1996, while we find substantially lower suspicion among all private sector and male

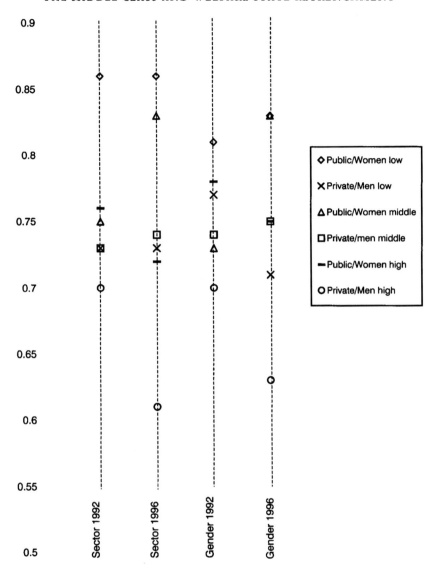

Figure 3.5 Finance index. Values in different groups.

groups, the result is convergence, so that group differences are almost negligible in 1996.

As a summary of group differences among the non-manual employees, Table 3.5 describes index value differences among the non-manuals between women and men, between public and private sector employees, and between lower and higher levels. Positive values thus indicate that women, or public sector employees, or lower-level employees are more supportive of the welfare state than their counterparts; negative values indicate the opposite.

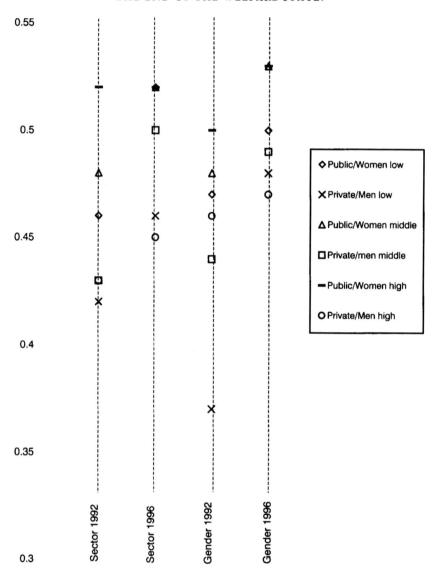

Figure 3.6 Suspicion index. Values in different groups.

As shown in Table 3.5, we find significant level differences only on the finance index, where differences also became wider from 1992 to 1996. On the other two indices, differences between higher- and lower-level non-manuals were insignificant already in 1992, and disappeared almost completely in 1996. Sector differences show a clearer and more persistent pattern, where public sector employees are more supportive of the welfare state than private sector non-manuals. The same goes for gender differences, where attitudinal

Table 3.5 Sector, gender and level differences in index values among non-manual employees in 1992 and 1996.

	Service index		Finance index		Suspicion index	
	1992	1996	1992	1996	1992	1996
Sector differences	0.086‡	0.114‡	0.067†	0.108‡	0.062‡	0.043†
Gender differences	0.049†	0.059†	0.043*	0.118‡	0.054†	0.037*
Level differences	0.040	–0.016	0.063*	0.131‡	–0.036	0.003
Index value for all non-manuals	0.80	0.85	0.76	0.76	0.45	0.50

Significance: ‡p = 0.001-level; †p = 0.01-level *p = 0.05-level

differences between men and women on how to finance welfare policies became larger from 1992 to 1996.

If we compare the three indices we find that sector, gender and level differences are largest on the Finance index in 1996, and smallest on the Suspicion index. Both these findings could be expected from what was found in the diagrams above. We also find (from the total index values) that support for the welfare state is strongest among non-manuals when it comes to issues of service delivery, it is somewhat weaker on issues of collective financing, and it is at its weakest in issues of suspicion of abuse. On none of the three indexes, however, do we find any signs of weaker middle class support for the welfare state in 1996 compared to before the welfare state crisis.

Conclusion

Coming back to the three scenarios in which the chapter took its departure, what may be said about how middle-class support for the Swedish welfare state has changed in the crisis? The first scenario, about a growing polarisation between workers and non-manuals, hardly received any support from the analysis. Middle-level non-manuals actually became more similar to the workers in their attitudes from 1992 to 1996. Lower-level non-manuals were not very different from workers in 1992 and stayed quite similar. Higher-level non-manuals became more similar to workers on the service issues, but diverged from them in issues about financing.

The latter fact means that the second scenario, on convergence, does not get wholesale support either. While there is clearly convergence between middle-level non-manuals and the workers, evidence is more mixed concerning the higher-level non-manuals. Furthermore, the distance between the small elite group and the workers is clearly widening. The elite group changed their attitudes, contrary to the population at large on all three indices.

This shows that there is clearly some support for the third scenario, on a growing split within the middle class. While support for the welfare state

47

increases considerably among middle-level non-manuals, it decreases in the elite group. Even if this result is very fragile, since the elite group is so small, it is at least indicative of a possible split among the non-manual groups.

Splits along sector and gender lines and between different levels of non-manual employees clearly exist, but with the exception of the elite group there are no unequivocal signs that such splits became wider in the welfare state crisis. Such differences became larger regarding financing issues, but they remained stable regarding service delivery issues and suspicions of abuse. In general, attitudinal differences between various levels of non-manuals seem to be somewhat smaller than sector and gender differences. In particular, among the higher non-manuals, public sector employees and women are considerably more supportive of welfare policies than their private sector and male counterparts.

How could we explain these changes and differences in welfare state support in the middle class? As been emphasised by several authors referred to above, it is clearly the case that the institutionalisation of welfare policies have broadened their support far beyond the confines of the working class. Both lower- and middle-level non-manuals, and public sector employees and women among the higher non-manuals, display considerable support for welfare policies. Among middle-level groups this support has grown stronger in the welfare state crisis. This could probably to a large extent be explained by growing insecurity among middle-level employees. Fear of unemployment and ensuing problems with economic sustenance are in the 1990s no longer confined to workers and lower-level clerical workers. Furthermore, effects from the crisis are clearly visible among family members and in the social networks, even among people who have no fear of unemployment or poverty themselves. Both in their own interest and on behalf of other people, the middle layers have turned towards stronger welfare state support in the welfare crisis.

Among the top-level employees things look different. Many of them have gained considerably during the 1990s in terms of rising incomes and consumption standards (Halleröd 1996). Perhaps the effects of the economic crisis are also less visible in their circle of friends and acquaintances. Judging from the elite debate, as conducted in editorial columns, TV debates or expert judgements, it is also in these elite groups we find greater support for neo-liberal ideas and ideals (Boréus 1994, 1997; Hugemark 1994; Svallfors 1996: ch. 9), while the impact of these ideas in the population at large has been small. The impact of such a neo-liberal turn within the public debate may have had more influence among political decision-makers than among a wider public.

From an electoral point of view, the development in the 1990s nevertheless look highly problematic for politicians looking for possible welfare state retrenchments. As Pierson (1996: 156) points out, the 'broad and deep reservoirs of public support' for the welfare state, extending far into the middle class, constitutes a formidable obstacle to radical welfare state retrenchment. The results from the analysis conducted in this paper clearly supports this. What is suggested by Pierson's (1994) own analyses, furthermore, is that such obstacles

48

may be effective, at least to some extent, even in more residual welfare states than the Swedish one.

It should nevertheless be highly interesting to extend the analysis conducted here to countries in other 'welfare regimes' than the one found in Sweden, to see whether developments in middle-class support for the welfare state differ in countries where public sector employment is smaller and welfare policies are less encompassing than in Sweden. As suggested by Esping-Andersen, 'middle-class welfare states', such as the Swedish one, 'forge middle-class loyalties' (Esping-Andersen 1990: 33). It is by no means clear that middle-class reactions to cutbacks will be the same in other more residual welfare states. Comparative time series at the level of detail presented here are, unfortunately, hard to come by.[8]

In the meantime, observations on middle class resistance against welfare cut-backs over most of Western Europe seem to indicate that the tendencies dis-cussed in this chapter are not only present in the heartland of social democracy. Such resistance will without doubt add to the problems for politicians in power to adjudicate between the exigencies of a global finance economy and public demands for security and employment. Present-day politicians may know a great deal more than Macmillan about who the middle classes are and what they want. It remains to be seen how willing they will be to give it to them.

Notes

1 As reported by Lord Fraser of Kilmorack (Hall and Taylor 1994: note 1).
2 The response rate was 66.3 per cent, 76.0 per cent and 68.7 per cent respectively (details of sampling and non-responses are found in Svallfors 1989: Appendix A; Svallfors 1992: 5, Appendix; Edlund *et al.* 1996). It transpires that the structure of non-responses looks fairly similar in all 3 years, with a slight under-representation of high-income earners and a slight over-representation of people living in Stockholm among non-responses. Age and gender differences are small. The biases therefore seem to be rather constant over the period, with a probable weak 'right-wing' bias in the sample due to the higher response rate among high-income earners.
3 When this question was posed in 1986 and 1992, a small minority preferred several alternatives, in spite of the question format. These combination answers were subsequently given separate codes. In 1996, these combination answers virtually disappeared, due to clearer questionnaire instructions. For every area, two rows of percentage counts are therefore supplied. One where all combination answers are included in the 'Other' category, and one (within parentheses) where every combination answer that contains 'State or local authorities' are included in that category. While the first row probably over-estimates change from 1992 to 1996 somewhat, the second row probably under-estimates it somewhat.
4 In the Socio-economic classification (SEI), lower non-manuals consist of codes 33 and 36, middle non-manuals are code 46, higher non-manuals are code 56 and 'upper-level executives' are code 57 (SCB 1982).
5 The term 'abacus plots', and the idea to use them, has been taken from Hout *et al.* (1996). They have picked the plots from Cleveland (1994), who calls them 'dot plots'.

6 The distinction between vertical and horizontal divisions clearly mirrors Bell's distinction between *status* and *situs*, in his forecast about the post-industrial society (Bell 1976: 376–7).
7 The results reported in Figures 3.4–3.6 and Table 3.5 are virtually identical to those found if the elite group is excluded from the analysis.
8 The best available data in this respect come from the third replication of *The Role of Government*, fielded within *The International Social Survey Program* in 1996. But they are still not as detailed as the data analysed here.

References

Ahrne, Göran and Håkon Leiulfsrud (1984) 'De offentligt anställda och den svenska klasstrukturen' *Häften för kritiska studier*, 17(1), pp 48–66.
Baldwin, Peter (1990) *The Politics of Social Solidarity. Class Bases of the European Welfare State 1875–1975*, Cambridge: Cambridge University Press.
Bell, Daniel (1976) *The Coming of Post-Industrial Society*, 2nd edn, New York: Basic Books.
Blomberg, Helena, Kroll, Christian, Suominen, Sakari and Helenius, Hans (1996) 'Socialklass och attityderna till nedskärningar i välfärdssystemet i Finland' *Sociologisk forskning*, 33(4), pp 57–78.
Boréus, Kristina (1994) *Högervåg. Nyliberalismen och kampen om språket i svensk debatt 1969–1989*, Stockholm: Tiden.
Boréus, Kristina (1997) 'The Shift to the Right: Neo-Liberalism in Argumentation and Language in the Swedish Public Debate since 1969, *European Journal of Political Research*, 31: 257–86.
Cleveland, W. S. (1994) *The Elements of Graphing Data*, Murray Hill, NJ: Hobart Press.
Edlund, Jonas, Sundström, Eva and Svallfors, Stefan (1996) *ISSP96. Role of Government III*. Codebook for Machine-Readable Datafile. Department of Sociology, Umeå University.
Erikson, Robert and Goldthorpe, John H. (1992) *The Constant Flux. A Study of Class Mobility in Industrial Societies*, Oxford: Clarendon Press.
Esping-Andersen, Gøsta (1985) *Politics against Markets: The Social Democratic Road to Power*, Princeton: Princeton University Press.
Esping-Andersen, Gøsta (1990) *The Three Worlds of Welfare Capitalism*, Cambridge: Polity Press.
Goul Andersen, Jørgen (1985) 'Offentligt ansatte i klassestrukturen' in Hoff, Jens (ed) *Stat, Kultur og Subjektivitet*, København: Politiske studier.
Hall, Peter and Taylor, Rosemary C. R. (1994) 'Political Science and the Four New Institutionalisms'. Paper presented at the Annual Meeting of the American Political Science Association, New York, September 1994.
Halleröd, Björn (1996) 'När har Sverige blivit nog ojämlikt? De svenska hushållens ekonomi 1985 och 1992' *Ekonomisk debatt*, 24: 267–79.
Hout, Michael; Manza, Jeff and Brooks, Clem (1996) 'Class Voting and the Politics of Redistribution: Inferences from Seven Political Cultures'. Paper presented at the Annual Meeting of the International Social Survey Program (ISSP), Portoroz, Slovenien, 5–8 May 1996.
Hugemark, Agneta (1994) *Den fängslande marknaden. Ekonomiska experter om välfärdsstaten*, Lund: Arkiv.

King, Desmond S (1987) 'The State and the Social Structures of Welfare in Advanced Industrial Democracies', *Theory and Society*, 16: 841–68.

Korpi, Walter (1980) 'Social Policy and Distributional Conflict in the Capitalist Democracies. A Preliminary Comparative Framework', *West European Politics*, 3: 296–316.

Korpi, Walter (1983) *The Democratic Class Struggle*, London: Routledge and Kegan Paul.

Pierson, Paul (1994) *Dismantling the Welfare State. Reagan, Thatcher and the Politics of Retrenchment*, Cambridge: Cambridge University Press.

Pierson, Paul (1996) 'The New Politics of the Welfare State', *World Politics*, 48: 143–79.

Rothstein, Bo (1995) 'Political Institutions – An Overview', in Robert E. Goodin and Hans-Dieter Klingemann (eds) *A New Handbook of Political Science*, Oxford: Oxford University Press.

SCB (1982) *Socio-ekonomisk indelning (SEI)*. Meddelanden i samordningsfrågor 1982:4. Stockholm: Statistics Sweden.

Stephens, John D. (1996) 'The Scandinavian Welfare States: Achievements, Crisis, and Prospects' in Gøsta Esping-Andersen (ed.) *Welfare States in Transition. National Adaptions in Global Economies*, London: Sage.

Svallfors, Stefan (1989) *Vem älskar välfärdsstaten? Attityder, organiserade intressen och svensk välfärdspolitik*, Lund: Arkiv.

Svallfors, Stefan (1992) *Den stabila välfärdsopinionen. Attityder till svensk välfärdspolitik 1986–92*. (Working paper, Department of Sociology, Umeå University.)

Svallfors, Stefan (1995) 'The End of Class Politics? Structural Cleavages and Attitudes to Swedish Welfare Policies', *Acta Sociologica*, 38: 53–74.

Svallfors, Stefan (1996) *Välfärdsstatens moraliska ekonomi. Välfärdsopinionen i 90-talets Sverige*, Umeå: Boréa.

Svensson, Torsten (1994) *Socialdemokratins dominans. En studie av den svenska socialdemokratins partistrategi*, Uppsala: Acta Universitatis Upsaliensis.

Thelen, Kathleen and Steinmo, Sven (1992) 'Historical Institutionalism in Comparative Perspective', in Sven Steinmo, Kathleen Thelen and Frank Longstreth (eds) *Structuring Politics. Historical Institutionalism in Comparative Analyses*, Cambridge: Cambridge University Press.

Wilensky, Harold (1975) *The Welfare State and Equality*, Berkeley: University of California Press.

Wright, Erik Olin and Cho, Donmoon (1992) 'State Employment, Class Location and Ideological Orientation: A Comparative Analysis of the United States and Sweden', *Politics and Society*, 20: 167–96.

51

4

WHO WANTS TO PRESERVE THE 'SCANDINAVIAN SERVICE STATE'?

Attitudes to welfare services among
citizens and local government
elites in Finland, 1992–6

Helena Blomberg and Christian Kroll

One of the main characteristics of the welfare system in the Scandinavian/
Nordic countries is the important role of the public social and health services
offered to all inhabitants, regardless of income or place of residence. Because of
this fact, these countries have also been named 'service states' as opposed to
'distribution states' in which public social expenditures are mainly used for
social transfers (OECD 1994; Kosonen 1995). Although the aim has been to
guarantee a uniform standard of services for all, the provision[1] of these services
is entrusted to the local governments in all Nordic countries (Anttonen and
Sipilä 1996). After the second world war, this task has resulted in the development of a special type of local government, in which the provision of welfare
services plays a central role; in this welfare state model of local government 'the
value of efficient service delivery, linked with national norms concerning equity
and redistribution, has shaped the growth and functions of local government', a
development which has been influenced by the possibilities and wishes of the
strong central governments in these countries to (re)define the role of local
government from time to time according to the state's wishes (Kangas 1995:
341; Kröger 1997).

The universal welfare services have in many ways contributed to the goals of
the Scandinavian welfare model concerning economic and social equality; as a
result, the use of services has been dependent mainly on need and not on means.
These public services have also furthered a more equal income distribution and
facilitated women's participation in working life (Bryson *et al.* 1994; Anttonen
and Sipilä 1996; Uusitalo 1997). The fact that all citizens, rich and poor, have
access to and also use welfare services offered by the same system, has at the
same time been thought to lead to a widespread wish within the population to

direct resources precisely to these municipal services. Since the municipalities have a far-reaching, independent right to impose tax (mainly concerning personal income), inhabitants in the municipalities have also been assumed to have good means to demand the services they want and to organise the collective financing of these services through the municipality (Alber 1995: 136, 143; Sipilä 1995: 15–16). With reference to similar arguments, it has also been assumed that politicians are reluctant to suggest too far-reaching plans concerning cuts in welfare services, if popular opinion is against such ideas (Pierson 1994).

Previous studies of attitudes towards the welfare services have supported the hypothesis about the high level of popular support in the Nordic countries for this type of service-provision while, at the same time, attitudes have varied more concerning other dimensions of the welfare system (Svallfors 1989; 1995). Many of the more detailed studies of different aspects of welfare policy have concerned one point in time only and often these have not been primarily concerned with (municipal) welfare services (but see also Svallfors 1996). Research into the attitudes of elites and comparisons between their attitudes and the attitudes of the population have been even more scarce. Since politicians and administrators at the municipal level play an important role in the development of welfare services in the Nordic countries, the importance of their attitudes, alongside of the attitudes of the population, has perhaps been underestimated where the future of the 'Scandinavian service state' is concerned.

To pay attention also to the attitudes of these elites is especially interesting today, considering that the public debate since the latter half of the 1980s has been marked by a critique of the Scandinavian welfare model and especially of the public, municipal welfare services (Sipilä 1995; Ervasti 1996; Svallfors 1996), and by ideas and aspirations to decentralise and to lessen the state regulations and control in general (Olsson 1990; Kangas 1995; Sipilä 1995; Albæk et al. 1996). These trends happened to coincide with the economic crisis of the early 1990s, which resulted in an unprecedented need for cuts in the public economy, regardless of ideological considerations.

Even though the situation is in many ways similar in other Nordic countries, and especially in Sweden (Bergmark 1997; Sipilä et al. 1997: 44), Finland makes an interesting example, since many of the earlier mentioned trends of development in the 1990s that could be assumed to be reflected in the attitudes of both the population and the elites have been particularly strong in the Finnish society; far-reaching administrative reforms have been carried through, giving the municipalities (of whom there are about 450) more autonomy at the expense of state control over the organisation of welfare services. Although the formal position of local self-government in the Finnish municipalities has been very strong all the time, state control over the majority of functions was in reality very tight during the time of intensive welfare state construction. At the same time, the state subsidies for these activities were considerable (Niemi-Iilahti 1995); as a result of reforms,[2] for instance in the system of state subsidies in 1993, which for example abolished the system of 'earmarked' grants for different types of services, the means of the central government to steer and control municipal service-provision were at once heavily reduced (Kröger 1995: 79; Albaek *et al.* 1996).[3] At the same time, ideas of 'managerialism' have become popular within the administration of the welfare services which, among other things, has resulted in an increased influence of the administration on the practical management of the services at the expense of the political level (Lehto 1995: 306–7).

In addition to administrative reforms, the effects of the economic depression of the early 1990s – among OECD countries only Finland was hit harder in the 1990s than in the depression of the 1930s – resulted in a previously unknown situation as far as welfare services are concerned and, so far, the recovery of the national economy has not resulted in a stop in cuts in the public sector. The relative share of public welfare services of the total social expenditure has decreased significantly during the 1990s, which means that Finland, according to this measure, has moved in the direction of 'distribution state'. Even though this mainly is due to increased transfers in connection with sharply increased unemployment, various types of cuts in the welfare services have also been made. Different services have been affected differently and conditions vary greatly between municipalities. One factor conducive to this development, beside decreased state control, is the fact that the state increasingly has disclaimed its former economic responsibilities vis-à-vis services through substantial cuts in state subsidies to the municipalities (Albaek *et al.* 1996; Lehto 1997; Uusitalo 1997). At least partly forced to by this development and also by decreased tax revenues because of unemployment, the municipalities utilised their increased right of self-government mainly to make cuts in municipal expenditures (Kröger 1995: 79). This policy has continued despite some signs of an improved economic situation in the municipalities in the middle of the 1990s.[4] Means applied to cut expenditures have been for instance reducing personnel costs, reorganising services, changing the quality of services, and also transferring costs to the clients (Lehto 1995: 307–10), of which especially the last has been said to result in that the principles of universalism and the right to services are losing their meaning (Anttonen and Sipilä 1996: 96). According to some estimates, basic welfare services have despite these measures (still) been prioritised in comparison to other municipal activities (Eronen *et al.* 1995).

How, then, have the attitudes of the population developed in this new situation, in which services are no longer enhanced, but instead cuts are made in these services? Is there a growing resistance against (further) cuts when more and more cuts are implemented, or are a growing number of people instead ready to abandon the system altogether if standards are lowered? Is there a variation in attitudes towards cuts depending on type of service, and if so, why? And to what extent is there concordance between the attitudes of the municipal political and administrative elites and the attitudes of the population and how should possible differences in attitudes between these groups be understood? Is there evidence in support of the assumption that municipal government elites in a service system of the Scandinavian type are sensitive to the wishes of the population regarding the level and financing of services?

In this chapter, the intention is to investigate the development of attitudes towards public services, with special regard to cuts in welfare services, in the period of 1992–6 among representatives of the municipal political and administrative elites, as well as the inhabitants in the Finnish municipalities. The development of these attitudes could be assumed to be of interest also from a broader, more theoretical perspective. Possible changes in attitudes during the 1990s, and the way in which attitudes develop among elites and population in relation to each other, could reveal something about the factors that generally determine attitudes in these groups. Thus, the 'dynamics' of attitude development between (municipal) elites and the population will also be of interest.

The presentation begins with a discussion about different assumptions concerning the impact of an economic crisis on attitudes of the population. After that, the focus will be on theories concerning the relationship between the population and elites that could be of interest for attitude formation and transference of attitudes between these groups. Then, the hypotheses of the study are presented. Following a presentation of material and methods used, results from the empirical analyses are presented and, finally, results and their possible implications are discussed against the background of the theoretical framework.

Reasons for changes in the attitudes of the people

In order to be able to discuss reasons for changes in attitudes, a definition of the concept of attitudes is necessary. By defining an attitude as the view of an individual on a specific phenomenon, a state of things or an object in real life (Allardt 1983: 51; Miegel 1990: 8), it is possible to make a distinction between the concept of attitudes and the concept of values, something which is not always done (Hofstede 1980: 22), but has been common within various scientific disciplines. Values, then, are seen as fewer, more fundamental and constant ideas about what is desirable in principle, and are not connected to any specific phenomena in real life. Although it still can be difficult to make a clear distinction between the concepts of attitudes and values, it is clear that a view can be more or less general and more or less tied to a specific phenomenon or state of things in real life (Allardt 1983: 55; Oftedal 1992). The distinction is important, since it can be assumed that the view on a certain phenomenon in real life – the attitude – arises as a consequence of the ideas of the desirable – the values – internalised by the individual. Thus, attitudes can be seen as expressions of underlying values (Rokeach 1973: 11; Inglehart 1977: 29; Williams 1979: 16). At the same time, the relationship between attitudes and values is asymmetric; attitudes have their origin (partly) in values, while values are not to any noteworthy degree influenced by attitudes. What other factors, besides values, there are that can be assumed to influence attitudes, is often left undealt with, sometimes the impact of emotional and cognitive factors is mentioned (Suhonen 1988). In the research related to welfare policy it has been common, in addition to stressing value-related factors, to interpret attitudes towards the welfare system as expressions of the aspiration of individuals and groups to maximise their (usually objectively defined) self-interests (Knutsen 1988; Pöntinen and Uusitalo 1988; Martinussen 1993). While this latter interpretation is based on rational choice-theory (Hollis 1989; Blomberg et al. 1996), the assumptions about the impact of values on attitudes are based on socialisation theory (Blomberg and Kroll 1995). Despite their very different points of departure, it seems fruitful to let the two approaches complement each other as explanations of the formation of attitudes; it seems realistic to assume that the individual, when taking up a position on a certain issue in real life, takes into consideration his/her values (one of which might be that every-one should first and foremost further his own interests), as well as his/her self-interests (Sears et al. 1979: 371; Hadenius 1986; Kangas 1997). This approach (combining the two above approaches), used below, could help explain why a majority of the population might support benefits they do not personally need, or why some groups might not approve of benefits that should be in their (objective) self-interest.

Both theories that emphasise the influence of values on attitudes and theories based on assumptions about the impact of self-interest on attitude formation presume that attitudes may change over time. When you look at theories explaining attitudinal change, it is possible to discern theories which stress the effects on attitudes of slow and gradual changes in the structure of industrial-ised societies (because of effects on both values and on self-interests) on the one hand and theories that emphasise the effects on attitudes of more sudden and temporary changes in the economy on the other. This, of course, does not mean that the two kinds of factors could not interact, but since it could prove difficult to predict the effects of such interaction, there seem to be reasons for keeping the two perspectives apart – something which is not always done. When changes in attitudes are studied over a shorter period of time, however, it should be possible to make such a distinction, since the kinds of changes in attitudes that are due to changes in the values of (parts of) the population (among other things) could be assumed to be relatively stable over such a period, despite economic fluctuations.

Sihvo and Uusitalo (1995: 252–3) discuss different theoretical approaches that stress the impact of an economic crisis on the attitudes of the population towards the welfare system. One approach stresses the consequences of the people's perception of economic decline; if a person feels that his/her personal economic situation is being threatened (directly or through increased taxation) this is thought to affect negatively his/her willingness to take the common good into consideration through contributing to the financing of the welfare system. In the light of the discussion about the impact of values and self-interests on attitudes, this would imply that economically hard times should result in considerations based on self-interest becoming more important than value-based considerations. Testing this assumption would require data from economically prosperous as well as less prosperous times.

A second theoretical approach is concerned with the impact on the attitudes of the population of influential groups such as politicians, political parties and other organisations, mass media, etc. and their interpretation of the state of the economy and their views on the interplay between social policy and economy. Here, it is assumed that those within these groups that point at growing social expenditures and stress the importance of making cuts, activate themselves to try to convince others of their view on the situation, which is assumed to have an influence on public opinion. This perspective is further discussed in Chapter 5, which deals with the question of the relationship between the population and the elites in general.

A third approach deals with the impact on attitudes of actual changes in the welfare system. Here, considerations of self-interests are taken to be the major reason for changes in attitudes. Sihvo and Uusitalo (1995) assume that the synchronous effects of more people using the system and a lowering of the level of social security that can be the result of an economic crisis, might lead to changes in attitudes towards the system. Since studies have shown that different parts of the welfare system enjoy different levels of support – universal benefits and services enjoy a higher level of support than those which are aimed at marginal groups (especially if the situation of the people in these groups can be considered to be self-caused) (Coughlin 1979; Taylor-Gooby 1985, 1988; Papadakis 1992: 31) – one could assume that different services would be affected differently by such a change in attitudes. Other assumptions not unlike this last one have been presented with special regard to welfare services. Cuts in services are thought to result in a 'vicious circle of cutback policies': the lowered standard of public services results in growing dissatisfaction, which in turn leads to more positive attitudes towards alternative service-providers and a growing pressure to privatise, which results in further lowering of the standard of public services and, thus, to even greater dissatisfaction and negative attitudes towards the public services. Especially people well off that have the means to use private services have been assumed to react in this way, while groups dependent on public services do not regard the lowered standard of services as an incentive to change their attitudes (Johanson and Mattila 1994).

This last type of assumption does also have some similarities with the scenarios that have been presented by Sihvo (1994) about cuts in public social services, based on Hirschman's (1970) theory of the population's reactions to changes in systems to which they belong and on which they depend. Expected reactions to changes are: 'exit', i.e. to stop utilising the services and turn to alternative service-providers, 'voice', i.e. to show dissatisfaction with the changes in the services either through protesting, voting or in opinion polls, etc. and, finally, 'loyalty', i.e. to accept the new situation and remain loyal to the public service system. Since there has been little research so far on possible changes in the utilisation of public social services, it is difficult to make statements about the relationship between attitudes and the consumption of services.

The relationship between the attitudes of the people and the attitudes of elites

Attitudes held by political and administrative elites are usually of interest because it is thought that comparing them with the attitudes of the people can reveal to what extent elites will act in accordance with the people's wishes. In other words, the assumption is, that it is possible to say something about the future actions of decision-makers, and even about the future political development, on the basis of their attitudes. However, since the relationship between attitudes and non-verbal actions is a complex one (Oftedal 1992), it is difficult to tell to what extent the attitudes of elites, as they come out in attitude surveys, will correspond to their behaviour in the decision-making process. Despite this reservation, a comparison between the attitudes of the population and the elites can be thought to shed some light on the relationship between these groups when it comes to attitude formation and the transference of attitudes.

Different theoretical approaches concerning the relationship between the people, political elites and administrative elites have been presented, which imply different consequences concerning the development of attitudes over time in the three groups. The above assumption, that the people – in a system with welfare services provided by the municipalities – have good possibilities to influence the level of the services through the democratic process, seems to correspond with the classical doctrine of democracy, based on the assumption of popular sovereignty; politicians make decisions according to the popular will and these decisions are then carried out by the administration. This implies that politicians and administrators are thought to be altruistic in the sense of only seeking the common good and that they are not influenced by personal interests that might arise out of their capacity as politicians. This idea of a passive and unselfish role attributed to the two elite groups has been criticised by public choice theory (Downs 1957; Niskanen 1971; Lewin 1988; Udehn 1996). That line of thought, based on economic theory, assumes that the relationship between the involved groups is instead characterised by the aspiration of everyone to promote their respective self-interests. On the political market, politicians try to maximise the number of votes given to them, administrators act to maximise their power and influence, and the voters to maximise their (economical) well-being. In public choice theory, the relationship between the different actors on the political market is usually assumed to be asymmetric; for instance, politicians are thought to be able to manipulate the voters, through creating 'political business cycles' or through providing information or misinformation furthering their goals. Thus, in contrast to the classical doctrine of democracy where attitudes are thought to be transferred 'from the bottom upwards', in public choice the assumption seems to be rather the opposite, although opinions vary on this point. Some theorists within public choice, dealing with the self-interests of administrators, presume that these are able to manipulate the politicians into acting according to the administrators' self-interests (mainly in maximising their budgets) and the public choice-approach has been criticised for not offering any comprehensive view on the relationship between all three groups, that is the population, political elites and administrative elites (Udehn 1996).

Both the above approaches can be assumed to be rather simplified and one-sided regarding the factors thought to determine actions and attitudes, as well as concerning the direction of attitude transference, and there are theories other than public choice that might lead us to conclude that the attitude transference goes mainly 'from the top down'. For example, Svallfors (1989), Papadakis and Bean (1993) and Sihvo and Uusitalo (1995) have discussed the question of how societal institutions, such as political parties, pressure groups, labour market organisations, the mass media, etc. influence the population's attitudes. Here, it is thought that attitudes are influenced both through changing people's interests and values. For example, political parties and their representatives have been thought to try either to change or strengthen the population's apprehension of what its self-interests are. Also, individuals who identify themselves with a party are thought to become socialised to the values advocated by the party (Pöntinen and Uusitalo 1988). If one presumes that members of elites should be seen first and foremost as representatives of political parties and/or other institutions, as the assumptions mentioned might imply, their attitudes could be expected primarily to reflect the values of the respective institutions.

What is said above shows that assumptions concerning the direction of attitude transference imply that elites see their roles in relation to the population and to each other in a certain way (Lewin 1988: 99–125). Some studies about elites (Niiranen 1995; Jacobsen 1996) have focused on these roles that elites have internalised, that is, how they in practice see their role in the democratic process. Depending on how the elites perceive their role, different factors achieve varying importance for their attitudes towards any given issue which, in turn, could further help to explain why differences in attitudes can exist between elites, and between elites and the population.

What then, are possible roles perceived by elites that could influence their attitudes towards certain issues, such as public welfare services? Concerning the administrative elite at the municipal level, Jacobsen (1996: 47) names some thinkable ideal roles, the first one, consistent with the classical doctrine of democracy, being the role as a loyal implementer of democratic decisions made by the politicians. A second possible role is the one of the autonomous administrator, characterised by scepticism towards both political decisions and

59

popular will. This role could originate, on the one hand, in the type of factors suggested by public choice – the wish for more personal power and influence – or, on the other hand, in the professional code and notions of expert knowledge, that is, in professional values. In addition to these, there is a third role, 'the citizens' advocate', which implies that leading administrators through direct contact with the 'consumers' of the services administered first and foremost seek to fulfil the wishes of the population, even in cases where these wishes are in conflict with political decisions or (other) professional values.

What is particularly interesting about these roles, is that they are assumed to vary *within* one administrative elite, depending on external factors, such as the size of the social entity administered. The smaller the entity, the more likely it is for the elite to have contact with the 'consumers' and thus to be sensitive to their wishes. Another factor that could influence the perceived role is the administrator's time of service within the organisation; here, the assumption is that administrators adopt existing political values as time goes by. This process of socialisation is thought to go both ways; administrators become more 'politicised' and politicians become more 'bureaucratised' (Peters 1987; Jacobsen 1996: 48–52). The assumption that varying roles could exist within one elite could probably also be extended to political elites.

Concerning roles within political elites, there has – in addition to problems in connection with determining the will of the people through the democratic process – elsewhere been a discussion about whom the elected political elite, given that they see as their basic role to represent (the will of) the voters, feel that they primarily represent: their own supporters or the entire population? On the other hand, as touched upon above, the political elite, too, has by some been assumed to try to influence or manipulate the public rather than to be guided by public opinion, either in the pursue of personal power, or for the purpose of furthering the values of one's party (see Forma 1996 for a further discussion).

Research on organisations, in turn, has emphasised the importance of the working environment for the attitudes of elites. At the municipal level this could mean that elites to a large extent would be influenced by existing directives, regulations, available (financial) resources and also by prevailing norms and strategies within the organisation (Argyris and Schön 1978). Although the people, too, probably have been forced to consider what is economically feasible and effective, such questions can be assumed to be of greater importance for the elites (Niiranen 1991).

The above discussion shows that there is a large variety of factors that might influence the attitude transference between (municipal) elites and the population. Some earlier Finnish research about municipal elites seem to confirm the assumption that different elites consider different aspects; administrators more often emphasize the municipal organisation, while the leading politicians more often refer to the attitudes of the population (Oulasvirta 1992).

Hypotheses

Our intention is to analyse the development of the attitudes of the population and of the municipal political and administrative elites in Finland towards economy measures and cuts in municipal services, with the main focus on welfare (social and health) services, over the period 1992–6. First, the changes in the attitudes of the population will be analysed with regard to the scenarios (section 2) concerning changes in attitudes due to the lowered standard of services. Second, the relationship between the population and the elites will be examined in the light of what was assumed (section 3) concerning the formation of attitudes and the transference of attitudes.

To begin with, attitudes towards what could be called the 'general municipal service strategy' are analysed. Attitudes regarding this more general issue are measured by the statements 'Municipal services should henceforth be increased rather than reduced' and 'If necessary, it is better to raise municipal taxes than to reduce services'.[5] After that, we examine attitudes concerning the acceptability of some types of economy measures regarding services, in the case that the economy of one's own municipality has to be strengthened in the future, namely whether one approves of reductions in service provision and in the number of service-providing personnel respectively.[6] It should be noted that the above statements/questions are about municipal services in general, not about welfare services only.[7,8] Also included are some questions concerning the attitudes towards cuts in a number of separate municipal services on condition that the municipalities have to reduce their spending.[9] Here, the attitudes towards cuts in 'core' welfare services will be of special interest, and attitudes towards cuts in day care, services provided by the health-care centres, care for older people and means-tested social assistance (which is regarded as part of the welfare services) will be analysed in more detail.

Where changes in the attitudes of the population are concerned, it might be assumed that if all the cuts in expenditures and consequently in services that have been made in the 1990s would result in an increasing proportion of the population wanting to 'exit' the present system, i.e. due to a growing dissatisfaction with what the system offers, the acceptance of (further) cuts should have increased among the population over the time period. This desire to 'exit' the service system could be assumed to be extended to most kinds of municipal services and, thus, a growing proportion of the population could be expected to oppose ideas of increased services. The trend could be expected to be even stronger when a raise in taxes in order to preserve the present services is concerned. The same might be expected also concerning the named types of economy measures regarding services. If the cuts and reductions of services have *not* resulted in an increased 'exit', the development of attitudes should be the opposite, especially if services are perceived as having deteriorated. In other words, a growing proportion of the population could be expected to use its 'voice' by opposing further cuts and economy measures regarding services.

Even though our data on attitudes do not extend to the time before the economic crisis, it is reasonable to expect that if the assumption is true (section 2) then the willingness to take the common good into consideration through contributing to the financing of the welfare system is negatively affected by a feeling that one's personal economic situation is being threatened (directly or through increased taxation). This willingness should have decreased during the 1990s, since the economic situation of citizens on average probably has not changed for the better in any considerable way. If the 1990s are thus charac- terised by a growing emphasis on self-interests, this should, as far as services are concerned, result in the population opposing cuts in health-care services the most from the beginning of the studied period – since more people use these services than the other services included – and the proportion of the population that resists cuts precisely in these services should furthermore have been growing throughout the 1990s.

Below, we consider the possible relationship between the population and the political and administrative elites. If there are any noteworthy differences between the attitudes of the population and of the elite(s) it seems reasonable to believe, on the basis of what was said above about the sudden crisis in the (public) economy, that the attitudes of the elites are more permissive of cuts and reductions on all questions. If the attitudes of the elites, despite this, are affected by the attitudes of the population, the elites' attitudes should have developed in the same direction as the population's concerning all questions but also have come nearer the population's attitudes over time, as the population's attitudes have become known to the elites. Depending on how the two elites perceive their roles, the attitudes of the administrators could be expected to be either closer to ('The citizens' advocate') or further from ('The autonomous administrator') the population's attitudes than the attitudes of the political elite. On the other hand, if the assumption that it is the elites that influence the attitudes of the population is true, we could expect that the attitudes of the population have changed more and moved in the direction of the attitudes of the elites.

Target groups, data and methods

The analyses below are based on data from two annual (1992–6) surveys by Finnish Gallup done for the Development Fund of the Finnish Municipalities; one of the sets of data, which include various questions on municipalities and their activities, represents inhabitants aged 15 years and above in all Finnish municipalities (excluding the self-governed province of Åland), and was gathered through c. 1000 annual interviews conducted in the respondents' homes. The other set of data is based on anonymous questionnaires mailed annually to chairs of the executive boards and the chief executive officers of all Finnish municipalities (excluding Åland).

Finnish local government consists of the Municipal council, elected by the citizens for a period of 4 years, which is the highest political decision-making body, deciding in all matters of greater importance (budget, appointments, planning). The council appoints the members of the executive board on political basis (often from among themselves). The board prepares and executes the decisions of the council, and decides autonomously on a great number of matters (Modeen 1995: 287; Niemi-Iilahti 1995: 276). The council also appoints – officially on the basis of meritocratic principles – the chief executive officer, that is, the leading municipal administrator. Until 1995, the executive officers, who in practice usually are political appointees, were always elected for lifelong service and could not easily be removed (Modeen 1995). The chief executive officers constitute a very homogeneous group, education- and genderwise; nearly 80 per cent have an academic degree in political sciences (about half of them even from the same university) and only 2 per cent of the executive officers are women (Pikkala 1997). Since the same political party, the non-socialist Center Party of Finland (formerly Agrarians), is the leading party in 273 out of 455 (1992–6) Finnish municipalities – of which a majority are rural and have a small population (Niemi-Iilahti 1995: 278) – a large number of executive officers should in practice enjoy the confidence of this party. The chief executive officers have a central and – in comparison with, for example, Sweden or Denmark – a very independent role in preparing and presenting matters to the executive board and in administering municipal personnel and economy (Modeen 1995; Pikkala 1997). According to Modeen (1995: 287) an ambitious chief executive officer is able to conduct governmental affairs according to his/her wishes, and political decisions only rarely differ from the propositions made by the chief executive officer.

Turning to a closer description of the empirical data, the number of respondents in the data representing the population has been about 1000 a year ($n =$ 960 in 1996, $n = 1024$ in 1995, $n = 1010$ in 1994, $n = 989$ in 1993 and $n = 1029$ in 1992). Data were gathered through a stratified multi-step sample (a new one for every year) with regard to age, gender, type of municipality and province. About 10 per cent of the interviewees were afterwards contacted by telephone and background data and answers on some items were double-checked. Drop-out analyses with reference to gender, age and education indicate no signs of systematic distortions in the data. Concerning the data on elites, the response rate has varied somewhat over the years; in 1996, 246 chairs of the executive boards returned the sent out questionnaires. The number was 247 in 1995, 264 in 1994, 253 in 1993 and 228 in 1992, resulting in a response rate of c. 60 per cent, except for 1992 (c. 50 per cent).[10] The corresponding figures for the chief executive officers were 334 in 1996, 341 in 1995, 361 in 1994, 413 in 1993 and 309 in 1992 (response rate c. 80–90 per cent except in 1992 when it was 69 per cent). In other words, drop-out rates in these data could be considered low with regard to the administrators, while it is considerably higher in the case of politicians. Separate analyses, however, do not point at any systematic distortions with reference to size of municipality or province.

In presenting the results we first display the distribution in percentages of the attitudes of the population on various questions over the time period of 1992–6. When attitudes towards cuts in different types of welfare services are presented, the existence of possible statistically significant differences in the support for these services at the beginning and the end of the time period respectively are tested using McNemar's test. Here, answers are recorded into dichotomous variables ('against cuts' and 'in favour of cuts', while those who answered 'I do not know' are excluded).[11] When results concerning elites are presented, we again first display the distributions in percentages of the attitudes of the respective elite between 1992 and 1996. Whether there are significant differences between the attitudes of the two elite-groups is tested using the chi-square test. Finally, differences in attitudes between the population and the elites over the period of 1992–6 are displayed in a number of figures.

The development of the attitudes of the population

To begin with, we study whether the changes in the attitudes of the population indicate an increasing will to 'exit' the present service system, or whether there instead is an increasing 'voice' of protest against (further) cuts over the time period studied and, also, whether there are signs of increased selfishness within the population as a whole and/or in some groups concerning the support for different welfare services.

In Table 4.1, we first study the attitudes concerning more general questions on 'service-strategy' (whether one would prefer services to be increased rather than reduced, and whether one would prefer raised taxes to reduced services). Second, attitudes towards two questions on service-related economy measures of improving municipal finances (whether one accepts reductions in service-provision and in the number of service-providing personnel respectively, in order to improve the economy of one's own municipality) are displayed. Third, Table 4.1 also shows the distribution of attitudes on some more specific questions about cuts in various types of municipal services.

The results in Table 4.1 show that the proportion of respondents that protest (raise their 'voice') against cuts and reductions in services and expenses seems to vary according both to the level of abstraction – for instance, the proportion of respondents who accept cuts or reductions is larger when the question is about 'services' in general than when specific welfare services are mentioned – and to the 'framing' of the question (if cuts or reductions in the service-state are explicitly tied to the question of municipal economy or not) (Kangas 1997). Furthermore, results point at a clear trend concerning the changes in attitudes over time. The proportion of respondents that resist reductions in services in general, in service-providing personnel and cuts in specific, named services has as a rule increased over time. Likewise, attitudes on the question of whether services should be increased rather than reduced have changed significantly; the proportion of respondents that would prefer services to be increased has grown

Table 4.1 Attitudes of the population towards cuts and reductions in public services. Proportion (%) of respondents

	1992	1993	1994	1995	1996
Agreeing with the following 'service strategies':					
Prefer services to be increased rather than reduced***	41	42	48	56	61
Prefer raised taxes instead of reduced services**	51	55	53	59	55
Not accepting the following measures in order to improve the economy of one's own municipality:					
Reductions in service-provision***	34	37	42	45	—
Reductions in the number of service-providing personnel***	52	59	61	60	—
Resisting cuts in:					
Child day care**	76	75	75	78	81
Health care***	60	68	72	74	76
Elderly care	85	85	85	87	84
Social assistance***	41	48	46	44	52
Education***	67	72	77	81	77
Public transport	55	59	59	61	60
Library services***	35	37	37	47	41
Sports and recreation services***	22	22	27	35	35
Cultural services*	22	18	19	23	23
n =	1029	989	1010	1024	960

Asterisks indicate that the change in attitudes on the responding question is statistically significant (Chi-square test): *** = $p < 0.001$, ** = $p < 0.01$, * = $p < 0.05$

over time. Attitudes towards raised municipal taxes to guarantee the present level of services, on the other hand, do not follow an equally clear trend.[12]

Moreover, people seem to be much more ready to accept cuts in non-welfare-related services than in health and social services. This fact is not very surprising, either from the point of view of self-interests or from a viewpoint stressing the importance of values. On the one hand, everyone needs care at some point in life, while the need of public activities in the areas of sports or culture seldom is as fundamental or acute. On the other hand, it might also be assumed that people regard cuts in welfare-related services – which would affect vulnerable groups, the sick, the old, families with children – as less acceptable than cuts in non-welfare-related services (Papadakis 1992: 259; Sihvo and Uusitalo 1995). Furthermore, it should be noted that the resistance against cuts also varies between different welfare services, especially at the beginning of the 1990s. The resistance against cuts has been lowest over the whole time period concerning the most 'universal' benefit, health-care services, in comparison to both elderly care (McNemar's test, probability 0.001 in 1992, 1996) and day care (McNemar's test, probability 0.001 in 1992, 1996).

The growing resistance against cuts within the population as a whole does not exclude the possibility of changed relationships between the attitudes of different groups (for example age- or income groups) within the population. Both self-interest and value-related factors could be assumed to have resulted in a growing resistance in some groups, while the opposite trend might be found in some other groups. On the basis of the distribution in percentages of the attitudes of different groups towards cuts in welfare services (see Appendix 4.1), the trend between 1992 and 1996 seems to be that, as a rule, all groups included have become less sympathetic to cuts in welfare services.[13] However, this trend does not hold good for the attitudes towards means-tested social assistance, where the attitudes of respondents with a university education and older respondents (50 years of age and above) have not changed over time.

A comparison between the attitudes of the population and of the elites

Below, the focus will be on the attitudes of the municipal political and administrative elites and the relationship between them and the attitudes of the population. How alike are the attitudes of these groups? How have they changed over time? First, the annual distributions in percentages of the attitudes of the two elite-groups are displayed.

On the basis of Table 4.2, we can conclude that both elites are critical of raising municipal taxes in order to preserve the existing level of services and, even more, of the idea of increasing services. What is interesting to note is that the two elite groups show a very similar attitude-pattern when it comes to these 'service-strategy' questions, although there are some differences between the groups on the question about increasing services, concerning which the political elite has become somewhat more sympathetic to the idea of increased services. Furthermore, both elites seem to accept a reduction of services as well as reductions in service-providing personnel in order to improve municipal finances.

With regard to the latter question, the attitudes of the two groups have diverged over time; chairs of the executive boards have become more critical of reductions in service-providing personnel, while this is not the case concerning the chief executive officers. When it comes to the more detailed questions about cuts in various named municipal services, a large proportion of both elites are ready to accept cuts in all mentioned services, but the willingness is greatest concerning non-welfare-related services. Further, the differences in attitudes between the two elites are smallest at the end of the period studied, that is, in 1996, when there are statistically highly significant differences between the two groups only concerning cuts in elderly care.[14]

Turning to the relationship between the attitudes of the population and of the elite groups, Figures 4.1–4.8 highlight a number of interesting results. In the figures, the attitudes of the population have been set as the point of reference and thus been given the value of zero (0), against which the attitudes

Table 4.2 Attitudes of the administrative and political elites towards cuts and reductions in public services.
Proportion (%) of the chief executive officers (administrators) and the chairs of the executive boards (politicians)

	1992 Adm/Pol	1993 Adm/Pol	1994 Adm/Pol	1995 Adm/Pol	1996 Adm/Pol
Agreeing with the following 'service strategies':					
Prefer services to be increased rather than reduced	5/6	4/5	6/10	7/15***	10/16*
Prefer raised taxes instead of reduced services	26/22	37/35	29/31	28/31	28/30
Not accepting the following measures in order to improve the economy of one's own municipality:					
reductions in service-provision	1/3	2/1	3/4	4/7	—
reductions in the number of service-providing personnel	15/22*	19/29**	16/31***	17/30***	—
Resisting cuts in:					
Child day care	8/22***	10/17*	20/32***	27/29	37/41
Health care	11/24***	18/29**	30/45***	28/40**	42/53*
Elderly care	27/47***	33/52***	40/64***	44/59***	53/71***
Social assistance	20/17	29/25	30/23	27/18**	28/23
Education	3/14***	9/21***	23/40***	22/33**	36/41
Public transport	32/42*	31/36	26/39***	37/42	39/45
Library services	7/9	9/11	16/15	26/20	32/22*
Sports and recreation services	2/4	2/5	5/6	11/12	17/14
Cultural services	6/9	5/7	9/6	13/9	17/12
n =	295/214	388/234	350/251	322/242	318/228

Asterisks indicate that the attitude differences between chief executive officers and the chairs of the executive boards is statistically significant (Chi-square test): *** = p <0.001, ** = p <0.01, * = p <0.05.

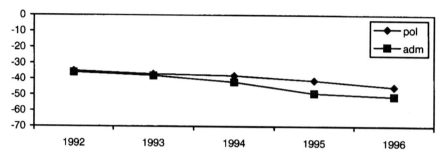

Figure 4.1 The difference (in percentages) between the proportion of the population, the chairs of the executive boards and the chief executive officers respectively, in favour of the claim that municipal services should in the future be increased rather than reduced.

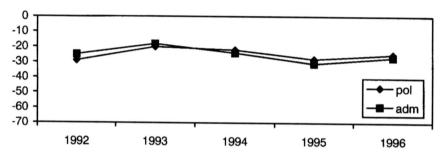

Figure 4.2 The difference (in percentages) between the proportion of the population, the chairs of the executive boards and the chief executive officers respectively, in favour of raised taxes instead of reduced services.

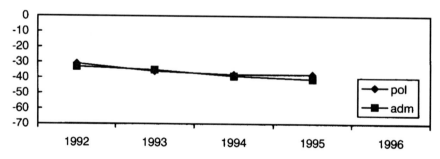

Figure 4.3 The difference (in percentages) between the proportion of the population, the chairs of the executive boards and the chief executive officers respectively, not accepting a reduction of services in order to improve the economy of the municipality.

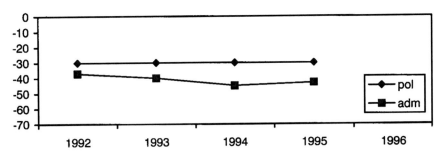

Figure 4.4 The difference (in percentages) between the proportion of the population, the chairs of the executive boards and the chief executive officers respectively, not accepting reductions in the number of service-providing personnel in order to improve the economy of the municipality.

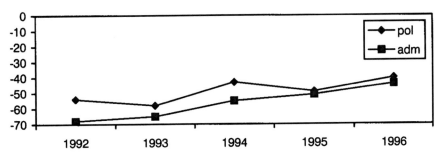

Figure 4.5 The difference (in percentages) between the proportion of the population, the chairs of the executive boards and the chief executive officers respectively, not accepting cuts in day-care services.

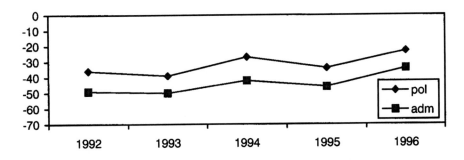

Figure 4.6 The difference (in percentages) between the proportion of the population, the chairs of the executive boards and the chief executive officers respectively, not accepting cuts in health care.

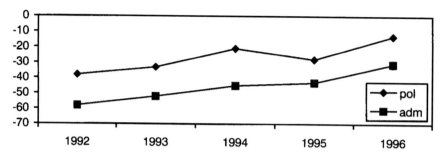

Figure 4.7 The difference (in percentages) between the proportion of the population, the chairs of the executive boards and the chief executive officers respectively, not accepting cuts in elderly care.

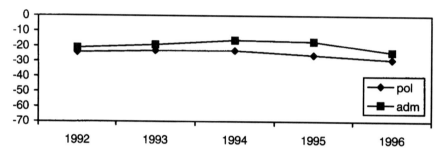

Figure 4.8 The difference (in percentages) between the proportion of the population, the chairs of the executive boards and the chief executive officers respectively, not accepting cuts in means-tested social assistance.

of the two elite groups are then compared. A negative value for an elite indicates that the proportion of this elite *resisting* cuts is *smaller* than the respective proportion within the population.

Figures 4.1 and 4.2 show that with regard to the questions about 'service-strategy', there is a big difference between the attitudes of the population and of the elites. Where the majority of the population prefers a raise in municipal taxes to reductions in services and is inclined to think that services should be increased rather than reduced, only a small minority of the elites share this view. Moreover, there are no signs of a convergence of the attitudes of the population and the elites over time.

Results concerning the questions about the service-related measures of improving municipal finances show a similar pattern; the differences in attitudes between the elite groups and the population are significant, the elites accepting reductions in services and in service-providing personnel to a much larger extent than does the population and the differences have remained relatively unchanged over time (Figures 4.3 and 4.4).

Finally, Figures 4.5-4.8, show the differences in attitudes when it comes to the questions directly related to cuts in different welfare services.[15] As can be

70

seen, the elite groups are much more inclined to accept cuts in the mentioned welfare services than the population is. Despite the remaining differences, the gap between the population's and the elites' attitudes still has become smaller over the time period. The differences are greatest concerning day care and smallest concerning elderly care. Also, with regard to the question on means-tested social assistance, it is the elite groups who are more inclined to accept cuts, but in contrast to the questions about welfare services, the differences in attitudes between elites and population have here remained relatively un-changed over time.

What could explain the differences in attitudes?

As the previous chapter showed, the differences in attitudes between the elite groups and the population remain substantial over the first half of the 1990s. In other words, it does not seem as if the municipal elites to any decisive extent are influenced by the attitudes of the population, nor as if the attitudes of the elites are of any vital importance when it comes the the formation of the population's attitudes. The attitudes of the two elite groups, however, seem to be very simi-lar. How should this be understood? One explanation could perhaps be found in the roles of politicians and administrators discussed above, which can be assumed to affect their notions of the economic situation of the municipality and/or their values; this fact, in turn, would then result in dissentient attitudes between the elites and the population concerning our questions. In addition, it could be assumed that the factors connected with the attitudes of the elites are different from those that underlie the attitudes of the population.

The data at hand offer the possibility to test towards the end of the period studied, the covariance between some very general notions and the question of the readiness to accept cuts in various municipal services in a situation where the municipalities have to reduce their expenses.[16] Despite the limitations set by the fact that the data is from one point in time only, it can be assumed that the type of factors dealt with give an intimation of what kind of questions that are important regarding attitudes towards cuts in services in the different groups. First, we will investigate, whether it seems to be the same kind of factors that influence the attitudes of the two elite groups. A corresponding analysis will then be made concerning the population.

Considering what has been said above about the economic state of the Finnish municipalities as well as about the predominant ideological climate, one thinkable explanation of the fact that such a large proportion of the elite groups accept cuts in the municipal social and health services could be that the elites perceive the economic state of the municipalities as gloomier than does the population (see p. 54; also see note 4) and that the majority of the elites because of this fact consider that cuts are necessary, regardless of other consider-ations. At the same time, this type of question could be assumed to be of relatively greater importance for the attitude of the elites than for the attitude of the population. On the other hand, differences in attitude may be dependent on differing ideological/political values between the elites and the population concerning the municipalities' responsibility for the welfare of the citizens. In that case, it would be the normative ideas that 'underlie' the attitudes concerning cuts in specific services that differ between the elites and the population. Thus, the fact that the majority of the elites accept cuts could be seen to indicate that they think the principles of the service system should be altered.

An additional explanation of our results could, in principle, be found in differing personal self-interests in services between elites and the majority of the population (Forma 1997: 23–6). For instance, the elites (with a higher socio-economic position) could be less dependent on municipal welfare services than the population on average. On the basis of the results regarding differences between groups within the population (see Appendix 4.1), the groups with a higher socio-economic position (those with high incomes, the highly educated) do not differ considerably from other groups as far as attitudes towards cuts in services are concerned. Thus, it seems unlikely that the higher socio-economic position *per se* would be an important explanatory factor regarding the major difference in attitudes between the population and the elites.

Below, the possible connections between the attitudes of elites towards cuts in welfare services (including means-tested social assistance) and indicators of the 'perceived state of the municipal economy' as well as the 'principles of the service state' are analysed. The explanatory variable of 'perceived state of municipal economy' is measured by the statement, *'Economy measures in municipal services and administration are no longer necessary, since the necessary measures have been carried through and the worst economic strait is over'*, and the explanatory variable 'principles of the service state' is measured by the statement, *'Citizens have a right to free or almost free basic services provided by the municipality regardless of what it costs to provide them'*, a statement that could be regarded as representing one of the principles of the present system.[17,18]

According to the assumption of the importance of the 'perceived state of municipal economy', those respondents who think that economy measures are still required and that the economic strait in the municipalities is not over should more often than other respondents accept cuts in *all* the named social and health services. If the assumption concerning the importance of the 'principles of the service state'[19] variable is correct, respondents who do not agree with the principle of the right to basic municipal services for all regardless of costs should more often than other respondents accept cuts in *all* the named services.

The connections between the attitudes towards cuts in certain welfare services and some explanatory variables are tested by using multivariate logistic regression models. By studying various explanatory variables simultaneously in these models, the aim is to discern the 'independent' explanatory power of each variable. If the connection between the explanatory and the dependent variable is statistically significant (the limit is set at $P < 0.05$), the odds (and 95 per cent confidence intervals) for the different classes of the explanatory variable are calculated. The odds show the probability of the respective class of the explanatory variable to be opposed to cuts in the named welfare services in relation to the class of reference (odds = 1.00). In the logistic models we have included, in addition to the two explanatory variables mentioned above, the 'structural' variables of 'size of municipality'[20] and 'province', which were also included in the questionnaire. Each dependent attitude variable is made dichotomous; respondents who have answered that expenditures can be cut 'a lot' or 'somewhat' constitute one group, while those who think that expenditures can not be cut at all constitute the other. The proportion of respondents who had no opinion concerning these questions was small (c. 1–5 per cent depending on the service and elite-group in question) and has, due to both theoretical and practical reasons, been excluded in the analyses.

However, to begin with the distribution in percentages of the answers of the elites and of the population concerning the explanatory variables measuring the 'perceived state of municipal economy' and the 'principles of the service state' are displayed in Table 4.3. Results show that a large majority of the two elite groups do not think that the economic strait in the municipalities is over, nor that citizens have a right to basic services regardless of what it costs to provide them. As with many of the questions discussed above, the distribution of answers in the two elites is very similar.

The results from the above-mentioned logistic models are presented in Table 4.4. Now, the picture of the very similar attitudes of the elites is somewhat altered. First, the view on the economic situation of the municipalities does not have the same effect within the administrative elite as it has within the political elite. In other words, politicians who think that the economic strait is over show higher odds for resisting cuts in the different welfare services than those who believe that the economic strait is not over, while different views on the economic situation of the municipalities are not generally important for the administrators' attitudes towards cuts in the welfare services. This fact is especially clear concerning cuts in day-care services. Second, the view on the question about the right to basic services regardless of costs is also of importance

Table 4.3 The respective proportion of the elite-groups and the population (in percentages, 1995) who think that the economic strait in the municipalities is not over and that citizens do not have a right to basic services, regardless of costs to provide them

	Administrative elite	Political elite	Population
Economic strait in municipalities not over	82	81	50
Citizens do not have a right to basic services regardless of costs	83	82	39
n =	322	242	1024

Table 4.4 Connections between the 'perceived state of municipal economy', the 'principles of the service state', size of municipality, county and the attitudes of the administrative and political elites respectively towards cuts in welfare services. Logistic regression analysis. The odds show the probability of the respective group to be opposed to cuts in the named welfare services in relation to the group of reference (odds = 1.00)

	Child day care		Elderly care		Health care		Social assistance	
	Adm.	Pol.	Adm.	Pol.	Adm.	Pol.	Adm.	Pol.
Economic strait is ...	0.6598	0.0000	0.8249	0.0235	0.0202	0.0586	0.1229	0.3357
over		1.00		1.00	1.00			
not over		0.21*		0.41*	0.46*			
Citizens ... have a right to basic services regardless of costs:	0.1912	0.0207	0.4799	0.0143	0.2598	0.0121	0.0591	0.0114
do		1.00		1.00		1.00		1.00
do not		0.43*		0.39*		0.42*		0.36*
Size of municipality:	0.1618	0.5961	0.1108	0.9172	0.0219	0.0990	0.0588	0.0437
<4000 inhabitants					1.00			1.00
4000–8000					0.80			1.80
8000–30 000					2.21*			3.36*
>30 000					1.31			3.99*
County	0.3160	0.4638	0.6075	0.4177	0.3903	0.5472	0.6455	0.3105

*p <0.05.

regarding the attitudes towards cuts in different welfare services, mainly within the political elite. Those within the political elite who think that citizens have a right to basic services regardless of costs show higher odds for opposing cuts in the named welfare services. With regard to the explanatory variable of 'size of municipality', results show that the political elite in large municipalities show higher odds for opposing cuts in means-tested social assistance.

What, then, do the results concerning the population look like? Are the same factors connected to variations in attitudes as within the elite groups? The results in Table 4.3 show that (only) about half of the population think that the economic strait in the municipalities is not over, and roughly 40 per cent think that citizens do not have the right to basic services regardless of the costs – figures that differ remarkably from those of the elite groups. Logistic regression analyses (Table 4.5) show that those within the population who think that the economic strait in the municipalities is over show higher odds for being opposed to cuts in the various services. Also, those who think that citizens are entitled to basic services regardless of costs show higher odds for being opposed to cuts in services; moreover, it can be noted that the connection between this question and the attitudes towards cuts in services seems to be stronger than regarding the prior question of the economic state of the municipality. The attitudes towards care for elderly people however, are not differentiated by either of the two explanatory variables, a fact that could indicate that people defend these services regardless of the considerations discussed here.

Finally, it should be noted that even though attitudes towards cuts in services are connected with the 'perceived state of municipal economy' and the 'principles of the service state' (first and foremost within the political elite and the population), separate analyses (Table 4.6) show that the differences in attitudes towards cuts in services are still in general statistically very significant

Table 4.5 Connections between the 'perceived state of municipal economy', the 'principles of the service state', and the attitudes of the population towards cuts in welfare services. Logistic regression analysis, results are controlled for gender, age, income, education and size of municipality. The odds show the probability of the respective group being opposed to cuts in the named welfare services in relation to the group of reference (odds = 1.00)

	Child day care	Elderly care	Health care	Social assistance
Economic strait is . . .	0.0154	0.7379	0.0035	0.0010
over	1.00		1.00	1.00
not over	0.64*		0.61*	0.61*
Citizens . . . have a right to basic services regardless of costs:	0.0013	0.2298	0.0016	0.0000
do	1.00		1.00	1.00
do not	0.53*		0.58*	0.45*

*p <0.05

75

Table 4.6 Differences in attitudes towards cuts in welfare services between the population and the political and administrative elite respectively. Logistic regression analysis. Results are controlled for 'perceived state of municipal economy' and the 'principles of the service state'. The odds show the probability of the respective group to be opposed to cuts in the named welfare services in relation to the group of reference (odds = 1.00)

	Child day care	*Elderly care*	*Health care*	*Social assistance*
Group:	0.0000	0.0000	0.0000	0.0001
population	1.00	1.00	1.00	1.00
political elite	0.14*	0.25*	0.34*	0.44*
administrative elite	0.14*	0.14*	0.20*	0.79

*$p<0.05$

between the different groups even when these two explanatory variables are controlled for. However, concerning the attitudes towards cuts in social assistance, the attitudes of the administrative elite – when their views about the economic strait and the right to basic services are controlled for – do not differ significantly from the attitudes of the population, while this is the case with the attitudes of the political elite.

Conclusions

Even though the theoretical perspectives discussed (in sections 2 and 3) above stress different factors, they should not necessarily be seen as mutually exclusive. How, then, should the results concerning the development of attitudes in the 1990s be interpreted?

Our analyses allow us to make at least the following observations. First, there are no signs within the Finnish population, at least at the level of attitudes, pointing at an 'exit' from, i.e. an abandoning of, the service state, despite the negative effects on services of economy measures and cuts in the 1990s and the simultaneous rise in municipal taxes. Instead, the population seems to be using its 'voice' by showing a growing resistance against further cuts in services and a growing demand for an increase in services in general. Second, concerning cuts in welfare services, the population has shown the weakest resistance against cuts in health-care services, despite the fact that its larger proportion has to be assumed to have a self-interest in these services than in, for example, day care or care for older people. This seems to speak against the assumption that economically less favourable times have a negative effect on people's readiness to take the needs of others into consideration. Instead, results could be interpreted to indicate that people consider it wrong, from a normative viewpoint, to make cuts that affect the elderly and (families with) children – the elderly and the children are weak and vulnerable groups, while all cases treated at the health-care centre are not necessarily considered very severe. Another possible explanation could be that the services arouse different associations, for instance, concerning efficiency and 'cut-back margins'. The fact that the resistance against cuts in means-tested social assistance is lower in comparison to the universal services, combined with the fact that there is a strong connection between the view that the economic strait in the municipalities is not yet over and a readiness to accept cuts in social assistance, could be interpreted to mean that people during an economic crisis are more inclined to accept cuts in services that they do not benefit from personally. However, since a similar trend can be seen also regarding the most universal service, health care, results do not necessarily reflect the influence of self-interests.

Can the results, then, provide an intimation as to the relationship between the attitudes of the population and of the elites? In consideration of the more general questions concerning increases and (means of) cuts in services in general, the differences in attitudes betwen the population and the elites have not decreased, but rather, in some cases, even grown slightly during the 1990s. The attitudes of the population and of the elites concerning cuts in specific welfare-related services, on the other hand, have become more alike, which mainly is due to changed attitudes within the elites. Despite this, the differences in attitudes remain substantial with regard to all questions; even at the end of the period studied, the elites are much more willing to accept cuts in services than the population is, which seems to indicate that the elites are not, to any considerable degree, influenced by the attitudes of the population.[21] On the other hand, it does not seem as if any possible efforts by the elites to influence the attitudes of the people would have been successful, that is, that they would have got people to see the need for cuts from a different point of view. How can this continuous discrepancy in attitudes be explained?

The much more negative views on the economic state of the municipalities within the political elite as compared to the population can partly, but only partly, explain the willingness of this elite to accept cuts in the welfare-related services. Results also indicate a prevalence of differences in more fundamental values between the municipal political elite and the population, since so few within the elites and such a large proportion of the population think that citizens have a right to free basic services provided by the municipality, regardless of the costs of providing them, a fundamental principle that, in turn, is connected with the attitudes towards cuts in welfare-related services. Thus, the attitudes of the political elite and of the population can be assumed to be (partly) influenced by the same factors – the perception of the economic state of the municipalities and (one of) the basic principles of the service state – but the views on these questions differ significantly between the two groups. This, to some extent, seems to explain the difference in attitudes towards cuts in services. Why the political elite is not influenced more by the wishes of the people is, of course, difficult to determine. Perhaps the members of the political elite regard themselves as having been authorised by the people to make decisions that they – on the basis of their expert knowledge – consider to be necessary (Forma

1996)? Another possibility is that the attitudes of the political elite reflect future political interests; it might be felt that it is politically more advantageous in the long run, for example, to reduce the municipal debt or to refrain from raising taxes, than to listen to the demands of the people not to make cuts in welfare-related services. In any case, our results seem to point at a lack of a commonly constructed belief system or sense of social and political reality without which, it has been said, even meaningful communication between political elites and the people about an issue is not likely to occur (Miller *et al.* 1995: 2).

At the same time, it should be noted that the attitudes of the political elite concerning many of our questions are somewhat closer to the attitudes of the population than are the attitudes of the administrative elite. Moreover, apart from being farthest from the attitudes of the population, the attitudes of the administrative elite do not have a connection with our indicators of the perception of the economic situation of the municipalities and one of the basic principles of the service state. This provides some support both for the assumption that factors other than the attitudes of the population are of primary importance when it comes to the attitudes of this elite and also for the assumption that those factors are different from the ones that explain the attitudes of the population. The fact that the administrative elite does not see a connection between the economic situation of the municipalities and/or one of the basic principles of the service state on the one hand, and the cuts in welfare services on the other, gives rise to some interesting questions. What are the 'motives' behind the administrative elite's attitudes towards cuts in welfare services? Is the readiness to accept cuts connected to a more general notion of uncertainty regarding the development of the municipal economy, such as further cuts in state subsidies etc.? And why does the question about the principles of the service state not have any connection with the administrative elite's attitudes towards cuts in services? Political appointees as they often are, should they not have a 'political' view of that issue? Is it perhaps the educational homogeneity of this group (see section 5) and similar professional values that lead to the undifferentiated attitudes towards cuts in the service state? In any case, it is clear that the members of the administrative elite do not see themselves as 'citizens' advocates' regarding these issues. These results seem to be in agreement with the conclusions drawn from an earlier, empirical study on municipal administrative elites in the Nordic countries, where it was found that chief executive officers do not want an expanding administration with more personnel; instead, they want less state control, they are sympathetic to privatisation, and they regard the demands of the people as a problem – all opinions that present a challenge to the traditional views on the Scandinavian welfare state model (Ståhlberg and Hansen 1997: 90).

Concerning the relationship between the two elite groups, some interesting conclusions can be drawn. For example, the readiness within the administrative elite to accept economy measures and cuts is hardly in line with the assumptions about the administrators' striving to get more personal influence through maximising their own budget. Perhaps administrators do not, under the present circumstances, think that striving to maximise the budget is a way of gaining more influence? Or perhaps they are guided by values, professional or other, that influence their attitudes. Further, the strikingly similar attitudes between the elite groups on many of our questions indicate, despite some differences in the factors that are connected with the attitudes of the respective elite, that the two groups are still very much influenced one by another. Perhaps it is the administrative elite – that traditionally has played a central role in municipal decision-making (Modeen 1995; Pikkala 1997) – that has been able to influence the political elite's thinking about the necessity of cuts in services. Of course, attitudes might have been transfered in the opposite direction also. The fact, however, that the attitudes of the politicians seem to be (partly) justified with either economic or normative arguments, while the attitudes of the administrators are not, speaks against this interpretation. A third possible explanation of the similar attitudes of the elite groups over the studied period could be the often very long time of cooperation between the leading politician and administrator in the municipal organisation, which may have resulted in a socialisation to similar views on the necessity of certain measures (or certain politics), even though the attitudes of the political elite are more connected to 'ideology' and the administrative elite's attitudes are more 'down-to-earth'.

However, it has to be remembered that the results of this study should not be generalised too much, and that our questions have concerned a limited number of issues only. Still, it seems clear that the municipal elites, at least on the level of attitudes, are ready to accept further cuts in the service state if the economic situation should require it, and that they are unwilling to increase services. Attitudes are of course not always transformed into political decisions, but since a majority of both municipal elites think that the economic strait in the municipalities is not over even by the mid-1990s, there seems reason to believe that the economy measures and cuts in the Finnish service state will continue.

Finally, one might wonder how it transpires that the Finnish population continues to show such a strong resistance against cuts. The answer can probably be found in the universal character of the Scandinavian service state, that is, the fact that such a large proportion of the population uses the system. It also seems as if a large part of the population has internalised the values behind the service state (Blomberg and Kroll 1995), which leads to the notion that welfare services should not be cut in any radical way, even in economic straits. However, a majority of the municipal elites seems not to agree with this view and, thus, the consequences of the recent reforms extending the autonomy of local government – which were said to be carried through in order to improve the possibilities of the inhabitants of each municipality to adjust services to the local needs – have not necessarily had the desired effect. Results are interesting also from a wider perspective considering that a similar trend of local government reforms also prevails in other Nordic countries. Thus, if differences in attitudes between local government elites and the people in all Nordic countries are as significant as in Finland, the future of the Scandinavian service state looks rather uncertain, in spite of considerable popular support for its preservation.

Appendix 4.1 Opinion changes in various population groups: education, income, gender and age. Proportion (%) of respondents who are opposed to cuts in child day care, health care, elderly care and social assistance when compared to those who accept cuts in 1992 and 1996 respectively

	Child day care		Elderly care		Health care		Social assistance	
	1992	1996	1992	1996	1992	1996	1992	1996
Education:								
No vocational education	75	82	85	83	68	78	48	58
Vocational course	80	90	88	93	65	82	43	57
Vocational school	76	84	86	86	58	76	42	58
College	77	83	87	91	56	75	39	47
University	72	78	82	78	49	75	36	37
Income (FIM/year):								
< 90 000	76	84	87	86	64	78	50	63
90–150 000	79	84	86	90	61	78	43	56
150–240 000	77	84	87	83	59	74	37	46
> 240 000	62	82	76	87	46	75	27	30
Gender:								
Women	81	86	88	90	62	81	44	58
Men	73	81	83	82	59	73	41	50
Age-group:								
15–24 years	76	82	79	78	64	75	43	56
25–34 years	80	92	87	89	56	77	39	60
34–49 years	78	83	88	86	59	74	40	55
50–65 years	75	76	89	90	63	81	45	48
65 +	69	84	87	90	64	87	50	52

N = 1029 in 1992, 960 in 1996.

Notes

1 Local government has a central role in the funding and planning of social services but voluntary organisations and family child-minders are also involved in service production, while commercial services play a very minor role.
2 It should be noted that administrative reforms that have come into force in the 1990s were planned under the economic upswing of the 1980s – a time characterised by a rapidly expanding municipal sector, a fact that was feared to result in a shortage of skilled labour in the private sector (Heikkilä and Lehto 1992).
3 Despite this, municipal authority is still limited *inter alia* by the fact that some services are defined as subjective rights by national legislation (acute health care,

day care and some services for gravely disabled persons) and that also other important items of expenditure such as means-tested social assistance and home-care allowance are regulated by national legislation and norms. Furthermore, some of the more expensive services are produced by regional unions of municipalities which limits the authority of one single municipality (Lehto 1995: 305–6).

4 After a rapid decline of the economy of the municipalities at the beginning of the 1990s, the situation in the middle of the decade – according to some indicators – was in many respects as good as it was before the depression. Since this was achieved mainly through raised municipal taxes and various cuts – some of which were meant to be of a temporary nature – the recovery might be seen as 'artificial' and a continuous uncertainty has dominated the economic debate at the municipal level (cf. Helin 1996), although there are big differences in how municipalities have coped with the depression.

5 The respondents were asked to react to the statements on a five-degree scale: 1) I completely agree; 2) I somewhat agree; 3) I somewhat disagree; 4) I completely disagree; 5) I cannot say.

6 The respondents were asked to choose betwen the options of: 1) I completely approve; 2) I approve to some degree; 3) I do not approve at all; 4) I cannot say. These questions were included in the questionnaires in 1992–5 only.

7 Statements/questions were selected from a large number of statements about municipalities and different means to improve the municipal economy respectively. A criterion was that the statements should be about the municipal service-sector only and should involve some type of reductions.

8 It can be noted that the expenses for social and healthcare services constitute c. 37 per cent and the expenses for education and cultural services constitute c. 22 per cent of total municipal expenses (cf. Statistics Finland, 1995). Out of the total expenses of social and health-care services, day care constitutes the biggest single item of expenditure (41 per cent), elderlycare being the second biggest (c. 27 per cent), while the proportion of expenditures on means-tested social assistance is c. 14 per cent. Figures are for 1993.

9 The question used is 'In which of the following items of expenditure do you think cuts could be made if the municipalities have to reduce their spending?' On each item, respondents were asked to choose between the alternatives of [Expenditures can be cut]: 1) A lot; 2) Somewhat; 3) Not at all; 4) Cannot say. A number of items of expenditure were named. Some items, which were not regarded as 'services' (e.g. financial support to enterprises) were excluded from the analysis.

10 With regard to the data on chairs of the executive boards, it should be noted that the target population in 1992 is partly different from that in 1993–6, since local government elections were held in 1992.

11 In our study, McNemar's test for correlated proportions in a 2×2 table (cf. Everitt 1977: 20–1) is used to compare the data of two (dichotomous) variables (e.g. attitudes towards cuts in health-care services and elderly care), each representing the number of persons accepting or resisting cuts in a certain welfare service in a certain year (1992 and 1996 respectively). The test establishes whether there is a statistically significant difference between the number of observations in the category of respondents that resist cuts in one of the services but not in the other, and the number of observations in the category where the opposite situation is true. If there is no significant difference between these categories, the resistance against cuts does not differ as regards the two services involved.

12 On this question, the proportion of respondents who choose the 'I cannot say' option has increased over time. If these are excluded from the analyses, 54 per cent agreed with the statement in 1992 while the figure for 1996 is 60 per cent.

13 This does not hold for attitudes towards elderly care, concerning which resistance against cuts has been very strong over the whole time period.

14 Results in Table 4.2 do not include information on whether the changes in attitudes within the respective elite group are statistically significant. However, separate analyses show that the attitudes of the elites have not changed appreciably between 1992 and 1996 with regard to the more general questions concerning 'service-strategy' and means of improving municipal finances (with the exception that the politicial elite has become more inclined to think that services should be increased rather than reduced). Considering the more specific questions about cuts in various types of services, however, the attitudes of the elites have in general changed in a statistically very significant way; both elites have become less ready to accept cuts in the different services, except for the unchanged attitudes of the political elite towards public transports and cultural services.

15 Over the whole period studied, the two elites are more inclined to accept cuts also in other earlier mentioned services than is the population. With regard to attitudes towards cuts in public transport and in sports and recreation services, the differences have not diminished over time. Concerning library and cultural services, differences in attitudes have diminished mainly between the administrative elite and the population.

16 Analyses concerning the other types of questions used were not feasible due to the very uneven distribution of answers in the data on elites.

17 Regarding both questions, respondents could choose between the alternatives: 1) Completely agree; 2) Somewhat agree; 3) Somewhat disagree; 4) Completely disagree; 5) Cannot say. In the statistical analyses, those that agree with the statement are included in one group and those who do not agree with the statement in another. Respondents without an opinion have been excluded from the analyses.

18 The connection between norms/values and attitudes towards cuts in services could, in principle, also be tested by using information concerning the political affiliation of the elites. However, unfortunately there are no questions about the political preferences nor on any other more detailed background data such as the name of the respondent's municipality. These questions were deliberately omitted because it was assumed that they would negatively affect the willingness to answer the questionnaire.

19 Regardless of whether the elites emphasise the principle 'per se' or the aspects of cost, the question still remains an issue of principles, since the right to (basic) services has always been taken to imply 'regardless of costs'.

20 'Size of municipality' is based on a question in which the respondent was asked to indicate whether he/she represented a municipality with under 4,000, 4,000–8,000, 8,000–30,000, 30,000–80,000 or with more than 80,000 inhabitants. Since the number of respondents in the last-mentioned category was (of necessity) very low, the last two groups were combined in the analyses. Concerning the impact of this variable, it could be assumed that the elites in small municipalities contact the population more easily and, thus, would more easily be influenced by their attitudes (cf. section 3). On the other hand, a majority of the small, rural municipalities are dominated by the Centre Party of Finland (former Agrarians) while the 'wage-earners' parties (that traditionally have considered child care and elderly care to be more important than the Centre Party does) have a stronger position in urban municipalities. Thus, the variable of size of municipality could also be an indicator of 'differences in ideology' or even of differences in values between urban and rural areas. The variable of 'province' has been created by including the Finnish provinces in one of four categories (South, East, West and North) mainly on the basis of their geographical location.

21 It should be noted that the attitudes of the population most likely were known to the elites, *inter alia* through the study in question.

References

Albæk, E., Rose, L., Strömberg, L. and Ståhlberg, K. (1996) *Nordic Local Government*. The Association of Finnish Local Authorities, Helsinki: Kuntaliiton painatuskeskus.

Alber, J. (1995) A Framework for the Comparative Study of Social Services. *Journal of European Social Policy*, 5 (2): 131–49.

Allardt, E. (1983) *Sosiologia I* [Sociology I]. Porvoo: WSOY.

Anttonen, A. and Sipilä, J. (1996) European Social Care Services: Is It Possible to Identify Models? *Journal of Europan Social Policy*, 6 (2): 87–100.

Argyris, C. and Schön, D. A. (1978) *Organisational Learning: A Theory of Action Perspective*, Massachusetts: Addison-Wesley.

Bergmark, Å. (1997) From Reforms to Rationing? Current Allocative Trends in Social Services in Sweden, *Scandinavian Journal of Social Welfare*, 6 (2): 74–81.

Blomberg, H. and Kroll, C. (1995) Välfärdsvärderingar i olika generationer – från kollektivism mot en ökad individualism? [Welfare Values in Different Generations – From Collectivism Towards Increased Individualism?] *Sosiologia*, 32(2): 106–21.

Blomberg, H., Kroll, C., Suominen, S. and Helenius, H. (1996) Socialklass och attityderna till nedskärningar i välfärdssystemet i Finland [Social Class and Attitudes Towards Cuts in the Welfare System in Finland]. *Sociologisk forskning*, 4: 57–79.

Bryson, L., Bittman, M. and Donath, S. (1994) 'Men's Welfare State, Women's Welfare State: Tendencies to Convergence in Practice and Theory?', in Sainsbury, D. (ed.) *Gendering Welfare States*. London, Thousand Oaks, New Delhi: Sage Publications.

Coughlin, R. M. (1979) Social Policy and Ideology: Public Opinion in Eight Rich Countries. *Comparative Social Research*, 2: 3–40.

Downs, A. (1957) *An Economic Theory of Democracy*, New York: Harper & Row.

Eronen, A., Hokkanen, L., Kinnunen, P., Lehto-Pusa, P., Rönneberg, L. and Särkelä, R. (1995) *Hyvinvoinnin verkostoja näkyvissä* [Networks of Well-being in Sight]. Sosiaaliturvan Keskusliitto, Helsinki: Gummerus Kirjapaino.

Ervasti, H. (1996) *Kenen vastuu? Tutkimuksia hyvinvointipluralismista legitimiteetin näkökulmasta.* [Whose Responsibility? Studies on Welfare Pluralism from the Perspective of Legitimacy] Research Report: National Research and Development Centre for Welfare and Health (STAKES). Helsinki: Gummerus Oy.

Everitt, B. S. (1977) *The Analysis of Contingency Tables*, London: Chapman and Hall.

Forma, P. (1996) *The Politics of Interest Mediation. The Case of Universalistic Social Policy in Finland*, University of Turku, Department of Social Policy. Series B:7/1996.

Forma, P. (1997) *Citizens, Elites and the Welfare State. Opinions on Pension Policy in Finland*, National Research and Development Centre for Welfare and Health, Themes 5/1997, Helsinki.

Hadenius, A. (1986) *A Crisis of the Welfare State? Opinions About Taxes and Public Expenditure in Sweden*, Stockholm: Almqvist & Wiksell.

Heikkilä, M. and Lehto, J. (1992) *Sopeuttaminen vai kriisi?* [Adaption or Crisis?] Sosiaalija terveyshallituksen raportteja 74. Helsinki: VAPK-kustannus.

Helin, H. (1996) *Kunnilla menee hyvin, kuntalaisilla huonommin* [The Municipalities Are Doing Well, the Inhabitants Are Doing Worse] Helsingin kaupungin tietokeskuksen tutkimuksia 1996:1. Helsinki: Tietokeskus.

Hirschman, A. (1970) *Exit, Voice and Loyalty. Responses to Decline in Firms, Organisations and States*, Cambridge, MA: Harvard University Press.

Hofstede, G. (1980) *Culture's Consequences: International Differences in Work-Related Values*, Beverly Hills: Sage.

Hollis, M. (1989) *The Cunning of Reason*, Cambridge: Cambridge University Press.

Inglehart, R. (1977) *The Silent Revolution. Changing Values and Political Styles among Western Publics*, New Jersey: Princeton University Press.

Jacobsen, D. I. (1996) The Role of the Public Manager: Loyalty, Autonomy or Advocacy? *Scandinavian Political Studies*, 19 (1): 45–63.

Johanson, J.-E. and Mattila, M. (1994) The Vicious Circle of Cutback Policies: Citizens' Attitudes Toward Cutbacks in Finnish Welfare Services. *Scandinavian Political Studies*, 17 (4): 289–303.

Kangas, A. (1995) Finnish Municipal Cultural Policy in Transition. *Finnish Local Government Studies*, 4/95: 340–7.

Kangas, O. (1997) *Self-Interest and the Common Good: Impact of Norms, Selfishness and Context in Social Policy Opinions*, University of Turku, Department of Social Policy, Series B:10/1997.

Knutsen, O. (1988) The Impact of Structural and Ideological Party Cleavages in Western European Democracies: A Comparative Empirical Analysis, *British Journal of Political Science*, 18: 323–52.

Kosonen, P. (1995) *Eurooppalaiset hyvinvointivaltiot* [European Welfare States], Tampere: Gaudeamus.

Kröger, T. (1995) 'Kunnat valtion valvonnassa?' [Municipalities under State Supervision?] in J. Sipilä, O. Ketola, T. Kröger and P.-L. Rauhala (eds) *Sosiaalipalvelujen Suomi* [Finland – the Country of Social Services], Juva: Werner Söderström Osakeyhtiö.

Kröger, T. (1997) 'Local Government in Scandinavia: Autonomous or Integrated into the Welfare State?' in J. Sipilä (ed.) *Social Care Services: The Key to the Scandinavian Welfare Model*, Aldershot: Avebury.

Lehto, J. (1995) Adaption or a New Strategy? Finnish Local Welfare State in the 1990's. *Finnish Local Government Studies*, 4/95: 303–13.

Lehto, J. (1997) 'Rahoituksen ja rakenteen muutoksia sosiaali- ja terveyspalveluissa' [Changes in the Financing and Structure of Social and Health Care Services], in H. Uusitalo and M. Staff (eds) *Sosiaali- ja terveydenhuollon palvelukatsaus 1997* [Report on Social and Health Services 1997], STAKES: Reports 214, Helsinki: Gummerus Kirjapaino Oy.

Lewin, L. (1988) *Det gemensamma bästa* [The Common Good], Borås: Carlssons Bokförlag.

Martinussen, W. (1993) 'Welfare State Support in Achievement Oriented Hearts: The Case of Norway' in E. J. Hansen, S. Ringen, H. Uusitalo and R. Erikson (eds) *Welfare Trends in the Scandinavian Countries*, New York: M. E. Sharpe.

Miegel, F. (1990) *Om värden och livsstilar. En teoretisk, metodologisk och empirisk översikt* [On Values and Lifestyles'. A Theoretical, Methodological and Empirical Overview]. Sociologiska institutionen Lunds Universitet.

Miller, A. H., Hesli, V. L. and Reisinger, W. M. (1995) Comparing Citizen and Elite Belief Systems in Post-Soviet Russia and Ukraine. *Public Opinion Quarterly*, 59: 1–40.

Modeen, T. (1995) Politicians-Professionals – The Power Structure of Finnish Local Government. *Finnish Local Government Studies*, 4/95: 286–90.

Niemi-Iilahti, A. (1995) The Structure and Finance of Finnish Local Government – In European Perspective. *Finnish Local Government Studies*, 4/95: 272–85.

Niiranen, V. (1991) *Sosiaalitoimi vapaakuntakokeilussa*. [The Social Sector in the Free-Commune Experiment], Itsehallintoprojektin julkaisuja 1, Sisäasiainministeriö: Helsinki.

Niiranen, V. (1995) *Sosiaalitoimen moniuloitteinen johtajuus* [The Multidimensional Management of Social Services] Sosiaaliturvan keskusliitto, Helsinki: RT-paino.

Niskanen, W. A., Jr (1971) *Bureaucracy and Representative Government*, Chicago: Aldine-Atherton.

OECD (1994) *National Accounts 1979–1992*, Paris: OECD.

Oftedal, E. (1992) Holder holdningar? Om forholdet mellom holdninger og semiotikk [On the Relationship Between Attitudes and Semiotics], *Sosiologi i dag*, 1992: 3.

Olsson, S. E. (1990) *Social Policy and Welfare State in Sweden*, Lund: Arkiv förlag.

Oulasvirta, L. (1992) *Kunta, valtio ja talous. Kuntien ja valtion suhteita, valtionapujär-jestelmää ja kuntien talousongelmia koskeva tutkimus* [The Municipalities, the State and the Economy. A Study of the Relationship Between the State and the Municipalities, the System of State Subsidies and the Municipalities' Financial Difficulties] Tampereen yliopiston kunnallistieteiden laitoksen julkaisusarja 1. Tampere.

Papadakis, E. (1992) Public Opinion, Public Policy and the Welfare State, *Political Studies*, XL: 21–37.

Papadakis, E. and Bean, C. (1993) Popular Support for the Welfare State: A Comparison Between Institutional Regimes. *Journal of Public Policy*, 13(3): 227–54.

Peters, B. G. (1987) 'Politicians and Bureaucrats in the Politics of Policy Making' in J.-E. Lane (ed.) *Bureaucracy and Public Choice*, Modern Political Series, Vol. 15, London: Sage.

Pierson, P. (1994) *Dismantling the Welfare State?* Cambridge: Cambridge Univeristy Press.

Pikkala, S. (1997) 'Kommundirektörers ställning och bakgrund' [Position and Background of Chief Executive Officers], in L. Rose (ed.) *Kommuner och kommunala ledare i Norden* [Municipalities and Municipal Leaders in the Nordic Countries] Meddelanden från Ekonomisk-statsvetenskapliga fakulteten vid Åbo Akademi. Institutet för jämförande nordisk politik och förvaltning. Ser. A:469, Åbo: Åbo Akademis tryckeri.

Pöntinen, S. and Uusitalo, H. (1988) Stability and Change in the Public Support for the Welfare State; Finland 1975-1985. *International Journal of Sociology and Social Policy*, 8: 1–24.

Rokeach, M. (1973) *The Nature of Human Values*, New York: The Free Press.

Sears, D. O., Hensler, C. P. and Speer, L. K. (1979) Whites' Opposition to 'Busing': Self-interest or Symbolic Politics? *The American Political Science Review*, 73: 369–84.

Sihvo, T. (1994) Väestön tuki hyvinvointivaltiolle vahvistumassa [Citizens' Support for the Welfare State Is Increasing]. *Dialogi*, 8: 4–5.

Sihvo, T. and Uusitalo, H. (1995) Economic Crises and Support for the Welfare State in Finland 1975–1993. *Acta Sociologica*, 38(3): 251–62.

Sipilä, J. (1995) 'Aluksi' [Introduction], in J. Sipilä, O. Ketola, T. Kröger and P.-L. Rauhala (eds) *Sosiaalipalvelujen Suomi* [Finland- the Country of Social Services], Juva: Werner Söderström Osakeyhtiö.

Sipilä, J., Andersson, M., Hammarqvist, S.-E., Nordlander, L., Rauhala, P-L., Thomsen, K. and Warming Nielsen, H. (1997) 'A Multitude of Universal, Public Services – How and Why Did Four Scandinavian Countries Get Their Social Care Service Model?' in J. Sipilä (ed.) *Social Care Services: The Key to the Scandinavian Welfare Model*, Aldershot: Avebury.

Statistics Finland (1995) *Public Economy*, 1995: 3.

Ståhlberg, K. and Hansen, J. O. (1997) Problemlösningar och förändringar [Solutions to Problems and Changes], in L. Rose (ed.) *Kommuner och kommunala ledare i Norden* [Municipalities and Municipal Leaders in the Nordic Countries] Meddelanden från Ekonomisk-statsvetenskapliga fakulteten vid Åbo Akademi. Institutet för jämförande nordisk politik och förvaltning, Ser. A:469, Åbo: Åbo Akademis tryckeri.

Suhonen, P. (1988) *Suomalaisten arvot ja politiikka* [The Values of the Finns and Politics], Juva: WSOY.

Svallfors, S. (1989) *Vem älskar välfärdsstaten?* [Who Loves the Welfare State?] Lund: Studentlitteratur Arkiv.

Svallfors, S. (1995) The End of Class Politics? Structural Cleavages and Attitudes to Swedish Welfare Policies. *Acta Sociologica*, 38 (1): 53–74.

Svallfors, S. (1996) *Välfärdsstatens moraliska ekonomi. Välfärdsopinionen i 90-talets Sverige* [The Moral Economy of the Welfare State. Opinions on Welfare in Sweden in the 90's], Umeå: Borea.

Taylor-Gooby, P. (1985) *Public Opinion, Ideology and State Welfare*, London: Routledge and Kegan Paul.

Taylor-Gooby, P. (1988) The Future of the British Welfare State: Public Attitudes, Citizenship and Social Policy under the Conservative Governments of the 80's. *European Sociological Review*, 4 (1): 1–19.

Udehn, L. (1996) *The Limits of Public Choice. A Sociological Critique of the Economic Theory of Politics*, London: Routledge.

Uusitalo, H. (1997) 'Sosiaali- ja terveyspalvelut sosiaaliturvan osana' [Social- and Health Care Services as a Part of Social Security], in H. Uusitalo and M. Staff (eds) *Sosiaali- ja terveydenhuollon palvelukatsaus 1997* [Report on Social and Health Services 1997]. STAKES, Reports 214, Jyväskylä: Gummerus Kirjapaino Oy.

Williams, R. M., Jr (1979) 'Change and Stability in Values and Value Systems: A Sociological Perspective', in M. Rokeach (ed.) *Understanding Human Values*, New York: The Free Press.

5

WELFARE STATE OPINIONS AMONG CITIZENS, MP-CANDIDATES AND ELITES

Evidence from Finland

Pauli Forma

The welfare state is clearly an institution of the citizens. Social policy programmes, income-transfer schemes and social services provide shelter and security against hardships and accidents in life, and act as sources of income after active working life, during sickness or unemployment. However, the welfare state is also of interest to the elite of society. Since social politics is, at the macro-level, the politics of big money, the elite are also interested in social political programmes, their organisation, financing and administration. Furthermore, the development of the welfare state is a political process in which citizens are not the main players, but representatives of the different social groups, political parties and interest groups which are making decisions about the welfare state.

Although the welfare state interests citizens on the one hand and the elite on the other, earlier studies have almost without an exception operated at one level only (Kangas 1995a: 52). Studies that have analysed which political parties or interest groups have battled for this or that social political reform, have almost without exception dealt with the elite level. For example, the power-resource approach (Stephens 1979; Korpi 1983; Esping-Andersen and Korpi 1987) which is one of the most frequently utilised perspectives in explaining the development of the welfare state, has not been interested in discussing the citizen–elite connection. As Korpi (1989: fn. 5) has stated, this discussion is beyond the scope of the power-resource perspective. Thus, we have plenty of information about which political parties have battled for different social political reforms. However, we do not know what ordinary people at the grassroots level have wanted or thought about these reforms. We do not know whether the will of the citizens has been similar or different to that of the elite.

The citizen-level, then, has been analysed in public opinion studies. The main focus in these studies focusing on opinions on the welfare state has been whether, and to what extent, people support the welfare state. However, in almost all of these studies, the elite level has been absent. Although knowledge about opinions of the citizens is important in itself, we cannot say much about public policy or further development of the welfare state when the analysis is restricted to this level. The reason for this is that there is no straight and clear connection between public opinion and public policy. Although the problem dealing with the link between the elite and the citizens has been identified (Papadakis 1992: 22) and some theoretical frameworks have been developed (Whiteley 1981; Wilensky 1981; Kuran 1995) empirical studies where both the citizens and the elite are included have been surprisingly few.

This article aims to overcome the weaknesses of the power-resource approach and public opinion studies by analysing both the welfare state opinions of the ordinary citizens and groups that are closer to political decision-making and power in Finnish society. It is assumed that the opinions of the elite groups are better predictors when trying to estimate the future development of welfare policy. Thus, the strategy of the study is as follows: First, we examine the opinions of the ordinary citizens. This is the level where opinion studies usually operate. Second, since in a representational democracy parliament is the most important institution in mediating the will of the people to political decision-making, we examine the opinions of the candidates of the 1995 parliamentary elections in Finland. Third, since not all power is located in parliament, we also examine the 'elite-level' of Finnish society; civil servants, members of parliament, directors of the largest companies, researchers and journalists.

The article is organised as follows. First, we look at studies dealing with connections between public opinion and public policy. After that, issues attached to the measurement and influencing on public opinion are discussed. In the empirical analysis, we first take an overview of the opinions in levels being studied. After that, we will control some background variables in order to see whether differences in opinions of the citizens and the elite are smaller when this measure is taken. In the final section, the results are summed up and their wider implications to the research field are discussed.

From public opinion to public policy

In Fishkin's (1995) words, public opinion is 'the voice of the people'. It gives a picture about the views of ordinary citizens. This picture is interesting in itself, but it is obvious that political decisions are not based solely on the opinions of the citizens. One example of this with regard to the welfare state is that in spite of strong popular support for the it (Ervasti and Kangas 1995; Svallfors 1995; Taylor-Gooby 1995), welfare programmes have been rolled back in several countries and more cut-backs are to come. Thus, it seems that popular support for the welfare state does not stop governments implementing cut-backs and therefore the relationship between public opinion and public policy have to be examined more closely.

Among researchers, there is no consensual understanding about the impact of public opinion on public policy. Some researchers have assumed that public opinion is a strong and influential factor when it comes to policy-making: public opinion sets the agenda for political actions, it limits choices and legitimates policies (Whiteley 1981). From this perspective, public opinion indeed is an important and strong determinant of public policy. The other pole, though, is less optimistic. For example, Wilensky (1981) states that public opinion is so complex and includes so many dimensions that politicians and parties can mobilise just those sections of it which are suitable for their interests. Edelman (1977: 49–55) puts it even more straightforwardly: according to him, the elite can 'create public opinion' and use it to support their policies. From these perspectives it is much more important to study power structures and the views of the political parties and politicians than public opinion in order to make predictions about public policy.

There are studies which have examined empirically the relationship between public opinion and public policy (for a review of this theme, see Jacobs and Shapiro 1994). In these studies, a correlation between public opinion and public policy has been found (Erikson 1976; Monroe 1979). However, despite the correlation, it is difficult to be sure whether changes in public preferences cause changes in policies, or whether public policy affects opinions. In this latter case, people adapt to implemented policies. However, there is also clear evidence that public opinion has an influence on public policy. According to Page and Shapiro (1983: 186), policy shifts followed changes in public opinion, which indicates that public opinion was a cause for policy change and not vice versa.

However, the link between public opinion and public policy is not straightforward, nor is it clear. The main reasons for this are two-fold: First, there are problems with the measurement of public opinion. Because of these problems, it might be difficult to be sure exactly what the will of the citizens is. Needless to say, if there is uncertainty about this, not so much can be said about its impact on public policy either. The second source of dispute is that public opinion can be influenced. If public opinion is not the 'genuine' will of the citizens, i.e. it is a result of manipulation, considering its impact on public policy is meaningless. These two themes are focused on in the following sections.

Measuring public opinion

Kuran (1995: 295–6) raises several reasons why public policy does not necessarily follow public opinion: legislative procedures, election laws, the ambitions of the individual politicians and irresponsibility of executives may lead to policy decisions that differ from public opinion. One point that Kuran raises is that policy makers receive information from their constituencies through symbols subject to interpretation. These symbols are votes, words, statistics and images which leave room for manipulation. Public opinion is among those symbols which can be interpreted differently. It can be argued that one source of confusion between public opinion and public policy is that public opinion is not a sharp and clear-cut issue.

In a way, there is a parallel between social choice problems and public opinion. As the literature dealing with social choice has indicated, there is no method which can be used to aggregate unquestionable outcomes (Arrow 1951). As Riker points out in his *Liberalism against Populism* (1982), when aggregating preferences of the people the outcome is always somehow determined by the method used. The same individual preferences might produce different common wills when different methods are used. Furthermore, even the same aggregating procedures may lead to different outcomes if manipulation takes place. Since public opinion is an aggregated will of the citizens, these problems are also relevant regarding it. Studies focusing on survey methodology have pointed out that results of opinion studies are sensitive to the wording of the question (Hadenius 1985; Smith 1987; Kangas 1997). This means that the frame in which the question is presented has an impact on results. Because different wordings lead to different results one can say that there is no such thing as the 'right' public opinion. Public opinion is not a genuine 'will of the citizens', it only tells how people have responded to the questions asked. Public opinion might also be manipulated, which is more closely focused on in the following section.

Information also plays a fundamental and relevant role here. Opinion studies have been criticised because citizens are assumed not to be capable of forming an opinion toward issues on the political agenda. For example, Converse (1964) claims that most of the citizens do not have enough information to evaluate options available and make their decisions. According to him, most opinions revealed in surveys are 'meaningless doorstep opinions', they are not formed after serious consideration based on hard facts. From this point of view, certainly, we have to admit that for an average survey respondent most of the welfare state issues are highly tricky and complex. As an example of that, when answering questions dealing with cutting back the welfare state, a lot of background information should be available: the respondent should be aware of the organisation and finance of social security schemes. Furthermore, the present state and future development of the national economy should be known in order to decide whether cut-backs are needed. This kind of information is hardly available to experts – and it is obvious that an average citizen may lack expertise and the information needed in these kind of questions.

Regarding the link between public opinion and public policy, the lack of information at the citizen level gives more freedom to decision makers to disparage the opinions of the citizens. They can claim that there is no need to follow the opinions of the people because citizens do not have enough information about issues on the political agenda. However, Page and Shapiro (1993) found evidence about rational bases of people's opinions. In their longitudinal study, this meant that most of the citizens had preferences about policy issues and, when the public opinion changed, it changed in a reasonable, regular and understandable way. Public opinion was also quite stable and formed coherent patterns which reflected the values and beliefs of American society. Thus, the work of Page and Shapiro indicates that citizens are capable of handling issues on the political agenda and forming reasonable opinions on them.

Manipulating public opinion

Although there can be correlation between public opinion and public policy it is obvious that the elite are not just passive realisers of the citizens' preferences. Of course, the elite can regard public opinion as the feelings of the citizens, but here they can also be active. In other words, the elite may actively try to affect public opinion. Above, it was considered that citizens need information in order to form their opinions on different issues. However, information is a scarce resource and different elite groups are certainly in a position where they can control the flow of information to citizen level. According to Page and Shapiro (1989: 307–8), information can be used to educate and manipulate the public. The former refers to situations where 'correct, helpful political information' is given to the public which helps them to make fully informed policy choices. Manipulation takes place when 'false, incorrect, biased or selective information is given to the public to mislead it'. Of course, the distinction between educational and manipulative information is far from clear: it is difficult to know whether efforts to manipulate public opinion have been made, or whether just information has been given to the public. However, the most important thing is to notice that information can be used actively to effect public opinion. Different elite groups indeed may be using this possibility which Zaller (1992: 313) calls 'elite domination'.

In the above section the framing of survey questions was discussed. These frames can also be used more widely, since political questions discussed in public can also be framed (Gamson et al. 1992; Zaller 1992). More precisely, when an issue is on the political agenda and there is tense public discussion about it, different parties who have interests to defend may try to introduce such frames which are favourable to them. For example, a stigma of 'old-fashioned' or 'reactionary' can be given to some options, while the other options can be labelled as 'modern' or 'fresh' ones. It is obvious that different elite groups have many possibilities to introduce these frames. Politicians, of course, may use framing in order to get support for their policies. Also different expert groups, researchers and civil servants are potential framers. Due to their position they have superior access to information. Although these groups are experts in their own field, they also have their own ideological orientations and views of what society should look like (Korpi 1996). Therefore, while the comments of the experts are often given great weight, one must be aware that they are not necessarily free from normative elements.

To conclude, the impact of public opinion on public policy is problematic since public opinion is not a clear-cut phenomenon. It is always influenced by the methods used in estimating it, and it may be difficult for citizens to gather information in order to form rational, well-thought-out opinions. Therefore, a genuine 'will of the citizens' does not exist. Partly due to these difficulties there is room for manipulation. The elite can try to manipulate public opinion in order to get support for their policies. If public opinion is a result of manipulation and not a genuine popular will, comparing it to public policy is meaningless. In the following we will move on to the empirical analysis.

Research questions and data-sets

In the empirical analysis, opinions on pensions are analysed. There are good reasons why focusing just on pensions can be fruitful: First, in every welfare state, pension schemes are large and dominate social security programmes which contain a lot of financial resources. Second, ageing, and financial security against the associated needs, concern every human being. Third, pension schemes can conveniently be used for examination of the most important institutional aspects of the welfare state since we can examine the entitlement rules of the benefits, the determination of the benefit-level, their financing and administration of pension funds. The issues which will be covered in this study include entitlement rules of the pensions, determination of the benefit level and the administration of pension funds. The research strategy is to compare welfare state opinions among citizens, MP-candidates of the 1995 parliamentary elections and five different elite groups of Finnish society.

In politology and sociology, there is a long tradition of elite studies (Mosca 1939; Pareto 1963; Michels 1966). According to elite theories, the elite should meet certain requirements. According to Putnam (1976: 3–4; see also Bottomore 1993: 1–15) the 'hard core' of the elite theories can be summarised as follows: Power, like all social goods, is distributed unequally and people fall into two groups: those who have power and those who have not. The former group are the elite and the latter group are masses. The elite, then, is homogeneous, unified and self-aware. It is also self-perpetuating and drawn from a very exclusive segment of society. For these reasons, the elite is essentially autonomous, answerable to no one else for its decisions. If taken very strictly, the elite groups in this study do not meet these requirements. However, this was not the aim when collecting the elite data. In spite of that, we aimed to receive information about opinions of those groups which are relevant when it comes to social political issues and decision-making in Finnish society. Furthermore, it is clear that each of our elite groups are the elite when compared to the citizens: they have power due to their position and they also have the means to influence public opinion via public discussion.

Thus, the opinions of the citizens are the starting point of our study. The citizen-data ($n = 1737$) were collected in late 1994 and at the beginning of 1995. The data represents the Finnish population between 18 and 70 years old (for a closer description of this data, see Forma and Kangas, Chapter 8, this volume). Since in a representative democracy, parliament is the most important institution which mediates the will of the citizens to political decision-making, we study the opinions of the representatives of the citizens. In this study, the opinions of the 1995 candidates of the parliamentary elections are analysed. The candidate data ($n = 529$) were collected just before parliamentary elections and include all the most important political parties of the Finnish political system. The response rate for these data was 49 per cent.

However, the candidates are only those who do not participate in political decision-making. Therefore we collected data also from the elite level of Finnish society. The elite data ($n = 388$) were collected at the beginning of the year 1996. *Members of parliament* ($n = 110$) represent the political elite in this study. However, as not all power resides in parliament, we also analyse some other important elite groups. *Civil servants* ($n = 70$) certainly have power due to their position (Heclo 1974: 301–4). Also *researchers* ($n = 53$) are an important group: like civil servants, their power is based on the information they have (Stryker 1990; Korpi 1996). *Directors* of the largest companies ($n = 107$) may have a say when it comes to social policy issues. In addition, they participate in decision-making via their interest groups. Finally, the *mass media* plays a central role since it gives, or does not give, room for viewpoints of different interest groups and raises issues to the political agenda (Gans 1979; Parenti 1989; Svallfors 1996). Therefore, it is relevant to include representatives of the media ($n = 48$) in the analysis. This groups consists mostly of editors of the biggest newspapers in Finland, but also includes columnists and other staff working in the media. Appendix 5.1 provides detailed information about the structure and collection of the data-sets.

Comparing opinions of the citizens, candidates and the elite

Presently, there are two main pension systems in Finland: the national pension, which is linked to residence in Finland, and employment pensions which are linked to employment. Earlier, the national pension included a basic amount which was paid to the retired person. The additional amount depended on, and was proportional to, other pension income, primarily employment pension. From the beginning of the year 1996 the basic amount disappeared and whole national pension became tested by pension income. The employment pensions are earnings-related, required by law, and it is the duty of the employer to take care of the employee's pension insurance. Currently, there is no upper limit for the benefits paid from the employment pension system. The state, employers and employees all contribute to the financing of the employment pensions and the funds are administered by private companies under the supervision of the government. In summary, the pension system in Finland is institutional in Palme's (1990: 87) classification of the pension schemes: the national pension provides an adequate minimum for everyone and employment pensions provide compensation for loss of income. According to Jäntti, Kangas and Ritakallio (1996), the present pension systems have been successful in diminishing poverty and equalising income differences.

In the following section we will move on to empirical analysis. The results will be reported so that we will first examine the aggregate opinions of the citizens, MP-candidates, members of the parliament, directors of the companies, researchers, civil servants and journalists. Tables provide percentage shares of positive attitudes and *P*-values for statistical difference (χ^2-test). The exact questions and alternative answers are given in Appendix 5.2. In the latter section of the empirical analysis, multivariate analysis is used to control the impact of different background variables.

Entitlement rules

Entitlement rules of social benefits are important since they determine who is and who is not covered by social security schemes. When the coverage is at its narrowest, only the poor are entitled to benefits. On the other hand, when the coverage is at its widest, every citizen is entitled to social benefits. The former refers to means-testing and the latter to universalism, which usually are regarded as polar-types when it comes to the entitlement rules of social security benefits. Entitlement rules have been central when looking at the history of the welfare state since they have been used to build political coalitions between social classes. As Esping-Andersen (1985) points out, widening the coverage of social security was an effort to include the middle classes in supporting the welfare state project. Now, as well as in the future, the importance of entitlement rules is in their impact on the legitimacy of the welfare state. As Korpi (1980; see also Forma 1997a) has emphasised, wide coverage of the social security programmes produces a wide support base for the welfare state, while relying more on means-testing as an entitlement rule may be harmful for the legitimacy of the welfare state. Table 5.1 provides results regarding entitlement rules of the national pension.

It seems that the citizens are strongly in favour of a universal national pension. Support for a targetive scheme is low. The opinions of the citizens and the candidates fit together quite well, although the candidates are more hostile towards targeting than the citizens. So far, the preferences of the citizens seem

Table 5.1 Opinions on entitlement rules of national pension. Percent shares of positive attitudes. (Values within parentheses are p-values)

	Citizens	Candid-ates	Politics	Business	Research	Admin-istration	Media
Means-testing (.000)	30	21	46	65	49	40	50
Universalism (.000)	76	78	67	52	60	67	59

to mediate well with the candidate-level, but when we look at the figures for other groups, clear differences begin to emerge. All elite groups are more in favour of a selective national pension than are the citizens. Targeting gets its highest support among businessmen, but researchers, journalists and members of parliament are also in favour of this option.

Determination of the benefit level

The level of social benefits is also a relevant question, since wide coverage does not help much if the level of the benefits is poor. A low level of benefits may also have some side-effects. For example, they may create incentives for the better-off to seek social security from the private sector, which may endanger equality among pensioners (Kangas and Palme 1989). There are many ways in which the benefit-level can be influenced. First, benefits can be flat-rate, the same for all, regardless of how much people have earned during their working life. In the opposite case, benefits can be strictly related to the previous earnings of the claimant. It is also possible to set an upper limit for the benefits, a ceiling which prevents benefits rising above a certain level. Even though almost every other western country has introduced such an upper limit (Palme 1990), there is no pension ceiling in Finland. Table 5.2 provides figures for opinions on flat-rate benefits, earnings-related benefits and the pension ceiling.

Approximately every third citizen has positive opinions on flat-rate benefits. At the MP-candidate level, support is lower, but flat-rate benefits still receive some support. At the elite level, in every group, opinions towards flat-rate benefits are extremely hostile. Earnings-related benefits, then, do not gain wide support at the citizen-level. This finding is in conflict with an analysis done by Ervasti and Kangas (1995), who showed support for the principle of relating pension benefits to previous earnings to be about 75 percent. However, this difference can at least partially be explained by the different wording of the questions. Here, the question emphasised differences in incomes (see Appendix 5.2) which easily turns negative in respondent's minds: they may feel sympathy towards people with low incomes and want their pensions to be good, too. The question used by Ervasti and Kangas referred to the contributions people have made. According to these two different questions dealing with relating the level of benefits to previous earnings, Finns dislike inequality (different levels of

Table 5.2 Support for flat-rate benefits, earnings-related benefits and pension ceiling. Percent shares of positive attitudes. (Values within parentheses are p-values)

	Citizens	Candid-ates	Politics	Business	Research	Admin-istration	Media
Flat-rate (.000)	32	22	5	2	6	3	2
Earnings-related (.000)	42	54	81	96	88	90	90
Pension ceiling (.000)	85	79	65	24	46	67	60

the benefits for the rich and for the poor), but they have positive opinions on such differences which are based on merit during working life. This is a good example of how differences in wording can lead to different results!

When comparing the groups with each other, MP-candidates express somewhat more positive feelings towards earnings-related benefits than the citizens; all the elite groups are extremely positive towards the principle of relating pension benefits to earnings. A pension ceiling receives a high level of support from both the citizens and the candidates. Also, members of parliament and civil servants want to restrict high pension benefits. Businessmen have the most hostile attitudes towards an upper limit in pension benefits: the simplest possible explanation here is that they have the highest incomes of all the studied groups and an upper limit would immediately cut their pensions. Out of the elite groups, the opinions of researchers towards a pension ceiling are most negative, the reasons for this perhaps being that they know best the problems attached to pension ceilings.

Administration of pension funds

Pension funds contain a lot of money and are therefore the object of great interest. One of the most fundamental questions relating to pension funds is their administration. Who should control these funds and by which rules? Studies focusing on pension reforms have shown that different interest groups have had strong views on how funds should be organised: in the Scandinavian countries, big business and rightist parties tried to get the funds controlled by private companies, while trade unions and political parties on the left wanted more centralised, governmental control (Salminen 1993). Table 5.3 shows results regarding the administration of pension funds.

Starting from the bottom of the table, it seems that none of the studied groups trust private companies so much that they are willing to give the administration of funds solely to them. On the other hand, the first option, funds administered by the government only, is quite strongly supported since 36 percent of the citizens are in favour of this option. Support falls down to 31 percent at the MP-candidate level and 23 percent at the level of MPs. Other

Table 5.3 Opinions on the administration of pension funds. Values are percentages

	Citizens	Candidates	Politics	Business	Research	Administration	Media
Only the government	36	31	23	6	12	15	7
Private companies under strict supervision	53	57	63	45	64	65	67
Private companies with broad guidelines	11	12	14	45	25	19	27
Private companies strictly on their own	1	1	1	4	0	2	0

groups do not have such positive feelings about governmental administration. The most favoured alternative here is the second one: in every group, the wish is for private companies to administer pension funds, but under the strict supervision of the government. The group of businessmen is willing to give more freedom to private companies in administration.

Multivariate analysis: controlling for differences in backgrounds

Previous studies which have analysed the elite have shown that these groups usually differ from citizens when it comes to their backgrounds (for example, Verba et al. 1987). This is also true with our data-sets: candidates and the elite are better educated than the citizens, they more often belong to white-collar classes, their average age is higher, their gender structure is skewed to men and although we did not have a question about incomes in the elite questionnaire, obviously they have higher incomes than the citizens. Are the differences in opinions shown in Tables 5.1–5.3 due to these differences in backgrounds? Do the opinions of the candidates and the elite differ from those of the citizens because they are better educated or older? Earlier research might tend to support this kind of hypothesis, since several studies (Hasenfeld and Rafferty 1989; Ervasti and Kangas 1995; Svallfors 1995; Forma 1997a) have shown that opinions towards the welfare state are influenced by social class, income and education of the respondents. Thus, the variance which is caused by differences in backgrounds should be controlled for.

Now, our data-sets allow us to control the effect of certain background variables. These variables are gender, age, education and political party. The method used here is regression analysis with dummy-variables which allows us to use independent variables measured in the ordinal level. The methodological strategy utilised here is the same as in comparative opinion studies (Papadakis and Bean 1993; Svallfors 1997; Forma and Kangas, Chapter 8, this volume) where 'regime-dummies' are used to catch variation in opinions between different welfare state regimes after the socio-economic position of the respondents is controlled for. Here, we will try to catch variation which remains between levels (citizens, candidates and the elite) after differences in gender, age, education and party affiliation are controlled for.

In order to avoid categories with only a few cases, we have to use quite large age groups and, for the same reason, the two lowest education levels were combined. The equations consist of the gender, education, political party and 'level' (citizens, candidates and elite) of the respondent. One category from each variable is left out from the models: these categories create a baseline against which all the other groups are contrasted. This baseline in our models is a male citizen below 40 years old who has completed a low education level (vocational schooling or less) and who votes for the Social Democratic Party. The constant gives an estimate about opinions of this kind of person and the regression coefficients indicate the difference from the value of the constant. Dependent variables have been constructed so that the more positive the opinions are towards the issue in question, the bigger is the value for the dependent variable. Regarding the administration of pension funds, the higher the value of the dependent variable, the tighter governmental control for administration of pension funds is wanted. Hence, negative coefficients mean more negative opinions and the positive sign indicates the opposite. Table 5.4 provides results of the regression analyses.

There are statistically significant differences between men and women, age-groups, education categories and party affiliations. Better-educated people and supporters of the rightist parties want earnings-related benefits and they also want to give more freedom to the administration of pension funds. They do not want flat-rate benefits, pension ceilings or government financing. Age is also an important determinant of the opinions in some questions: older people support means-testing and pension ceilings, and they also want stricter administration of pension funds.

Table 5.4 Regression analyses of pension attitudes in Finland. B-coefficients.

	Means-testing	Universal-ism	Flat-rate	Earnings-related	Pension ceiling	Admin-istration
Gender						
Man	—	—	—	—	—	—
Woman	−0.145*	0.013	0.098	0.247***	0.159**	−0.001
Age (years)						
below 40	—	—	—	—	—	—
40–49	−0.001	0.164	−0.005	0.018	0.240***	0.073*
over 50	0.286***	−0.033	−0.013	0.131*	0.276***	0.114***
Education						
No further schooling/ vocational education	—	—	—	—	—	—
College	−0.161	−0.118	−0.479***	0.355***	−0.094	−0.065
Academic schooling	−0.072	−0.148	−0.734***	0.712***	−0.263***	−0.157***
Political party						
National Coalition	0.068	−0.013	−0.523***	0.549***	−0.649***	−0.354***
Centre Party	−0.062	0.138	−0.065	−0.089	−0.018	−0.057
Social Democrats	—	—	—	—		
Left League	−0.128	0.174	0.427***	0.349**	0.372***	0.298***
Other Party	0.103	−0.098	−0.039	−0.067	−0.166*	−0.138***
Level						
Citizens	—	—	—	—	—	—
Candidates	−0.350***	0.106	−0.461***	0.032	−0.230***	−0.064
Elites	0.695***	−0.378**	−0.975***	0.943***	−1.230***	−0.328***
Intercept	3.643***	5.471***	2.950***	2.675***	4.349***	3.336***
Var explained (R²)	0.057	0.020	0.231	0.234	0.198	0.131

Levels of significance: *p ≤ 0.05; ** p ≤ 0.01; *** p ≤ 0.001.

However, coefficients and figures for statistical significance for different levels, candidates and the elite, are of main interest here. They tell us whether the opinions of the candidates and the elite differ from the opinions of the citizens after controlling for background variables. The results indicate that differences between candidates and citizens are without exception smaller than between citizens and the elite groups. There is a statistically highly significant difference between the opinions of the elite groups and the citizens in every issue studied. However, there are also differences between candidates and citizens: the candidates are more hostile towards means testing, flat-rate benefits and pension ceiling than are the citizens. All in all, the results in Table 5.4 indicate that opinion differences between citizens and candidates, on the one hand, and citizens and the elite, on the other, occur not only because of differences in their backgrounds.

Conclusions and discussion

The purpose of this article was to examine opinions towards institutional solutions regarding pension security in Finland. The speciality of the study was to examine not only the opinions of the citizens but also the opinions of the candidates of the 1995 parliamentary elections and five different elite groups of Finnish society. These elite groups were members of parliament, top civil servants, researchers and representatives of the business sector and the media. Previously, welfare state studies have operated at one analytical level only. For example, the famous power-resource approach which has examined the political forces behind welfare state development has focused on the elite and their actions. On the other hand, several opinion studies have examined the opinions of the citizens without linking them to the opinions of the elite or to political decision-making in general. Thus, studies where both the citizens and the elite are included have been absent.

This article aimed to contribute to welfare state research by discussing the connection between the opinions of the citizens and political decision-making. Theoretically, two main difficulties attached to this relationship were identified. First, public opinion is not a clear-cut phenomenon, while, for example, different wordings of the questions may lead to different results. Second, the elite can try to influence public opinion, which also questions the relationship between public opinion and public policy. Thus, it is not easy to aggregate the popular will from the preferences of the people and therefore its impact on public policy remains unclear. The main empirical result of the article was that the opinions of the elite are not the same as the opinions of the citizens. Opinion differences between citizens and the MP-candidates were smaller than the differences between citizens and the elite groups. The elite group whose opinions differed most from the opinions of the citizens were the representatives of the business sector.

But how about the substantial meanings of the results? Often the more or less explicit assumption has been that the citizens desire the continuation of the welfare state, while the elite are introducing cut-backs. In a way, the elite are supposed to act against the will of the citizens. If this is true, the opinions of the elite should be more negative towards the welfare state than the opinions of the citizens. Does our analysis give support for this kind of thinking? Not necessarily. When compared to opinions of the citizens, the opinions of the elite are slightly more positive towards the kind of national pension system which targets benefits to the poor only. Because a fundamental cornerstone of the Scandinavian welfare state model is universalism, this finding indicates criticism towards the present welfare state model. However, regarding the employment pension, the opinions of the elite are more hostile than the opinions of the citizens towards flat-rate benefits and they strongly want that the benefits are diversified according to earnings. They also have more negative feelings than the citizens towards a pension ceiling. Regarding administration of pension funds, the elite – even more than the citizens – are in favour of the present system where funds are administered by private companies under government supervision. Thus, it is not an exaggeration to say that the elite are defending the main principles of the Finnish pension system even more rigorously than are the citizens. Hence, according to our analysis, not only the citizens, but also the elite of Finnish society, support the existing institutional solutions regarding pension security.

The research strategy used in this article was to compare the opinions of the citizens, candidates of the parliamentary elections and different elite groups. What kind of weaknesses may this method have, if we are interested in the relationship between the popular will and political decision-making? At least three weaknesses can be identified: first, opinions do not always tell much about actual behaviour. Even though, for example, a member of parliament reveals an opinion that he/she is strongly in favour of universalism, there is no guarantee that he/she is actively trying to build or maintain universalistic social policy programmes in parliament. Second, political decision-making is not only preference or interest aggregation (Elster 1985). Opinions of the individual are only raw material in the process of political decision-making where bargaining and coordination of interests takes place (Saari 1996). Third, we cannot be sure how honest the opinions revealed in these kind of surveys are. For example, an elite respondent might decide to show how a good friend of the Scandinavian welfare state model he or she is, regardless of his or her true and honest preferences. However, there are also reasons why this kind of method could be used. Opinion studies, when they have several levels like this one, may serve as a good starting point when studying the mediation of interests of the citizens in political decision making (Forma 1997b). If the opinions of the citizens, their representatives and whatever elite group were the same, there would not be much to study. But, when studies report differences in opinions between the citizens and the elite, the need for closer examination of the relationship between the will of the citizens and political decision-making becomes more necessary.

The main conclusion of this article is that the opinions of the elite are not the same as those of the citizens. Moreover, since these two opinions can differ quite dramatically, public opinion is not necessarily a good predictor of public policy. However, according to the evidence found in this article, the elite groups also support the existing institutional solutions regarding pension security in Finland. Therefore, it should be emphasised that differences of opinion between the citizens and the elite are not necessarily bad news for the welfare state. However, regarding opinion studies, one should always be sure exactly what is the dimension of the welfare state which has been focused on (Kangas 1995b: 308). In this study the dependent variables measured support for different institutional solutions for pension security. The results could have been different had we studied, for example, whether pension benefits should be cut (Blomberg and Kroll, Chapter 4, this volume).

All in all, comparing opinions of the elite and citizens seems to be an important and fascinating research field for opinion researchers. At the time of welfare state retrenchment it is more important than ever to study how decisions about social policies are implemented. Because of scarce resources for social policies, the elite are forced to make hard political decisions regarding the welfare state, the outcomes of which are visible in the everyday lives of ordinary citizens. Opinion studies which utilise data both from the level of the citizens and the elite could be a fruitful approach in order to examine how the will of the citizens matters in contemporary society.

Appendix 5.1 Description of the three data-sets analysed

I. Citizens (*n* = 1737), response rate 56 %:

- Postal survey. Random sample representing Finnish citizens aged 18 to 70.

II. Candidates of the 1995 parliament elections (n = 529), response rate 49 %:

- Postal survey. Constructed from the lists delivered by political parties. Candidates which were left out from the sample were excluded systematically from the lists.

Number of cases and response rates among political parties: National Coalition (*n* = 73) 41%, Center Party (*n* = 82) 41%, Green League (*n* = 97), 65%, Social-democrats (*n* = 91) 46%, Left League (*n* = 95) 64%, Other parties (*n* = 91) 36%.

III. Elites (*n* = 388), response rate 57%:

- Postal survey. Constructed from various sources by using the following criteria:

Politics: All members of the parliament who were elected in 1995. *Business-men*: The top leaders of 100 biggest companies in Finland according to their turnover 1994. *Research*: leaders and researchers of the most central research institutes (economic and social ones). Includes also research material from some other relevant institutions: National Research and Development Centre for Welfare and Health, The Social Insurance Institution, Government Institution for Economic Research, Taxpayers Association of

Finland, The Central Pension Security Institute, The Confederation of Unions for Academic Professionals in Finland, Research Institute of the Finnish Economy, Center for Finnish Business and Policy Studies, Finnish Confederation of Salaried Employees, Central Organization of Finnish Trade Unions. *Administration*: top civil servants from the following institutions: Finnish Parliament, Ministry of Education, Ministry of Social Affairs and Health, Ministry of Finance, Bank of Finland, President's Office, Ministry of Labour and Prime Minister's Office. *Media*: Editors-in-chief of the 20 biggest newspapers in Finland (according to their circulation 1995) plus the main newspapers of the political parties, two afternoon newspapers and editorial staff from TV and radio news.

Response rates among groups: Politicians 55%, business-men 59%, research 52%, administration 70% and media 55%.

Appendix 5.2 Questions and answering alternatives used

I. Entitlement rules

What do you think of these government policies for providing income for retired people . . .

● *A government old age pension paid from taxes given only to poor people?* (Means-testing)
● *A government old age pension paid from taxes given to everyone over 65.* (Universalism)

Answering alternatives: 1. 'The best policy'; 2. 'Very good'; 3. 'Good'; 4. 'Neither good nor bad'; 5. 'Bad'; 6. 'Very bad'; 7. 'Terrible'.

II. Determination of benefit level

Should superannuation benefits be:

● *The same for all regardless of how much they have paid in.* (Flat-rate benefits)
● *Bigger for people who had high incomes when they worked, and smaller for the poorly paid?* (Earnings-related benefits)
● *Should there be a ceiling on benefits, a maximum that anyone can get regardless how much the have contributed?* (Pension ceiling)

Answering alternatives: 1. 'Yes, definitely'; 2. 'Yes, probably'; 3. 'Mixed feelings, yes and no'; 4. 'No, probably not'; 5. 'No, definitely not'.

III. Administration of funds

● Should superannuation schemes be run by the government, private companies or what?

Answering alternatives: 1. 'Government should run them itself'; 2. 'Private companies – like banks and insurance companies – should run them under strict government supervision'; 3. 'Private companies should run them under broad government guidelines'; 4. 'Private companies should run them entirely on their own'.

Acknowledgements

The author wishes to thank Helena Blomberg, Olli Kangas, Christian Kroll and Stefan Svallfors for their valuable comments for earlier versions of the article.

References

Arrow, Kenneth (1951) *Social Choice and Individual Values*, New York: Wiley & Sons.

Bottomore, Tom (1993) *Élites and Society*, London: Routledge.

Converse, Philip (1964) 'The Nature of Belief Systems in Mass Publics', in Luttbeg, Norman (ed.) *Public Opinion and Public Policy*, Homewood: The Dorsey Press.

Edelman, Murray (1977) *Political Language: Words that Succeed and Politics that Fail*, New York: Academic Press.

Elster, Jon (1985) 'The Market and the Forum' in Jon Elster and Aanud Hylland (eds) *Foundations of Social Choice Theory*, Cambridge: Cambridge University Press.

Erikson, Robert S. (1976) 'The Relationship Between Public Opinion and State Policy: a New Look Based on Some Forgotten Data'. *American Journal of Political Science*, 20(1): 511–35.

Ervasti, Heikki and Kangas, Olli (1995) 'Class Bases of Universal Social Policy: Pension Policy Attitudes in Finland'. *European Journal of Political Research*, 27(3): 347–67.

Esping-Andersen, Gösta and Korpi, Walter (1987) 'From Poor Relief to Institutional Welfare States: The Development of Scandinavian Social Policy', in Robert Erikson, Erik J. Hansen, Stein Ringen and Hannu Uusitalo (eds) *The Scandinavian Model. Welfare States and Welfare Research*, New York: M. E. Sharpe Inc.

Esping-Andersen, Gösta (1985) *Politics against Markets. The Social Democratic Road to Power*, New Jersey: Princeton University Press.

Fishkin, James S. (1995) *The Voice of the People: Public Opinion and Democracy*, New Haven: Yale University Press.

Forma, Pauli (1997a) 'The Rational Legitimacy of the Welfare State. Popular Support for Ten Income Transfer Schemes in Finland', *Policy and Politics*, 25(3): 235–49.

Forma, Pauli (1997b) *The Mediation of Class Interests in the Parliamentary Arena*, University of Turku, Department of Social Policy. Series B:12.

Gamson, William A., Croteau, David, Hoynes, William and Sasson, Theodore (1992) Media Images and the Social Construction of Reality, *Annual Review of Sociology*, 18(3), 373–93.

Gans, Herbert J. (1979) *Deciding What's the News*, New York: Vintage Books.

Hadenius, Axel (1985) 'Citizens Strike a Balance: Discontent With Taxes, Content With Spending', *Journal of Public Policy*, 5(3): 349–63.

Hasenfeld, Yeheskel and Rafferty, Jane A. (1989) 'The Determinants of Public Attitudes towards the Welfare State', *Social Forces*, 67(4): 1027–48.

Heclo, Hugh (1974) *Modern Social Politics in Britain and Sweden*, New Haven: Yale University Press.

Jacobs, L. R. and Shapiro, R. Y. (1994) Studying Substantive Democracy, *Political Science and Politics*, 27(1): 9–21.

Jäntti, Markus, Kangas, Olli and Ritakallio, Veli-Matti (1996) 'From Marginalism to Institutionalism: Distributional Consequences of the Transformation of the Finnish Pension Regime', *Review of Income and Wealth*, 42(4): 473–91.

Kangas, Olli and Palme, Joakim (1989) 'The Private–Public Mix in Pension Policy', in Jon E. Kolberg (ed.) *The Study of the Welfare State Regimes*, New York: M. E. Sharpe.

Kangas, Olli (1995a) 'Interest Mediation and Popular Will', in Stefan Svallfors (ed.) *In the Eye of the Beholder. Opinions on Welfare and Justice in Comparative Perspective*, Umeå: Scandbook.

Kangas, Olli (1995b) 'Attitudes on Means-Tested Social Benefits in Finland', *Acta Sociologica*, 38(4): 299–310.

Kangas, Olli (1997) 'Self-Interest and the Common Good: Impact of Norms, Selfishness and Context in Social Policy Opinions', *Journal of Socio-Economics*, 26(5): 475–94.

Korpi, Walter (1980) 'Social Policy and Distributional Conflict in the Capitalist Democracies. A Preliminary Comparative Framework', *West European Politics*, 3(3): 296–316.

Korpi, Walter (1983) *The Democratic Class Struggle*, Worcester: Routledge and Kegan Paul.

Korpi, Walter (1989) 'Power, Politics and State Autonomy in the Development of Social Citizenship: Social Rights during Sickness in Eighteen OECD Countries since 1930', *American Sociological Review*, 54(2): 309–29.

Korpi, Walter (1996) 'Eurosclerosis and the Sclerosis of Objectivity: on the Role of Values Among Economic Policy Experts', *The Economic Journal*, 106 (November): 1727–46.

Kuran, Timur (1995) *Private Truths, Public Lies*, London: Harvard University Press.

Michels, Robert (1966) *Political Parties*, New York: The Free Press.

Monroe, Alan D. (1979) 'Consistency between Public Preferences and National Policy Decisions', *American Politics Quarterly*, 7(1): 3–19.

Mosca, Gaetano (1939) *The Ruling Class*, New York: McGraw-Hill Book Company.

Page, Benjamin I. and Shapiro, Robert Y. (1983) 'Effects of Public Opinion on Public Policy', *American Political Science Review*, 77(2): 175–90.

Page, Benjamin I. and Shapiro, Robert Y. (1989) 'Educating and Manipulating the Public', in Michael Margolis and Gary A. Mauser (eds) *Manipulating Public Opinion: Essays on Public Opinion as a Dependant Variable*, Pacific Grove: Cole Publishing Company.

Page, Benjamin I. and Shapiro, Robert Y. (1993) 'The Rational Public and Democracy', in George E. Marcus, and Russel, E. Hanson (eds) *Reconsidering the Democratic Public*, Pennsylvania: The Pennsylvania State University Press.

Palme, Joakim (1990) *Pension Rights in Welfare Capitalism. The Development of Old-Age Pensions in 18 OECD Countries 1930 to 1985*, Stockholm: Swedish Institute for Social Research.

Papadakis, Elim and Bean, Clive (1993) 'Popular Support for the Welfare State: Comparison between Institutional Regimes', *Journal of Public Policy*, 13(2): 227–54.

Papadakis, Elim (1992) 'Public Opinion, Public Policy and the Welfare State', *Political Studies*, 40(1): 21–37.

Parenti, Michael (1989) 'News Media Bias and Class Control', In M. Margolis and G. A. Mauser (eds) *Manipulating Public Opinion: Essays on Public Opinion as a Dependent Variable*, California: Brooks/Cole Publishing Company.

Pareto, Vilfredo (1963) *The Mind and Society. A Treatise on General Society*, New York: Dover Publications.

Putnam, Robert (1976) *The Comparative Study of Political Elites*, New Jersey: Prentice

Hall Inc.

Riker, William (1982) *Liberalism against Populism*, San Francisco: W. H. Freeman and Company.

Saari, Juho (1996) *Sosiaalipolitiikka markkinariippuvuuden vähentäjänä*, Stakes, Research Reports 69, Saarijärvi: Gummerus.

Salminen, Kari (1993) *Pension Schemes in the Making*, The Central Pension Security Institute. Studies 1993:2, Helsinki: Hakapaino.

Smith, J. (1987) 'That Which We Call Welfare by any Other Name Would Smell Sweeter', *Public Opinion Quarterly*, 51(1): 75–83.

Stephens, John D. (1979) *Transition from Capitalism*, London: Macmillan.

Stryker, Robin (1990) 'Science, Class and the Welfare State: A Class-Centered Functional Account', *American Journal of Sociology*, 96(3): 684–726.

Svallfors, Stefan (1995) 'The End of Class Politics? Structural Cleavages and Attitudes to Swedish Welfare Policies', *Acta Sociologica*, 36(1): 53–74.

Svallfors, Stefan (1996) Välfärdstatens moraliska ekonomi. Välfärdsopinionen i 90-talets Sverige, Umeå: Boréa Bokförlak.

Svallfors, Stefan (1997) 'Worlds of Welfare and Attitudes to Redistribution: A Comparison of Eight Western Nations', *European Sociological Review*, 14(3): 283–309.

Taylor-Gooby, Peter (1995) 'Who Wants the Welfare State? Support for State Welfare in European Countries', in Stefan Svallfors (ed.), *In the Eye of Beholder: Opinions on Welfare and Justice in Comparative Perspective*, Stockholm: Bank of Sweden Tercentary Foundation.

Verba, Sidney, Kelman, Steven, Orren, Gary R., Ichoro, Miyake, Watanuki, Joji, Ikuo, Kabashima and Ferree, Donald G. (1987) *Elites and the Idea of Equality. A Comparison of Japan, Sweden and the United States*, Cambridge, MA: Cambridge University Press.

Whiteley, Peter (1981) 'Public Opinion and the Demand for Social Welfare in Britain', *Journal of Social Policy*, 10(4): 453–70.

Wilensky, Harold (1981) 'Democratic Corporatism, Consensus and Social Policy: Reflections on Changing Values and the "Crisis" of the Welfare State', in *Welfare State in Crisis*, Paris: OECD.

Zaller, John R. (1992) *The Nature and Origins of Mass Opinion*, Cambridge: Cambridge University Press.

6

PROGRESSIVE TAXATION
FAREWELL?

Attitudes to income redistribution and
taxation in Sweden, Great Britain
and the United States

Jonas Edlund

One of the major goals of the welfare state is to decrease market-generated inequalities. In the struggle of redistributing wealth, the personal income tax has been one of the most powerful tools available for governments. Only imposed on the very rich at the turn of the twentieth century, the personal income tax base gradually expanded, and by the end of the second world war a majority of income earners paid income tax. Since then, the personal income tax has been a familiar aspect of modern tax policy (Peters 1991).

During the 1980s, a wave of tax reforms swept over the Western world, all strikingly similar to each other. In virtually all countries, reforms aimed at widening the tax base, cutting back tax expenditures, increasing indirect tax revenues, and lowering tax rates on corporate and personal income. These reforms indicated a substantial shift in income tax policy, as cuts in statutory levels mainly affected the upper brackets in the tax scale.

Explaining the commonalities regarding the structure and timing of the tax reforms, Steinmo (1994a) suggests forces inherent to the increasing global-isation of the world economy. In order to attract mobile capital, countries have been forced to redesign their tax systems in a more regressive direction. Similarly, Whalley (1990) mentions tax competition as a possible explanation for lowering rates of corporate taxation. Explaining other conformities it is additionally suggested that these tax reforms may reflect common intellectual influences in tax policy-making. Not fully satisfied with these explanations, Musgrave (1990) suggests a third force underpinning tax reforms, particularly the abandoning of income tax progression. 'The major factor [behind tax reforms] has been a change in political climate toward a less egalitarian view of distributive justice' (Musgrave 1990: 317).

From a quite different perspective, Inglehart (1990) reaches a similar conclusion, as he argues that issues of economic inequality and distributive justice have increasingly lost their political significance for the Western electorate. The combination of economic prosperity and extensive welfare policies have in some areas 'passed a point of diminishing returns'. Welfare policies 'have largely solved the problems they are capable of solving most readily – and have thereby reduced the demand for more of the same' (Inglehart 1990: 257). Consequently, redistributive policies tend to get crowded out from the political agenda as political priorities among the public shift to other mainly non-economical issues.

Thus, while some of the above arguments propose that tax reforms are responses to changing economic environments forcing governments to adopt less progressive tax policies, others maintain – which is of particular interest in the perspective of this chapter – that progressive taxation and income redistribution for various reasons have increasingly lost political support among the electorate. Focusing foremost on the latter set of arguments, the first objective of this chapter is to examine to what extent redistributive tax policies receive public support in Sweden, Great Britain and the United States. While these three countries share apparent commonalities as advanced industrialised Western democracies, a closer inspection reveals significant differences with respect to their institutional frameworks.

First, while all three countries have experienced large and far-reaching tax reforms, the tax systems still differ substantially in terms of revenue yield and distribution of taxes. Indeed, analysing the historical trajectories of tax policies in Sweden, Great Britain and the United States, Steinmo (1993) argues that these tax systems have been shaped by the broader institutional contexts within which they are embedded, and thus have come to represent different models of tax policy-making.

Second, in the welfare state regime typology provided by Esping-Andersen (1990) – in which regime types are discerned according to their institutional characteristics and distributive outcomes – two archetypal cases of different types of welfare state regimes, the social-democratic and the liberal regime, have come to be represented by Sweden and the United States, respectively. Great Britain on the other hand may be seen as representing a border case, an 'odd mixture' of the liberal and the social-democratic welfare models (Ginsburg 1992: 23).

While numerous studies in comparative public policy have demonstrated that the institutional configurations upon which the welfare state is founded have substantial impact on living standards and the distribution of various goods, it has increasingly been recognised that 'institutions can be expected to significantly affect the definitions of interests within the population and to influence the patterns of coalition formation among interest groups' (Korpi and Palme 1995: 4). In this perspective, institutions are more than products of political struggles. Institutions are in themselves powerful forces in creating interests, political conflicts and shaping public preferences (Esping-Andersen 1990; Skocpol 1992; Pierson 1993, 1994; Steinmo 1994b).

These suggestions lead us into the second objective of this chapter. Acknowledging that the countries under study differ in important respects regarding their institutional characteristics, and that these distinctive ways of organising state activities are supposed significantly to affect popular beliefs concerning the role of the state in society, it is expected that attitudes to income redistribution and taxation will vary both cross-nationally and between different strata within each nation. Arguments underpinning these assumptions will be elaborated in forthcoming sections.

As the general argument is that institutions matter for public attitudes to welfare policies, the following section will briefly recapitulate the categorisation of welfare states based on the writings of Esping-Andersen (1990) and Korpi and Palme (1995). As we will see, the provided arguments are mainly founded on the institutional characteristics of welfare policies and the accompanying distributive processes and outcomes; less attention has been paid to designs of tax systems and to what extent levels and distributions of taxes may generate social controversies over progressive taxation. Therefore, a short description and some summary measures of the tax systems in question with emphasis on the personal income tax and its distributive profile will be included. This will be followed by a brief description of the data and methods used in this chapter. Thereafter, the assumed implications of the different institutional configurations upon popular attitudes to redistribution will be discussed and subjected to empirical analysis. In the final section, the suggested scenarios are evaluated and discussed in the light of the main results.

Welfare regimes and tax system characteristics in Sweden, Great Britain and the United States

A key assumption in the arguments following below is that institutions structure interests and preferences. The concept of institution is less than clear-cut (Hall and Taylor 1996). Most authors, however, rely on a definition similar to the one provided by Levi (1990: 405), in which institutions are defined as 'formal arrangements for aggregating individuals and regulating their behavior through the use of explicit rules and decision processes enforced by an actor or set of actors formally recognized as possessing such power'. With this definition tax systems and welfare state programmes, as well as the set of rules regulating the political system and state bureaucracy fall within the concept, while factors such as class structures, 'political culture' and informal norms are excluded.

The typology of welfare state regimes presented by Esping-Andersen (1990) attempts to conceptualise the different ways societies have organised the network of social protection, and discerns three distinct types of welfare regimes: the liberal, the social democratic, and finally the conservative which will not be covered in this chapter. In the liberal welfare regime, into which the United

States is classified, elements of market solutions predominate as those that are better off are supposed to protect themselves via various private forms of insurance. State benefits are generally means-tested and targeted at those worst off in society. Social spending and tax revenue levels are relatively low. In the social-democratic regime social protection is linked to citizenship. Encompassing welfare programmes dominate and benefits are either income-related, coupled with a rather high basic security level for those with low income, or provided as citizens' rights. Social spending levels are comparatively high and are mainly financed by tax revenues. The prime example of this regime is Sweden, but Nordic countries in general meet the standards of this regime concept. While Britain has frequently been classified as a 'weak' liberal regime type, others have (which is perhaps more appropriate) interpreted the British welfare state as a border case, possessing some characteristics reminiscent of the social-democratic regime type while other features fit well into the liberal regime concept (Ginsburg 1992).

Explaining to what extent redistributive policies tend to decrease market-generated income inequalities and poverty, the distribution and levels of taxes and transfers are essential (Åberg 1989; Korpi and Palme 1995). As shown in Appendix 6.1, the distribution of income is more unequal in the United States and Britain compared to Sweden. Using poverty rates among working-age citizens as a complementary measure, a similar picture emerges which in addition shows the relative inefficiency of the American transfer and tax systems to reduce poverty.

It is well documented that effects of welfare policies, not only with respect to income redistribution, vary substantially between different regime types. Almost regardless of which measurements are used for classification, the limited role of the American welfare state is evident. Britain is generally located in a middle stratum, whereas Sweden ranks among the most advanced and generous welfare states (Esping-Andersen 1990; Palme 1990; Fritzell 1991; Kangas 1991; Korpi and Palme 1995; McFate et al. 1995). Still, as noted by Steinmo (1993: 1), less is known about the ways governments finance their welfare policies.

In a thorough analysis of the British, American and Swedish tax systems, Steinmo (1993) demonstrates that governments have chosen different approaches to finance their welfare policies. While these tax systems show some similar patterns in terms of the types of taxes collected, the levels and distribution of particular taxes vary, as shown in Appendix 6.2. In all three countries the bulk of revenues are collected via three major taxes: the personal income tax, social security contributions, and taxes on goods and services.

The Swedish tax system is perhaps best characterised as a broad-based, fairly standardised, high revenue-collecting tax system. According to some commentators, taxes are distributed in a less progressive direction compared to Britain and the United States, due to the high rates of taxes paid by ordinary workers and few tax deductions available, as well as the significant amount of taxes collected via the broad-based goods and services tax, which virtually does not allow any exemptions (Rose and Peters 1978; Steinmo 1993). Recent changes in tax legislation have followed and even accentuated these patterns. Through consecutive reforms during the 1980s, which culminated in the 'tax reform of the century' in 1991, statutory tax rates were cut, tax expenditures were scaled back, revenue sources were widened and a significant part of revenues has been redirected from income taxes to consumption taxes (Åberg 1993: 9–12; SOU 1995: 104).

The American tax system, as it has been argued, is foremost distinguished by its equity orientation, complexity and low revenue yield. Tax policy-makers generally have tried to achieve tax equity via various sorts of tax allowances, which in turn have created a complicated, particularistic and low revenue-collecting tax system. Recognising the complexity and inefficiency of the tax system, the goals of the major tax reform enacted in 1986 were to simplify the tax code and obtain a more fair and economically efficient tax system. Changes in the tax system included overall personal income tax cuts, which were financed with expanded corporate taxes, while the distribution of personal income taxes was largely preserved. However, in many respects these attempts did not comply with the objectives of fairness and simplicity. Perhaps most important, the tax code remained complicated, as some gains in simplicity were seriously offset by the introduction of other complex tax measures (Slemrod 1990; Steinmo 1993). Thus, similar to tax reforms in Sweden, United States tax reforms during the 1980s more or less followed previous paths of tax policy-making. The American tax system is still distinguished by its complexity and low tax revenue yield.

Similarly to the classification of welfare regimes, in terms of tax revenues, Britain's tax system falls somewhere between the American and the Swedish. While the British tax system has been characterised as a system in constant change, a number of tax reforms introduced during the conservative era of the 1980s transformed the British into a more consistent and stable system. As in Sweden, tax rates and available tax deductions at the personal level have been reduced, while indirect consumption taxes have been increased (Whalley 1990). Taken all together, it has been argued that these tax reforms have redistributed the tax burden downwards (Steinmo 1993).

Acknowledging that the personal income tax is an important ingredient in modern tax policy and that it has been subject to change during recent reforms, we still have not analysed the level and distribution of the income tax among the public at large in Sweden, Britain and the United States. As already pointed out, a significant characteristic of the tax reforms carried out during the 1980s was the lowered marginal tax rates on high incomes. In the US, the previous multi-bracket tax scale ranging from 14 per cent to 70 per cent, was replaced with a two-bracket scale of 15 per cent and 28 per cent, complemented with an additional 5 per cent surcharge for some high-income earners. In Britain, during the Thatcher era, the number of tax brackets was reduced from 13 to two, and previous tax rates running from 30 per cent to 83 per cent were changed to 25 per cent and 40 per cent. Similar patterns also occurred in Sweden. By 1991, an 11-bracket tax scale running from 34 per cent to 80 per cent had gradually changed into a two-rate structure of 30 per cent and 50 per cent (Whalley 1990).

However, while statutory tax rates may play a significant role in political debate, they offer only a limited guidance as measures of tax progressivity as various sorts of tax allowances and deductions may substantially affect actual distribution of taxes. In making cross-national comparisons of the personal income tax distribution, a common strategy is to construct a model tax payer equal to an 'average production worker' (OECD 1991). Comparing OECD countries with this measure, Sweden scores among the highest according to taxes paid, while Britain and the United States are in the middle. Taking social security contributions into account, country differences decrease to some extent, but the take-home pay for a Swedish worker is considerably lower than in most other countries (Appendix 6.3).

Since two drawbacks of this approach are its limited scope and static treatment of tax reliefs, a second strategy is to compare the distribution of taxes using country-specific personal income data. Data were obtained from an OECD survey conducted in 1987–8. At that time, the United States and Britain had implemented the two-bracket tax rates set out above, while the Swedish tax system used a four-bracket tax schedule beginning at 35 per cent and ending with a top marginal tax rate at 72 per cent.

As actual distributions of taxes are determined both by statutory tax rates and the structure of tax allowances and exemptions, it is useful to apply different concepts of income. The broadest concept available is income subject to tax. The second concept applied is taxable income. In Table 6.1, some summary measures are applied.[1] The increased gini coefficients when moving from income subject to tax to taxable income, identify an element of progressivity in the way taxable income is defined, which in effect is substantially stronger in Sweden and Britain than in the United States. Further, income minus tax is more equally distributed than the other income measures, which indicates the effect of a progressive tax rate schedule. Finally, the distribution of taxes are clearly more progressive in the United States and Britain compared to Sweden.

Thus, a general trademark of the tax system studied is that the income tax is clearly progressive. It is not the 'relatively poor who generate the bulk of tax revenues' (Taylor-Gooby 1993: 90), at least not considering the income tax. On the contrary, especially in the United States and Britain, the distribution of taxes is definitely weighted towards higher income classes. Second, arguments asserting that the United States and Britain have 'more progressive tax systems than has "socialist" Sweden' (Steinmo 1993: 2), need to be qualified. If the emphasis is on the distribution of taxes, disregarding the size of the average tax rate, the British and American tax systems are far more progressive than the Swedish, which is indicated by the Suits measure in Table 6.1. However, if

Table 6.1 Tax system progressivity in Sweden, Great Britain and the United States. Income and tax distribution estimated with gini coefficients and tax progressivity measures. *c.* 1987

	Sweden	Rank*	Britain	Rank*	USA	Rank*
1. Distribution (gini) for:						
a. ... Taxable income	0.59	10	0.78	13	0.80	14
b. ... Income subject to tax	0.47	10	0.45	7	0.79	15
c. ... Income subject to tax						
minus taxes	0.42	5	0.42	5	0.78	15
d. ... Net taxes	0.59	2	0.84	13	0.88	14
2. Measures of progressivity[a]						
a. ... Musgrave[b]	1.08	1	1.06	7	1.03	13
b. ... Suits[c]	0.24	13	0.72	2	0.66	3

Source: OECD (1990). * Rank orders are among 15 major OECD countries. 1a–d: The higher the rank the more equal distribution. 2a–b: The higher the rank the more progressive tax system.

Notes
a   Using income subject to tax as income concept.
b   A measure of change in pre-tax income and post-tax income distributions based on gini coefficients.
c   A measure of gini coefficients for taxes set against pre-tax income.

progressivity is measured by the changes in income distribution, which the Musgrave measure does, by comparing post-tax and pre-tax distributions, the Swedish tax system is considerably more progressive than the American, while the British is somewhere in between. This is explained by another important component, the average tax rate.

Acknowledging that the institutional configurations of the welfare state differ between the countries in question, what implications may these differences have for attitudes to income redistribution and taxation among the public at large? This will be analysed in the following sections.

Data and methods

The data used in this chapter were collected within the frames of the International Social Survey Program (ISSP). The programme was established in the mid-1980s as an attempt to create truly comparable attitudinal data-sets. Since then, a wide range of topics have been surveyed, and the number of participating countries has grown considerably (Davis and Jowell 1989; Svallfors 1996).

The bulk of the data used for analysis comes from the 1992 ISSP module on Social Inequality, which was conducted in Britain and the United States in 1992, while the Swedish survey was fielded in 1991. The response rate for Britain is 56 per cent of a total net sample of 1,920 adult citizens. Corresponding figures are for Sweden 63 per cent and 1,453, while the American response rate is 84 per cent out of 1,517 individuals. All samples are nationally representative and weighted according to the principles described in the code-book (ISSP 1992).[2]

An analysis of the response rates for Sweden shows that non-responses are more frequent among the elderly, among those with low income, and among those living in large cities. Neither the British, nor the American sample seem particularly biased. Another problem is that the British sample lacks one of the items on progressive taxation. A similar item from the 1990 ISSP Role of Government module will be used as a substitute.

A final note of concern is the differences in coding schemes used for some of the background variables. This relates particularly to education and party pre-ference, as these systems almost by nature are nation-specific, and occupation. Five different occupational schemes have been reclassified – following the works of Erikson (n.d.), Goldthorpe and Heath (1992) and Ganzeboom and Treiman (1994) – in order to, as far as possible, meet the standards of the Erikson/Goldthorpe classification schema (Erikson and Goldthorpe 1992).[3]

The above remarks about response rates, time lags between surveys and differences in coding procedures, suggest cautious interpretations of data. We should not take gross percentage distributions on single items too literally, but instead pay more attention to patterns of correlations, both between different attitudinal items, and between structural factors and attitudes; a 'gestalt' as Scheuch (1989) puts it.

Methods used in the analysis range from simple frequency tables to multi-variate statistical techniques such as multiple classification analysis (MCA) and logistic regression. MCA is a method which suits multivariate analysis when the independent variables are categorical and the dependent variable is at least on the interval scale level. MCA estimates coefficients for bivariate relationships (empirical means and eta) as well as coefficients controlled for the impact of other independent variables (adjusted means and beta) (Andrews *et al.* 1973). In analysis in which the dependent variable is dichotomous, logistic regression is preferred (Tabachnick and Fidell 1996). The coefficient, often denoted as the odds ratio, is expressed as the ratio between the odds for a given category compared to a reference category to have a certain value in the dependent variable, e.g. how many times higher or lower the odds for women compared to men is to be in favour of progressive taxation.

Attitudes to income distribution and taxation

The brief description of the main characteristics of the American, British and Swedish welfare states revealed some clearly marked differences, but in what ways may these admittedly different welfare state regimes affect public attitudes to welfare policies?

According to some statements, the impact of institutions in this context appears to be negligible. As pointed out in the introduction, Musgrave (1990) asserts that there has been a shift in value preferences among Western nations,

in which support for state redistribution and progressive taxation has lost much of its popularity. As Musgrave does not present any data, it is not clear whether he refers to changing value patterns among political elites, the public at large, or both. Steinmo (1993: 193) is more specific and argues that variations among welfare states is less associated with dissimilarities in public attitudes than with policy choices made by political elites. Accordingly it is proposed that 'both Swedes and Americans like public spending and hate taxes'. Somewhat surprising from an institutional point of view, we would according to this argument not expect to find any significant cross-country differences concerning public attitudes toward redistribution and taxation. While it may be commonly assumed that 'citizens like the benefits they receive . . ., but do not like to pay the . . . taxes', there are, as readily admitted by Peters (1991: 152), nevertheless reasons to expect that attitudinal patterns vary cross-nationally.

Some authors disregard the normative impact of institutions – in the sense that institutions may exercise long-term influence on perceptions and interpretations of how various social affairs should be organised in society – and devote more attention to the relationships between levels of welfare state intervention and popular support for welfare policies. As summarised by Coughlin (1980), research within this tradition has stressed that public willingness to reduce welfare policies tend to appear when welfare state expansion has passed a certain point – a critical threshold beyond which the perceived necessity for increased spending fades away, while public opposition to the burden of taxes financing ambitious welfare policies tend to rise. Thus, one major consequence of the welfare state growth among Western nations in general and the Scandinavian in particular, is that 'the policies that dominated the agenda of the Left throughout most of this century are running out of steam' (Inglehart 1990: 256). Applying the argument in the context of this chapter it is expected that public support for income redistribution and progressive taxation will be quite modest. Furthermore, public support for redistribution will be negatively correlated with actual redistributive conditions.

Focusing more closely on taxation one of the most widespread arguments is Wilensky's (1976) familiar thesis that the composition of taxes constituting the tax system to a significant degree structures tax discontent. In short, it is argued that anti-tax sentiments have more to do with the visibility of taxes than with other features, including the gross level of taxes (Hibbs and Madsen 1981). As discussed by Peters (1991), the concept of tax visibility is somewhat unclear and empirically it has been assessed in various ways, but it is generally conceived as the balance between the personal income tax and property tax on the one hand and other taxes on the other. While some scholars more or less concur in the argument (Coughlin 1980: 153; Steinmo 1993: 195), others are less persuaded, as relationships between tax visibility and various forms of tax discontent in a number of studies – covering attitudes to different types of taxes, tax evasion and the emergence of tax protest movements and parties – have not received empirical support (Listhaug and Miller 1985; Hadenius 1986; Peters

1991). When it comes to progressive taxation, Newton and Confalonieri (1995) demonstrate that public support is negatively, albeit weakly, correlated with the top marginal tax rate. However, neither Sweden nor the United States is included in this seven-nation comparison. Assessing the general definition of tax visibility it is expected that tax discontent will be most significant in the United States, followed by Sweden and lastly Britain (Appendix 6.2).

Korpi (1980: 305), sceptical of the tax backlash thesis as it appears to 'imply that citizens do not want to pay high taxes, irrespective of what they receive in return for taxes paid', suggests that welfare state support is likely to vary with the outcomes of social policy which different welfare state regime types tend to generate (Esping-Andersen 1990; Korpi and Palme 1995). Committed to full employment and favourable treatment of both the working class and the middle class via universalistic social services and income-related policies, social-democratic welfare regimes are supposed to forge broad coalitions of actors with common interests and demands for extensive welfare policies. Further-more, it is argued that the universalistic earnings-related element maintains the necessary 'political consensus required to preserve broad and solidaristic support for the high taxes that such a welfare-state model demands' (Esping-Andersen 1990: 26). By contrast, in liberal regimes, in which programmes targeted at those worst off dominate, welfare policies and taxes tend to receive only modest support since large fractions of the electorate are excluded from state benefits. It is thus expected from this perspective that support for redistribution and taxation will be considerably stronger in Sweden compared to Britain and particularly the United States.

Before beginning the analysis, it may be fruitful to distinguish between attitudes towards principles and practices concerning income distribution and progressive taxation. While principles are the rules, practice refers both to the ways the principles are applied, and the outcomes (Confalonieri and Newton 1995). In Table 6.2, items 1 and 3 refer to redistributive principles, while the other items are concerned with perceptions of the actual distributions of incomes and taxes. The percentage distributions in the table reveal some cross-country similarities but also variations; some in accordance with the presented suggestions, others perhaps less expected. Generally there seem to be little evidence that public support for redistributive policies should be particularly solid in social democratic welfare regimes such as Sweden. If variations among countries should be emphasised, welfare state support appears to be most salient in Britain.

It is apparent that a large majority in both Britain and in the United States agree that income differences are too large, while Swedes seem less dissatisfied with the income distribution. This result may reflect the comparatively egalitarian income distribution in Sweden. Furthermore, when it comes to government intervention in this area, public support is substantially lower among Americans compared to Swedish and especially British citizens.

Taking into account the large cross-country variations of the distributions

Table 6.2 Attitudes to income redistribution and taxation in Sweden, Great Britain and the United States. Values are percentages

		Sweden	Britain	USA
1. It is the responsibility of the government to reduce the differences in income between people with high incomes and those with low incomes	agree	51	64	38
	neutral	16	14	19
	disagree	28	19	39
	balance*	+23	+45	−1
2. Differences in income in [Sweden] are too large	agree	59	80	76
	neutral	20	10	11
	disagree	18	8	11
	balance*	+41	+72	+65
3. People with high incomes should pay a (...) share of their income in taxes than those with low incomes	larger	74	83	71
	same	21	14	23
	smaller	1	1	1
	balance*	+73	+82	+70
4. For those with high incomes, taxes are...	too low	42	45	61
	about right	26	35	15
	too high	21	18	17
	balance*	+21	+27	+44
5. For those with middle incomes, taxes are...	too low	1	6	2
	about right	40	54	19
	too high	49	38	75
	balance*	−48	−32	−73
6. For those with low incomes, taxes are...	too low	0	1	2
	about right	15	17	21
	too high	77	81	71
	balance*	−77	−80	−69
(*n*) circa		(910)	(1025)	(1260)

Source: ISSP (1992), except item 3 for Britain (ISSP 1990). *Balance: percentage points difference between those agreeing and those disagreeing. Don't know response rates are not shown in table.

and levels of taxes, the similarities in the response patterns towards taxation are perhaps more striking than the differences. First, the principle of progressive taxation enjoys quite strong support across nations. It is thus apparent that suggestions derived from institutional differences in tax systems to a large extent fail to explain the observed pattern.

Second, public discontent with the distribution of taxes is widespread. A general characteristic, most accentuated in the United States, is that high-income earners are too lightly taxed, while taxes for middle-income and low-income earners are perceived as too high. In what ways characteristics in tax system may account for these patterns are not clear, as they can be interpreted in at least two ways. On the one hand, they may indicate public demand for increased tax progression. On the other hand it is possible that they announce popular opposition to taxes on 'normal' ordinary incomes. Viewing the observed patterns mainly as expressing tax resistance the tax visibility concept fits the data. If they on the other hand are interpreted as demands for increased progressivity, the visibility of taxes does not provide an adequate explanation.

Moreover, relating attitude patterns to the actual distributions of taxes a different picture emerges. Contrasting the United States with Sweden may be illustrative. In the United States, where the distribution of taxes is clearly progressive and tax rates for low- and middle-income earners are comparatively low, the public is largely dissatisfied with the distribution of taxes. In Sweden, a country with much higher tax rates and in which the tax burden is more evenly distributed, popular discontent is comparatively lower. While this result is at odds with most tax backlash theories, it supports arguments emphasising that outcomes of social policy matter for popular welfare state support (see Appendix 6.1).

Taking the analysis a step further, it would be advantageous to analyse whether the observed patterns tend to express general tax discontent or demand for expanded progressive taxes. While the data available do not allow a rigorous test, we may get some hints by an examination of the correlations between the attitudes to income redistribution and progressive taxation. As shown in Table 6.3, attitudinal patterns seem somewhat more integrated in Sweden than in the other two countries. In all three countries attitudes to income distribution are wedded together, but correlations between the taxation items are more prominent in Sweden. Finally, attitudinal links between income distribution and taxation are more apparent in Sweden compared to the United States.

While the British case is more difficult to judge since one item is missing, the cross-country variations in strength of correlations between taxation items and questions of income distribution may indicate that Swedes more frequently tend to interpret tax policy as a redistributive policy compared to American citizens. In addition, the stronger associations between the items in Sweden may suggest that discontent with the tax distribution has more to do with demands for increased redistribution via progressive taxes than with general tax resistance compared to the United States. However, arguments emphasising cross-national variations of the multidimensional character of the data should perhaps not be pushed too far, as we have not analysed whether social divisions over taxation tend to be manifested in different patterns compared to redistribution.

Structural cleavages and attitudes to progressive taxation

To reduce risks and inequalities has been one of the main objectives of the welfare state. From a power-resources perspective, the unequal distribution of socio-economic resources and risks attached to unemployment, sickness,

Table 6.3 Correlation patterns among attitudes to income redistribution and taxation in Sweden, Great Britain and the United States. Pearson's r × 100 (coefficients ≥ 30 are shown in bold type).

	1	2	3	4	5
Sweden					
1 Income differences too large					
2 Government reduce income differences	66				
3 Taxes on high incomes too low	45	42			
4 Taxes on middle incomes too low	08	08	44		
5 Taxes on low incomes too low	−28	−23	−14	45	
6 High incomes should pay a larger share in taxes	32	30	48	16	−21
Great Britain					
1 Income differences too large					
2 Government reduce income differences	57				
3 Taxes on high incomes too low	26	23			
4 Taxes on middle incomes too low	10	01	47		
5 Taxes on low incomes too low	−27	−32	−08	26	
6 —	—	—	—	—	—
United States					
1 Income differences too large					
2 Government reduce income differences	41				
3 Taxes on high incomes too low	28	07			
4 Taxes on middle incomes too low	−04	00	06		
5 Taxes on low incomes too low	−15	−19	00	27	
6 High incomes should pay a larger share in taxes	27	30	24	−10	−23

Source: ISSP (1992). All variables are five point scales running from −1 (less taxes and redistribution) to 1 (increase taxes and redistribution).

retirement and child caring, is in capitalist societies intimately connected with occupational positions (Korpi 1983; Esping-Andersen 1985). As those with weaker positions on the labour market are exposed to higher risks and less resources they are supposed to favour strategies which reallocate market outcomes in a more equal direction. The welfare state may therefore be seen as a major arena for class conflict, where the strongest supporters of welfare state policies are expected to be found among those with less marketable resources (Matheson 1993). In this chapter three indicators of the position within the social stratification system will be used: social class, education and income.

Social class will be measured in accordance with the Erikson/Goldthorpe classification of occupations, which is designated to derive classes on the basis of specific work and market conditions (Erikson and Goldthorpe 1992). While the class schema used here is not as detailed as the original classification, it distinguishes between unskilled workers, skilled workers, routine non-manuals, service classes II and I (lower- and higher-level controllers and administrators, respectively) and, finally, self-employed. An exception is the British 1990 sample. Due to a different occupational code only four categories – workers, lower non-manuals, higher non-manuals and self-employed – are extracted (Svallfors 1993a).

The second measure of social stratification is education, and problems of standardisation exist here too. Levels of education will be separated into three categories. The first is those with primary education; the second is more heterogeneous though, as it is comprised of those with some sort of secondary education; the third category includes those with a university education.

The third stratification variable is income. Due to different currencies and coding schemes, income will simply be divided into quartiles. Since income has been counted as household income, married and co-habiting couples' income has been divided by two.

In a comparative perspective it has been argued that class-related divisions over redistributive policies will vary systematically with the institutional configuration of the welfare state. In welfare states relying on selective policies aimed at those worst off in society, coalitions between poor and better-off citizens are likely to be discouraged (Korpi 1980; Korpi and Palme 1995). Targeting programmes as well as benefits at a low flat rate tends to split the working class and promote coalitions between better-off workers and the middle class against the poorer segments of the working class. Such a scenario is expected to be present in the United States and, to a lesser extent, in Britain. On the other hand, in welfare states which have institutionalised encompassing welfare policies, as in Sweden, class conflicts are supposed to be less severe since the working class as well as the middle class is included and covered by the same insurance programmes.

However, others have argued that in the transition from industrial to post-industrial societies, class divisions may be complemented or even superseded by other cleavage structures. In this context, one of the more prominent sources to conflict is gender (Orloff 1993; Sainsbury 1994). Arguments are built either upon self-interest, as women are seen as more dependent on the state both in terms of employment and in terms of benefits and services (Borchorst and Siim 1987; Hernes 1987), and/or different experiences of socialisation among men and women (Waerness 1987). Using similar arguments – self interest and socialisation experiences – others have maintained that private vs. public sector employment is a potential source of conflict over social policies (Hoel and Knutsen 1989), which may be enhanced in periods of welfare state retrenchment (Sears and Citrin 1985; Pierson 1994).

Esping-Andersen (1990) elaborates the above themes further and argues that changing occupational structures may give rise to other axes of conflicts which will replace or complement class divisions. Since 'the structure of the welfare state is a key feature in the contemporary process of social stratification' (Esping-Andersen 1993: 20), it is suggested that patterns vary across nations. In Sweden, class conflicts are supposed to be translated into gender and sector conflicts, due to the heavily gender-segregated labour market and the significant job expansion in the public sector. In the United States on the other hand,

119

cleavages tend to be expressed mainly as class conflicts, due to the decreasing segregation effects in the labour market (Esping-Andersen 1990: ch. 9). Thus, it is expected that class conflicts would be less severe in Sweden than in Britain, while class conflicts are supposed to be strongest in the United States.

Finally it has been suggested that slowly changing value patterns related to age cohorts may have substantial impact on politics. According to Inglehart (1990), questions of redistribution and inequality will gradually lose their political significance as older age cohorts are replaced by younger age cohorts. These effects may be expressed both in terms of generation differences – due to their different formative experiences concerning material well-being, younger people are expected to be less supportive of the welfare state than older people – and withering links between party preferences and traditional left–right political attitudes.

Analysing the links between party identification and attitudes to income redistribution, a general problem is that it is difficult to establish causal chains between political party identification and other political attitudes. Furthermore, if there exist strong links between political choice and in this case, attitudes to taxation, links between other variables rooted in structural conditions and attitudes to taxes may be distorted. The strategy in this chapter is to run separate analyses.

Examining group differences to the principle of progressive taxation, which are displayed in Table 6.4, there are little signs that this is a socially divisive issue. Although some income differences are present in Britain and Sweden, the most surprising finding is perhaps the negligible influence of class-related factors. Generally, both class and education show non-significant relationships with progressive taxation support, except in Sweden in which those with lower service class occupations and the self-employed are less supportive. The 'deviant' case of the higher service class may be noticed.

There are also indications of age differences in Sweden and the United States as older citizens are more in favour of progressive taxation than younger. Further, it can be noticed that sector and gender differences, with one exception are non-significant. In Sweden, contrary to the earlier-presented arguments, the odds for men to support progressive taxation is nearly twice as large compared to women. Finally, political choice exhibits a consistent pattern between nations, although it is more pronounced in Sweden than in Britain and the United States. Not surprisingly, those on the right are less sympathetic to progressive taxation than those on the left.

Moving on to Table 6.5, in which attitudes to the distribution of taxes are presented, less consensus is shown when we focus on class differences. In Sweden, the differences between classes, educational categories and income groups clearly point in the direction of divergent views concerning the distribution of taxes. Those in higher strata generally tend to favour lower taxes on high incomes compared to others, but are not claiming less taxes on low incomes to the same extent as those within lower social strata.

Table 6.4 Attitudes to the principle of progressive taxation by various structural determinants. Model I: Percentage agreeing. Bivariate analysis. Models II and III: Logistic regression. Multivariate analysis. Coefficients expressed as odds-ratios (OR)

	People with high incomes should pay a larger share of their income in taxes than those with low incomes								
	Sweden			Britain			USA		
	I	II	III	I	II	III	I	II	III
	%	OR	OR	%	OR	OR	%	OR	OR
All	74			83			71		
Class	***	***	***						
Service I [GB:1][a] (ref. cat.)	80	1.00	1.00	82	1.00	1.00	64	1.00	1.00
Service II	63	**0.43**	**0.40**	n.a.	n.a.	n.a.	69	1.19	1.11
Routine non-manuals [GB:2][a]	72	0.83	0.84	84	1.45	1.46	72	1.30	1.17
Skilled manuals [GB:3][a]	77	0.82	**0.63**	86	1.42	1.29	76	**1.67**	**1.64**
Unskilled manuals	83	1.31	1.17	n.a.	n.a.	n.a.	73	1.32	1.22
Self-employed [GB:4][a]	67	**0.30**	**0.35**	82	0.98	1.03	70	1.13	1.01
Education	*								
Primary	80	0.69	0.71	83	0.75	**0.71**	74	0.95	0.98
Secondary	71	0.71	0.71	83	0.84	0.80	71	0.97	1.01
University (ref. cat.)	72	1.00	1.00	83	1.00	1.00	67	1.00	1.00
Household income		*			*				
1st quartile	76	1.33	1.16	88	**2.00**	**1.78**	73	1.05	1.07
2nd quartile	80	**2.19**	**1.90**	86	1.34	1.25	72	1.01	1.05
3rd quartile	73	1.16	1.17	80	0.84	0.88	66	0.73	0.75
4th quartile (ref. cat.)	69	1.00	1.00	82	1.00	1.00	70	1.00	1.00
Gender		**	**						
Male (ref. cat.)	76	1.00	1.00	84	1.00	1.00	71	1.00	1.00
Female	71	**0.57**	**0.54**	83	0.89	0.94	71	0.98	1.02
Age	***						***	**	**
29 years or less (ref. cat.)	65	1.00	1.00	83	1.00	1.00	64	1.00	1.00
30-39 years	75	1.13	1.10	82	0.87	0.79	68	1.37	1.38
40-49 years	67	1.22	1.07	83	0.93	0.95	67	1.22	1.21
50-59 years	78	1.59	1.56	82	0.95	0.95	76	**1.74**	**1.81**
60 years or more	83	**2.14**	1.79	86	0.68	0.76	80	**2.24**	**2.30**
Sector							—	—	—
Public	73	0.85	0.79	86	1.33	1.27			
Private (ref. cat.)	75	1.00	1.00	83	1.00	1.00			
Political choice	***	—	***	***	—	***	**	—	*
Left	86		**3.60**	90		**2.39**	77		1.67
Centre	77		2.29	n.a.		n.a.	69		1.42
Right (ref. cat.)	60		1.00	75		1.00	66		1.00
No preference/other party	73		2.14	83		1.46	n.a.		n.a.
Constant		4.37	2.80		4.69	3.30		1.45	1.06
McFadden's R²		0.065	0.084		0.018	0.039		0.020	0.029

Source: ISSP (1992) except Britain (ISSP 1990).

Notes: a) Class variable values for Britain in brackets. 1 = Higher non-manuals (mix between service classes I and II). 2 = Lower non-manuals (mix between service class II and routine non-manuals). 3 = Manuals (Skilled and unskilled manuals collapsed). 4 = Self-employed.
Significance levels for variables: *** 0.001 level; ** 0.01 level; * 0.05 level. Coefficients in bold deviate significantly (p < 0.05) from the reference category. Variables not included in models are marked with —.

121

Table 6.5 Attitudes to the distribution of taxes by various structural determinants. Group means. Bivariate analysis.

| | For those with {. . .} incomes, taxes are too low | | | | | | | | |
| | Sweden | | | Britain | | | USA | | |
	High	Mid	Low	High	Mid	Low	High	Mid	Low
All	0.12	−0.29	−0.54	0.16	−0.18	−0.56	0.31	−0.48	−0.49
Class									
Service I	−0.15	−0.31	−0.42	0.21	−0.15	−0.45	0.29	−0.48	−0.40
Service II	0.01	−0.28	−0.47	0.22	−0.16	−0.53	0.35	−0.49	−0.42
Routine non-manuals	0.20	−0.30	−0.55	0.16	−0.19	−0.53	0.34	−0.47	−0.49
Skilled manuals	0.21	−0.28	−0.57	0.10	−0.23	−0.64	0.31	−0.46	−0.56
Unskilled manuals	0.22	−0.29	−0.61	0.14	−0.19	−0.61	0.28	−0.51	−0.55
Self-employed	0.08	−0.31	−0.58	0.16	−0.15	−0.56	0.33	−0.49	−0.45
Education									
Primary	0.26	−0.27	−0.65	0.11	−0.20	−0.63	0.19	−0.46	−0.57
Secondary	0.10	−0.30	−0.52	0.17	−0.19	−0.55	0.33	−0.49	−0.50
University	−0.07	−0.32	−0.45	0.21	−0.15	−0.48	0.35	−0.48	−0.37
Household income									
1st quartile	0.24	−0.25	−0.60	0.11	−0.21	−0.65	0.26	−0.44	−0.59
2nd quartile	0.20	−0.31	−0.59	0.21	−0.19	−0.58	0.39	−0.49	−0.47
3rd quartile	0.11	−0.29	−0.53	0.14	−0.18	−0.52	0.31	−0.49	−0.39
4th quartile	−0.11	−0.34	−0.48	0.18	−0.14	−0.46	0.33	−0.51	−0.49
Gender									
Male	0.11	−0.29	−0.56	0.16	−0.16	−0.54	0.34	−0.47	−0.47
Female	0.12	−0.30	−0.53	0.16	−0.21	−0.57	0.28	−0.49	−0.49
Age									
29 years or less	0.07	−0.33	−0.45	0.22	−0.22	−0.53	0.29	−0.45	−0.48
30–39 years	0.09	−0.32	−0.56	0.27	−0.09	−0.51	0.38	−0.50	−0.46
40–49 years	0.03	−0.34	−0.53	0.14	−0.19	−0.57	0.34	−0.54	−0.47
50–59 years	0.14	−0.27	−0.54	0.16	−0.23	−0.58	0.30	−0.57	−0.60
60 years or more	0.25	−0.21	−0.64	0.05	−0.21	−0.57	0.23	−0.42	−0.48
Sector							—	—	—
Public	0.14	−0.30	−0.54	0.22	−0.15	−0.56			
Private	0.07	−0.30	−0.54	0.13	−0.20	−0.56			
Political choice									
Left	0.32	−0.18	−0.62	0.26	−0.16	−0.64	0.36	−0.50	−0.57
Centre	0.04	−0.31	−0.52	0.21	−0.14	−0.58	0.33	−0.47	−0.47
Right	−0.21	−0.41	−0.50	0.04	−0.22	−0.45	0.22	−0.48	−0.42
No preference/other party	0.21	−0.29	−0.54	0.16	−0.22	−0.60	n.a.	n.a.	n.a.

Source: ISSP (1992). The tax distribution variables (five point scales) vary between −1 ('decrease taxes') and 1 ('increase taxes'), where 0 indicates that taxes are 'about right'. Variables not available are marked with —.

Class patterns in Britain seem to be different though. The service classes and those with university education are more prone to increase taxes on high incomes than workers and those with primary education. As a similar relationship can be observed concerning taxes on low incomes, the impression is that class conflicts over taxation have less to do with demands for changes in a more progressive direction than with tax resistance.

In the United States class divisions appear more vague. While there seems to be a tendency for increased tax progression among those in the working class compared to the higher service class, educational differences point in the same direction as those found in Britain. Finally, similar to Britain the impact of income is somewhat indistinct.

While both gender and sector differences appear to be small, and the impact of age seem to vary cross-nationally, attitudinal relationships between political preferences and tax levels seem to reflect conflicts over progressive taxation. This is perhaps most underlined in Sweden, due to the strong conflict between the left and the right on the appropriate tax level for those with high incomes, but similar divisions are also found in Britain and the United States.

So far it has been observed that social divisions over the distribution of taxes vary both in magnitude and between countries. There are indeed some signals of conflicting opinions on progressive taxation, but as some patterns are less easy to interpret it seems reasonable to enter the variables in a multivariate analysis in which the dependent variable is designed to capture demands for increased tax progression. As disagreements are almost non-existent when it comes to taxes on middle incomes, a somewhat rough measure of tax progressivity defined as the distance between the variable values for taxes on high incomes and low incomes respectively, will be applied.[4] The higher the value the more sympathetic of a progressive distribution of taxes.

In Table 6.6, the eta and empirical means in model I refer to bivariate relationships. The coefficients in models II and III are adjusted for the impact of other independent variables. As shown in the table, the patterns of social conflict vary largely between nations. Compared to the weak and, with one exception, non-significant influence of class-related factors on attitudes to progressive taxation, observed in Britain and in the United States, the sharp class cleavages that occur in Sweden are striking.

Comparing age patterns between nations, further differences can be noticed. In Britain the elderly are less prone to support further progressivity than other cohorts.[5] In Sweden, relationships are reversed, although not statistically significant, while in the United States, the youngest and oldest age groups are less appreciative than others.

While the expected sector cleavages are visible only in Britain, significant gender differences appear only in Sweden. Here too, men are slightly more in favour of progressive taxes than women. Finally, the impact of political preferences is similar across nations, as those sympathising with the left are more likely to endorse an augmentation of progressive taxation compared to right-wing supporters.

Conclusions

Some of the arguments set out in the introduction suggested that recent tax reforms may be seen as responses to public discontent with redistribution and

Table 6.6 Attitudes to progressive taxation by various structural determinants. Multiple classification analysis. Empirical and adjusted group index means; eta and beta coefficients

	Sweden			Britain			USA		
	I Eta Empirical means[a]	II Beta Adjusted means[a]	III Beta Adjusted means[a]	I Eta Empirical means[a]	II Beta Adjusted means[a]	III Beta Adjusted means[a]	I Eta Empirical means[a]	II Beta Adjusted means[a]	III Beta Adjusted means[a]
Grand mean	0.33	0.33	0.33	0.36	0.36	0.36	0.41	0.41	0.41
Class	**0.30**	**0.21***	**0.19**	**0.08**	**0.08**	**0.10**	0.08	0.07	0.06
Service I	-0.18	-0.12	-0.12	-0.03	0.01	0.02	-0.04	-0.04	-0.03
Service II	-0.09	-0.05	-0.05	0.02	0.04	0.05	-0.02	-0.01	-0.01
Routine non-manuals	0.06	0.06	0.05	-0.02	-0.03	-0.02	0.00	0.00	0.00
Skilled manuals	0.07	0.05	0.03	-0.01	-0.02	-0.02	0.03	0.02	0.03
Unskilled manuals	0.10	0.06	0.07	0.03	0.00	-0.03	0.04	0.03	0.03
Self-employed	-0.03	-0.08	-0.04	0.02	0.01	0.03	-0.02	-0.03	-0.03
Education	**0.27**	**0.14**	**0.12***	**0.05**	**0.06**	**0.05**	0.06	0.02	0.02
Primary	0.12	0.07	0.06	0.02	0.03	0.01	0.01	0.00	0.00
Secondary	-0.01	-0.02	-0.02	-0.01	-0.01	0.01	0.01	0.00	0.01
University	-0.15	-0.06	-0.05	-0.01	-0.01	-0.02	-0.04	-0.02	-0.02
Household income	**0.24**	**0.13***	**0.11***	**0.10**	**0.16**	**0.11***	0.09	0.08	0.07
1st quartile	0.07	0.03	0.01	0.03	0.06	0.02	0.02	0.02	0.01
2nd quartile	0.06	0.04	0.05	0.04	0.03	0.04	0.02	0.01	0.02
3rd quartile	0.00	-0.01	-0.01	-0.02	-0.04	-0.02	-0.06	-0.05	-0.04
4th quartile	-0.13	-0.07	-0.06	-0.04	-0.06	-0.04	0.01	0.02	0.01

Gender	0.03	0.08*	0.06	0.03	0.01	0.03	0.01	0.01	0.01
Male	0.01	0.03	0.02	−0.01	0.00	−0.01	0.00	0.00	0.00
Female	−0.01	−0.03	−0.02	0.01	0.00	0.01	0.00	0.00	0.00
Age	0.12	0.10	0.10	0.11	0.18***	0.11	0.10	0.12**	0.11*
29 years or less	−0.03	−0.07	−0.06	0.00	0.03	0.01	−0.03	−0.04	−0.03
30–39 years	0.00	0.02	0.02	0.04	0.04	0.03	0.03	0.03	0.02
40–49 years	−0.04	0.01	0.00	0.01	0.02	0.02	0.01	0.02	0.02
50–59 years	0.01	0.00	0.00	0.03	0.02	0.02	0.05	0.06	0.06
60 years or more	0.08	0.04	0.04	−0.06	−0.10	−0.06	−0.04	−0.05	−0.05
Sector	0.04	0.05	0.02	0.07	0.09**	0.09*	—	—	—
Public	0.01	0.02	0.01	0.03	0.04	0.04			
Private	−0.01	−0.02	−0.01	−0.01	−0.02	−0.02			
Political choice	0.30	—	0.23***	0.29	—	0.28***	0.17	—	0.15***
Left	0.12		0.09	0.10		0.09	0.06		0.06
Centre	−0.09		−0.06	0.04		0.04	0.01		0.00
Right	−0.16		−0.13	−0.11		−0.11	−0.09		−0.08
No preference/other party	0.05		0.03	0.04		0.03	n.a.		n.a.
R²		0.141	0.192		0.047	0.118		0.026	0.049

Source: ISSP (1992).

Notes: a) group means are expressed as deviations from the grand mean. Significance levels for variables (models II and III only): *** 0.001 level; ** 0.01 level; * 0.05 level. Variables not included in models are marked with —.

progressive taxes, while other suggestions pointed at the impact of institutions on public interpretations and preferences towards redistributive policies. Examining attitudes to taxation on the aggregate level in Sweden, Britain and the United States, it is rather the commonalities than the differences between nations, as well as the indications of strong public support for progressive taxation that characterise the data. The sizeable cross-national differences in institutional attributes have not left their imprint in distinctively divergent attitudinal patterns towards taxation. There is thus little empirical evidence for suggestions that support for redistributive policies should be more accentuated in social democratic welfare regimes compared to liberal regimes, at least when it comes to taxation. Emphasising variations among countries, it is in Britain rather than in Sweden that we find the strongest support for redistributive policies.

While the principle of tax progression is endorsed by a large majority of citizens in each country, perceptions and desires of the distribution of taxes show more cross-national variation. Public dissatisfaction with the tax distribution is prevalent. Citizens tend to favour increased taxes on those with high incomes, while they desire reduced taxes on those with lower incomes. This pattern is particularly evident in the United States. Swedes and Britons on the other hand appear to be less displeased. However, in interpreting these patterns, one major difficulty is to determine whether attitudinal patterns towards the distribution of taxes tend to express general discontent with taxes imposed on common incomes or increased tax progression. While there are reasons to believe that attitudes in this respect are interlaced, there are some indications that attitudes to taxation and redistribution are somewhat more tightly integrated in Sweden compared to the United States and Britain – a finding to which we will return later.

To what extent then may institutional arguments account for the attitudinal differences concerning the distribution of taxes? Interpreting them as indicators of tax discontent, Wilensky's tax visibility thesis seems to fit the data, as the share of visible taxes is more prominent in the United States compared to the others. Nevertheless, in comparing attitudinal patterns with tax measures concerned with levels and distributions of taxes, results are less than easy to interpret from a tax backlash perspective (c.f. Peters 1991). In this context, arguments emphasising the influences of social policy outcomes upon welfare state support, appear to fit data better.

Having emphasised the attitudinal commonalities on the aggregate level, social conflicts over progressive taxation are rather distinguished by cross-country differences than similarities. How then do the attitudinal patterns towards progressive taxation fare with the presented conflict scenarios? The most obvious result is perhaps the lack of fit between the suggested conflict patterns and the observed. Disagreements over progressive taxation based on different positions within the social stratification system vary in magnitude between the nations, but do not vary in accordance with the presented suggestions. Further, data also suggest that social divisions over the principle of progressive taxation appear to be less significant compared to the distribution of taxes – a pattern which is most clearly marked in Sweden and, to a lesser extent, in Britain.

Assumptions that divisions in Sweden should foremost be structured by other factors, such as gender and sector of employment, rather than social class cannot be corroborated, as demands for augmented progressivity are mainly expressed as distinctive class conflicts. Likewise, expectations that class conflicts should be particularly salient in liberal welfare regimes are not met. In the United States the lack of structural cleavages is perhaps the most significant remark, and in Britain, while some income differences can be noticed, class-based conflicts cannot be regarded as particularly strong.

Furthermore, sector and gender divisions seem to be of minor importance, with few exceptions. While there is some indication of divisions between public and private employees in Britain, gender differences appear solely in Sweden. However, as women are less sympathetic than men towards progressive taxation, expectations are not fulfilled.

The impact of age differs between countries. Generation theories receive some empirical support as both in Sweden and the United States older cohorts are more enthusiastic of the principle of progressive taxation than younger cohorts. However, the cross-country variations that are found towards demands for increased progressivity may be difficult to explain from a generation-theoretical perspective.

Moreover, there is little support for the claim that links between political party preferences and attitudes to welfare policies tend to be lessened in post-industrial societies. In fact, the relationships between political choice and attitudes to progressive taxation is the only observed pattern that is consistent both between nations and attitudinal items.

The brief summary of the results shows that there is less than solid support for the claims derived from institutional perspectives. However, on the basis of the evidence presented here, there is little reason to dismiss the idea that institutions influence and structure attitudes. By comparing the findings above with other research dealing with redistribution, some additional implications of the data may be considered.

Previous research has demonstrated that public support for government redistribution is more solid in Sweden and Britain compared to the United States, while conflict patterns have been shown to be similar across nations, and are mainly structured along class and gender divisions (Taylor-Gooby 1993; Svallfors 1993a, 1997). Contrasting these findings on the one hand, with the similar aggregate levels of progressive tax support, the variation of conflicting patterns associated with taxation, as well as the less than strong links between attitudes to taxation and income redistribution, on the other hand, may suggest that the forces and mechanisms behind the formation of attitudes are quite different when it comes to taxation compared to other forms of government redistribution.

In this respect one possible interpretation of the cross-national consensus towards the principle of progressive taxation, manifested both in rather strong aggregate support – which appears to be a common pattern among Western nations in general (Confalonieri and Newton 1995; Taylor-Gooby 1995) – and a relative non-appearance of social divisions, would suggest that progressive taxation has been a familiar ingredient in modern tax policy among Western countries for most of this century and to some extent has come to be taken for granted. A slightly different interpretation, supportive of the findings by Coughlin (1980), would suggest that cross-country attitudinal similarities are more likely to be found when concrete government policies are examined compared to more abstract and ideological issues of government intervention. However, regardless of which, if any, interpretation that may be more fruitful, they suggest that analysis should not be restricted to institutional configurations of modern welfare states, but also incorporate factors and processes shared by advanced capitalist nations in general (Pontusson 1995).

Furthermore, there are signs indicating that attitudes towards government redistribution are not one-dimensional, but to what extent matters of taxation are interpreted as redistributive policy seems to vary between nations. While it would be far beyond the scope of this chapter to acknowledge why attitudinal patterns, both in terms of aggregate levels and structural cleavages, towards government redistribution and progressive taxation appear to be more similar in Sweden than in the other countries, some arguments pointing at the decisive impact on attitude formation exercised by political parties and accompanying interest organisations may be noticed (Svallfors 1996).

Following these suggestions, explanations behind the observed attitudinal differences may be found in an analysis of the social bases of interest organisations and political parties, as well as in the ways these organisations have accomplished and articulated tax policy in public debate. Reviewing the debate surrounding the reformations of the Swedish tax system during the 1980s and onwards, it is obvious that arguments concerned with the distribution of the personal income tax played a major role in public debate (Hadenius 1981; Gilljam and Holmberg 1990; Feldt 1991; Åberg 1993). The more tightly integrated pattern concerning government redistribution in Sweden – as well as the observed divisions over taxation structured mainly along class and party lines – could then be interpreted as an effect of the political tensions caused by the comparatively high levels of taxes imposed on individuals, further encouraged and orchestrated by largely class-based organisations and parties. However, lacking comparative data in these respects, these suggestions may be considered as issues for further research, rather than empirical evidence.

The above remarks do however suggest, to paraphrase Greenberg (1994), that the linkages between components of institutions and attitudes cannot be taken as given or predetermined. The effects of each must be traced and demonstrated empirically. In this context, attitude research may be advised to incorporate both the commonalities as well as the differences in the frameworks surrounding modern societies in accounting for observed attitudes.

Appendix 6.1 Income distribution in Sweden, Britain and the United States. Selected indicators

	Sweden	Rank*	Britain	Rank*	USA	Rank*
1a Primary income *c.* 1986 (gini)[a]	36.6	8	34.0	6	38.6	11
1b Disposable income *c.* 1986 (gini)	22.0	2	30.4	9	34.1	12
2a Pretax and transfer poverty rate *c.* 1986 (percent)[b]	15.3	2	23.2	7	18.0	4
2b Post-tax and transfer poverty rate *c.* 1986 (percent)	8.6	3	12.5	5	18.1	7

Sources: 1a–b (OECD 1995); 2a–b (McFate *et al.* 1995). * Rank orders are among 12 major OECD countries (1a–b), or among 7 LIS countries (2a–b). The higher the rank the more equal income distribution.

Notes: a) The gini coefficient measures income inequality. The higher the coefficient, the more unequal income distribution. Primary income = income from work and property. Disposable income = Primary income + transfers – taxes – social security contributions. b) Poverty rate = percentage of households (heads aged 20–55 years) below 50% of adjusted median household income.

Appendix 6.2 Tax system composition in Sweden, Great Britain, United States, and OECD unweighted average. Selected taxes expressed as percentages of gross domestic product and total taxation.

	... as percentage of GDP				... as percentage of total taxation			
	Sweden	Britain	USA	OECD	Sweden	Britain	USA	OECD
Total tax revenue 1992	50.0	35.2	29.4	38.8	100.0	100.0	100.0	100.0
Visible taxes 1992 [a]	19.8	12.8	13.4	13.5	39.7	36.3	45.7	35.2
Personal income tax 1992	18.0	10.0	10.1	11.5	36.0	28.4	34.3	29.7
Corporate income tax 1992	1.2	2.7	2.1	2.5	2.4	7.6	7.2	6.8
Taxes on goods and services 1992	13.2	12.1	5.0	11.8	26.5	34.4	17.1	30.3
Social security contributions								
paid by employer 1992	13.9	3.7	4.9	5.7	27.7	10.5	16.8	14.3
paid by employee 1992	0.1	2.4	3.5	3.3	0.2	6.7	11.8	8.3

Source: OECD (1994).

Notes: a) Taxes on personal income and property.

Appendix 6.3 Personal income tax, employee's social security contributions, and take-home pay including cash transfers, expressed as percentages of gross earnings of an average production worker (mean 1987–90).

	Sweden	Rank*	Britain	Rank*	USA	Rank*
1. Personal income tax[a]						
a. Single people	36.3	2	19.3	10	18.8	11
b. Two-child families	35.0	2	15.8	8	11.9	13
2. Employee's social security contributions						
a. Single people	0.0	17	8.5	9	7.5	11
b. Two-child families	0.0	17	8.5	9	7.5	11
3. Take-home pay including cash transfers						
a. Single people	63.7	5	72.2	9	73.8	11
b. Two-child families	74.0	3	82.6	9	80.7	8

Source: OECD (1991). * Rank orders are among 18 major OECD countries. The higher the rank the higher the taxes.
Notes: a) Excluding the effects of non-standard tax reliefs.

Appendix 6.4 The personal income tax *c.* 1987. a) Tax rates in decile groups calculated on taxable income and income subject to tax. b) Distribution of income subject to tax and net taxes by decile groups. Values are percentages

Decile	−1	+1	2	3	4	5	6	7	8	9	10	
a) Tax rates												Average
Sweden												
Taxable income	—	54.0	40.6	37.9	37.1	36.8	38.6	39.7	41.3	42.9	53.3	43.3
Income subject to tax	—	4.6	11.4	19.0	27.4	29.7	31.5	32.4	33.0	32.9	39.2	32.2
Britain												
Taxable income	—	—	1.5	24.1	27.7	28.3	28.6	28.7	28.6	28.6	33.6	30.3
Income subject to tax	—	−4.1	0.1	5.6	10.6	12.8	14.6	15.8	16.0	17.2	24.7	17.1
USA												
Taxable income	—	0.0	−5.8	−9.2	4.3	10.9	14.1	15.1	16.2	17.1	24.2	19.7
Income subject to tax	−0.3	0.0	−0.2	−0.6	0.9	4.1	7.1	9.0	10.6	11.8	18.1	13.0
b) Distribution (row)												Sum
Sweden												
Income subject to tax	—	0.5	3.1	4.7	6.6	8.5	10.1	11.7	13.4	15.8	25.6	100.0
Net taxes	—	0.1	1.1	2.8	5.7	7.9	9.9	11.8	13.7	16.2	31.1	100.0
Britain												
Income subject to tax	−0.1	1.1	2.7	4.1	5.5	7.0	8.8	10.7	13.1	16.8	30.4	100.0
Net taxes	0.0	−0.3	0.0	1.4	3.4	5.3	7.5	9.9	12.2	16.8	43.9	100.0
USA												
Income subject to tax	−1.6	0.0	0.3	1.2	2.9	5.0	7.3	10.2	14.0	19.1	41.7	100.0
Net taxes	0.0	0.0	0.0	−0.1	0.2	1.6	4.0	7.1	11.4	17.4	58.4	100.0

Source: OECD (1990).

Acknowledgements

The research has been financially supported by the Swedish Council for Social Research (SFR) and by the Swedish Council for Research in the Social Sciences and Humanities (HSFR). I would like to thank Olli Kangas, Stefan Svallfors, Peter Taylor-Gooby and Rune Åberg for valuable comments on a previous draft.

Notes

1 A more detailed description is available in Appendix 6.4.
2 Additional analysis using unweighted data show negligible differences compared to the results presented here.
3 Classifying Sweden and the United States the algorithms provided by Svallfors (1997) have been used.
4 The tax progressivity measure (tpm) may be defined as: tpm $=$ (thi − tli)/2, in which thi is the variable value for taxes on high incomes, and tli is the variable value for taxes on low incomes. As the tpm is divided by two, it varies between −1 and 1. Measuring progressivity by creating a variable based on combinations of certain variable values, similar results regarding group differences as those presented in this paper are obtained.
5 It has also been observed that the elderly in Britain are more inclined to accept large income differences between different occupations compared to other age groups (Svallfors, 1993b). Explaining why and to what extent this 'neo-liberal' trait among the British elderly occurs, should be of particular interest for generational theorists.

References

Andrews F., Morgan, J. and Sonquist, J. (1973) *Multiple Classification Analysis*, Ann Arbor: University of Michigan.
Borchorst A. and Siim, B. (1987) 'Women and the Advanced Welfare State − A New Kind of Patriarchal Power?', in A. Showstack Sassoon (ed.) *Women and the State*, London: Hutchinson.
Confalonieri M. A. and Newton, K. (1995) 'Taxing and Spending: Tax Revolt or Tax Protest?' in O. Borre and E. Scarbrough (eds) *The Scope of Government*, Oxford: Oxford University Press.
Coughlin, R. (1980) *Ideology, Public Opinion and Welfare Policy*, Berkeley: Institute of International Studies.
Davis, J. and Jowell, R. (1989) 'Measuring National Differences: An Introduction to the International Social Survey Program (ISSP)', in R. Jowell, S. Witherspoon and L. Brook (eds) *British Social Attitudes. Special International Report*, Aldershot: Gower.
Erikson R. 'Kodningar av SEI och EGP i LNU91'. Stockholm: Swedish Institute for Social Research (mimeo).
Erikson R. and Goldthorpe, J. H. (1992) *The Constant Flux*, Oxford: Clarendon Press.
Esping-Andersen, G. (1985) *Politics Against Markets: The Social Democratic Road to Power*, Princeton: Princeton University Press.
Esping-Andersen, G. (1990) *The Three Worlds of Welfare Capitalism*, Cambridge: Polity Press.
Esping-Andersen, G. (1993) *Changing Classes*, London: Sage.
Feldt, K-O. (1991) *Alla dessa dagar . . . I regeringen 1982–1990*, Stockholm: Norstedts.

Fritzell, J. (1991) *Icke av marknaden allena: Inkomstfördelningen i Sverige*, Stockholm: Almqvist and Wiksell International.

Ganzeboom, H. B. G. and Treiman, D. J. (1994) 'Internationally Comparable Measures of Occupational Status for the 1988 International Standard Classification of Occupations', Dept. of Sociology, Utrecht University (mimeo).

Gilljam, M. and Holmberg, S. (1990) *Rött Blått Grönt*, Stockholm: Bonniers.

Ginsburg, N. (1992) *Divisions of Welfare*, London: Sage.

Goldthorpe, J. H. and Heath, A. (1992) 'Revised Class Schema 1992', *JUSST, Working Paper No. 13*, Oxford: Nuffield College (mimeo).

Greenberg, E. S. (1994) 'Macroeconomic Change and Political Transformation in the United States' in L. Dodd and C. Jillson (eds) *The Dynamics of American Politics*, Boulder: Westview Press.

Hadenius, A. (1981) *Spelet om skatten*, Lund: Norstedts.

Hadenius, A. (1986) *A Crisis of the Welfare State?*, Stockholm: Almqvist and Wiksell International.

Hall, P. and Taylor, R. (1996) 'Political Science and the Three New Institutionalisms' *Political Studies*, 44: 936–57.

Hernes, H. (1987) 'Women and the Welfare State: the Transition from Private to Public Dependence' in A. Showstack Sassoon (ed.) *Women and the State*, London: Hutchinson.

Hibbs, D. A. and Madsen, H. J. (1981) 'Public Reactions to the Growth of Taxation and Government Expenditure', *World Politics*, 33: 413–35.

Hoel, M. and Knutsen, O. (1989) 'Social Class, Gender and Sector Employment as Political Cleavages in Scandinavia', *Acta Sociologica*, 32: 181–201.

Inglehart, R. (1990) *Culture Shift in Advanced Industrial Society*, Princeton, NJ: Princeton University Press.

ISSP (1990) *Role of Government II*. Codebook and datafile compiled at the ZA, University of Köln.

ISSP (1992) *Social Inequality II*. Codebook and datafile compiled at the ZA, University of Köln.

Kangas, O. (1991) *The Politics of Social Rights. Studies on the Dimensions of Sickness Insurance in OECD Countries*, Stockholm: Almqvist and Wiksell.

Korpi, W. (1980) 'Social Policy and Distributional Conflict in the Capitalist Democracies. A Preliminary Comparative Framework', *West European Politics*, 3: 296–316.

Korpi, W. (1983) *The Democratic Class Struggle*, London: Routledge and Kegan Paul.

Korpi, W. and Palme, J. (1995) 'The Paradox of Redistribution and the Strategy of Equality', Stockholm: Swedish Institute for Social Research (mimeo).

Levi, M. (1990) 'A Logic of Institutional Change' in K. Schweers Cook and M. Levi (eds) *The Limits of Rationality*, Chicago: The University of Chicago Press.

Listhaug, O. and Miller, A. H. (1985) 'Public Support for Tax Evasion: Self-interest or Symbolic Politics?' *European Journal of Political Research*, 13: 265–82.

Matheson, G. (1993) *The Decommodified in a Commodified World*, Unpublished PhD Thesis, University of New England, Armidale.

McFate, K., Smeeding, T. and Rainwater, L. (1995) 'Markets and States: Poverty Trends and Transfer System Effectiveness in the 1980s' in K. McFate, R. Lawson and W. J. Wilson (eds) *Poverty, Inequality and the Future of Social Policy. Western States in the New World Order*, New York: Russell Sage Foundation.

Musgrave, R. A. (1990) 'Comments' in J. Slemrod (ed.) *Do Taxes Matter?*, Cambridge, MA: The MIT Press.

Newton, K. and Confalonieri, M. A. (1995) 'Politics, Economics, Class, and Taxation' in O. Borre and E. Scarbrough (eds) *The Scope of Government*, Oxford: Oxford University Press.

OECD (1990) *The Personal Income Tax Base*, Paris: OECD.

OECD (1991) *The Tax/Benefit Position of Production Workers 1987-1990*, Paris: OECD.

OECD (1994) *Revenue Statistics*, Paris: OECD.

OECD (1995) *Income Distribution in OECD Countries*, Paris: OECD.

Orloff, A. S. (1993) 'Gender and the Social Rights of Citizenship: The Comparative Analysis of Gender Relations and Welfare States', *American Sociological Review*, 58: 303–28.

Palme, J. (1990) *Pension Rights in Welfare Capitalism*, Stockholm: Almqvist and Wiksell.

Peters, G. (1991) *The Politics of Taxation*, Oxford: Blackwell.

Pierson, P. (1993) 'When Effect Becomes Cause: Policy Feedback and Political Change' *World Politics*, 45: 595–628.

Pierson, P. (1994) *Dismantling the Welfare State*, Cambridge: Cambridge University Press.

Pontusson, J. (1995) 'From Comparative Public Policy to Political Economy. Putting Political Institutions in Their Place and Taking Interests Seriously' *Comparative Political Studies*, 28: 117–47.

Rose, R. and Peters, G. (1978) *Can Governments Go Bankrupt?*, New York: Basic Books.

Sainsbury, D. (ed.) (1994) *Gendering Welfare States*, London: Sage.

Scheuch, E. K. (1989) 'Theoretical Implications of Comparative Survey Research: Why the Wheel of Cross-cultural Methodology Keeps On Being Reinvented', *International Sociology*, 4: 147–67.

Sears, D. O. and Citrin, J. (1985) *Tax Revolt. Something for Nothing in California. Enlarged Edition*, Cambridge: Harvard University Press.

Skocpol, T. (1992) *Protecting Soldiers and Mothers*, Cambridge: The Belknap Press of Harvard University Press.

Slemrod, J. (ed.) (1990) *Do Taxes Matter?*, Cambridge, MA: The MIT Press.

SOU (1995) *Skattereformen 1990–1991. En utvärdering. SOU 1995: 104*, Stockholm: Fritzes.

Steinmo, S. (1993) *Taxation and Democracy*, New Haven: Yale University Press.

Steinmo, S. (1994a) 'The End of Redistribution? International Pressures and Domestic Policy Choices', *Challenge*, 37: 9–17.

Steinmo, S. (1994b) 'Rethinking American Exceptionalism: Culture or Institutions?' in L. Dodd and C. Jillson (eds) *The Dynamics of American Politics*, Boulder: Westview Press.

Svallfors, S. (1993a) 'Policy Regimes and Attitudes to Inequality: A Comparison of Three European Nations' in T. P. Boje and S. E. Olsson-Hort (eds) *Scandinavia in a New Europe*, Oslo: Scandinavian University Press.

Svallfors, S. (1993b) 'Dimensions of Inequality: A Comparison of Attitudes in Sweden and Britain', *European Sociological Review*, 9: 267–87.

Svallfors, S. (1996) 'National Differences in National Identities? An Introduction to the International Social Survey Programme', *New Community*, 22: 127–34.

Svallfors, S. (1997) 'Worlds of Welfare and Attitudes to Redistribution: A Comparison of Eight Western Nations', *European Sociological Review*, 13: 283–304.

Tabachnick, B. G. and Fidell, L. S. (1996) *Using Multivariate Statistics*. 3rd edn, New York: HarperCollins.

Taylor-Gooby, P. (1993) 'What Citizens Want From the State' in R. Jowell, L. Brook and L. Dowds (eds) *International Social Attitudes. The 10th BSA Report*, Aldershot: Gower.

Taylor-Gooby, P. (1995) 'Who Wants the Welfare State? Support for State Welfare in European Countries' in S. Svallfors (ed.) *In the Eye of the Beholder*, Stockholm: Bank of Sweden Tercentenary Foundation.

Waerness, K. (1987) 'On the Rationality of Caring' in A. Showstack Sassoon (ed.) *Women and the State*, London: Hutchinson.

Whalley, J. (1990) 'Foreign Responses to U.S. Tax Reform' in J. Slemrod (ed.) *Do Taxes Matter?*, Cambridge, MA: The MIT Press.

Wilensky, H. (1976) *The 'New Corporatism', Centralization, and the Welfare State*, Beverly Hills: Sage.

Åberg, R. (1989) 'Distributive Mechanisms of the Welfare State – a Formal Analysis and an Empirical Application', *European Sociological Review*, 5: 167–82.

Åberg, R. (1993) *Århundradets skattereform?*, Stockholm: Fritzes.

134

7

WITHIN AND WITHOUT

Labour force status and
political views in
four welfare states

George Matheson and Michael Wearing

Prologue: the politics of post-industrialism

The claim is made from time to time that as industrial society gives way to post-industrial society, one consequence is going to be a fundamental reorientation of how people conceive of social differentiation and inequality, both in theory and in practice. In particular, a variety of theories of the post-industrial contend over the respective significance to be attached to paid work and state processes in understanding both who gets what and does what in life, and how people think, talk and write about such things (Gershuny 1978; Gorz 1983; Jones 1983; Frankel 1987; Esping-Andersen 1990; Pixley 1993; Offe 1994). Briefly, the core contention which we wish (sympathetically) to dispute, though it assumes many forms, goes something like this. Once, in the industrial society of times past, the most real, visible, felt and politicised lines of large-scale social distinction among individuals and kin groupings lay within the sphere of formal production – as management versus employees, owners versus wage-labourers, workers of varying power, prestige and remuneration. Now, however, things have changed, and the key political–economic–cultural fault line runs between those within the formal productive system and its labour market on the one hand and those outside them on the other: the 'job-rich' and 'job-poor' (Gorz 1983; Offe 1985; Van Parijs 1987). Thus, so the argument goes, while theories of social inequality based upon class conflict might have been appropriate to the capitalism of the nineteenth century, the world has changed a great deal since the times of Marx or Weber. The expanding role of the state, especially the set of economic and social policy institutions that have come to be known as the 'welfare state', combines with changes in the organisation of social production to locate the crucial social divisions of the modern era outside of the formal economy as such. As Zygmunt Bauman's account of 'new contradictions, new victims' in his influential *Memories of Class* (1982) has it:

> ... the field of the most drastic inequalities, conflicts and unresolved problems has shifted in late capitalist society from the disputed 'no-man's land' between the two powerful industrial class protagonists towards the deprived sectors of social life. The latter are causally related to the functioning of the system as a whole ... but they are not directly linked to the traditional repartition conflict between the industrial classes; if anything, they are more likely to be exacerbated rather than cured by the contestation arising from this conflict.
>
> Bauman (1982: 191)

With accounts of social differentiation tend to go corresponding readings, both positive and normative, of the politics of inequality, and this literature is no exception, typically offering something like a social movement politics around the distribution of time and the latter's free disposition via a guaranteed citizen's income (Keane 1988: 77–97; Van Parijs 1992) and perhaps some more convivial social infrastructure (Jones 1983; Gorz 1985, 1989).

As for what such a change in the social world of the developed countries would imply for the answering of questions in opinion surveys, one would presumably expect divisions between those employed and those not (for whatever reason) in employment over the popular acclaim they accord not only employment-related or benefit-related matters, but also more general questions of social differences and the appropriate role of government. Indeed, one would anticipate that such distinctions among categories would be a regular feature of late capitalist social orders and more apparent than traditional lines of ideological cleavage. Of course, one should not exaggerate the extent to which simple economistic views of individual or collective self-interest provide an adequate account of survey responses, let along motivational patterns in the surrounding real world. Even in the most seemingly unambiguous market-calculation situations, the driving forces of biopsychosocial interests are usually immersed in the fog of symbolism and signification which envelops them both in the survey/interview situation and in the wider social reality.

In fact, herein lies the main objection we wish to raise to the post-industrial utopian scenario. It attributes independent causal powers generative of political–economic ideas and actions to situations and positions as employed, unemployed, retired, housekeeping, etc. Yet these are inevitably always-already embedded in social processes which give both the material circumstances and associated subjective experiences their meaning. Less floridly, it is not necessarily at all the same thing to be unemployed or retired in Norway as it is in the United States, to be a retired share-cropper or a retired general in either place, or to be momentarily vs. semi-permanently out of work as a result of one's resources, relations and characteristics, and of where and when one has them.

Most significantly, not only the ground rules of employment and the administrative routines of claimant status, but the forms of life and consciousness which surround them, reinforce and proceed from them, could therefore be anticipated to vary with the sort of national welfare state system. The modern state offers constraints and opportunities, a symbol system and a lifeworld as much as protection and regulation. Expectations of work and job search come bundled together with social assistance or labour market programmes, each of these tailored to local conditions, whether overtly or otherwise. For the purposes of the present exercise, this means that a basis for classifying these national systems must be adopted: in what follows we use Esping-Andersen's (1990) tripartite categorisation of welfare states into liberal (historically market-oriented), social-democratic (labour movement domination of the state) and conservative (historically corporatist, etatist and Catholic). As one of the present authors has argued elsewhere (Matheson 1993), one of the main reasons why post-industrial-utopian insider–outsider models have been so popular in continental Europe has been because it is in France, Germany and neighbouring countries that conservative–corporatist policies have made this particular division into everyday social fact.

The focus of the empirical investigation is on the cross-national comparative dimension to political attitudes in Australia, West Germany, Norway and the United States. These countries are used to demonstrate such differences in prevailing ideologies of inequality, work and the state as might be expected to be associated with particular types of welfare state regime, as well as with different statuses vis-à-vis the labour force within each sort of national society. This chapter will briefly sketch out the difference in types of welfare state regimes while being acutely aware that the depth and breadth of opinion formation in these welfare states cannot be fully discussed. There are many dangers and pitfalls in adopting too general an explanation for policy development, and we are cautious about overplaying the role of singular explanations in the analysis. Quite apart from any possible intrinsic descriptive interest, the comparative analysis is also used to develop the theoretical arguments of the chapter. The main purpose of our comparative argument is to see how far conclusions drawn from country-specific evidence can be generalised beyond the specificity of national settings and located in the decommodifying processes of regime types.

What then is the empirical relationship between labour force status and political attitudes? Labour force status as employed, unemployed, retired, etc. represents a position in relation to the labour market and other means of survival at a point in time, and consequently may have some independent impact upon political consciousness, especially where the question at issue has an immediate relevance to a person's circumstances. In a recent study (Matheson 1993: ch. 6), for instance, the unemployed stand out as a case of a group whose attitudes tend to reflect their current situation as clients of the income support system much more than their various class backgrounds. This latter qualification points to the second, slightly higher level of abstraction at which the experience of inequality in the labour market over the lifespan and the socialising influences associated with paid work also shape one's views on the legitimacy of market society or its conceivable alternatives.

It should be noted that we are not criticising the notion of an underclass, or welfare classes or *Versorgensklassen* as such. There is much valuable work wherein it is recognised that there are a variety of situations and interests involved in being in a mode of life and subsistence that does not involve employment (Lepsius 1979; Alber 1984), that long-term or persistent benefit receipt is distinct in its consequences from mere labour force status at a point (Smith 1992; Willetts 1992) and where above all the purpose is analytical within a general sociological framework (Wilson 1987; Lawson 1992). Our objection in this regard is to the exaggeration of claims; to the belief that somehow these divisions by the extent of one's current labour force involvement are capable of interpretation in isolation from broader considerations of social structure or deserving of conceptual privileging above all matters of class or party.

Such considerations lend considerable weight to the importance of specific national regimes of employment and non-employment, and point toward the use of a classification such as Esping-Andersen's (1990) three-fold typology in making sense of these variations from country to country. A key issue is how far the model corresponds with the empirically observable world. In other words, to what extent does the 'three worlds' model adequately characterise the distinctiveness of the societies under scrutiny? Before proceeding to the empirical study, a prior requirement is to establish that the four countries under investigation, Australia, West Germany, Norway and the United States, have the sorts of properties that Esping-Andersen's typology asserts. The ambiguous nature of the Australian welfare state is established elsewhere (Wearing 1994). Australia possesses certain key characteristics of the liberal model (many of these were ascendant in the 1980s), yet retains a legacy of the anti-market stance pursued by its labour movement in the past. It is evident therefore that it is easier in some cases than others to fit countries into the 'three worlds' model (see also Cochrane and Clarke 1993). How then do the United States, Germany and Norway fare in this regard?

Rights, interests and life experiences in four welfare states

The selection of countries for the comparison is meant to provide contrasts among examples of each of Esping-Andersen's three welfare state types, and one – Australia – which does not fit very neatly into any of them. Thus, Germany is a conservative regime, the United States a liberal one, and Norway social-democratic. It is apparent in Esping-Andersen's own research that he has in mind for each of the three types a particular country which serves as its exemplar. Two of these, Germany and the United States, are included in the present sample, while due to lack of comparable data, the 'classic' social-democratic welfare state, Sweden, is replaced with Norway.

The German social order can be seen to fit the classification to which it is assigned, because it evidently served as the model for the classifier's conservative category. Moreover, that the Federal Republic of Germany possesses the characteristics of a conservative regime – an emphasis on the 'traditional' family, the graduation of social security entitlements by the status of the worker, and an exclusionary rather than inclusionary approach to labour force participation and employment – can be verified independently. Alber (1986: 4–5) observes that traditionally in Germany, 'social policy' tends to equal 'social insurance plus labour legislation' and that social security entitlements are generally earnings-related and based on contributory schemes financed by employees and employers, with the state taking a minor role in this process. In keeping with the conservative approach to family and gender roles, female labour force participation rates in the 1980s were consistently lower than in North America and even further below those prevailing in the Scandinavian countries (OECD, 1991). Perhaps most importantly in the light of preceding arguments, there is evidence also of the political importance of the insider/outsider split between the core workforce and the rest of the population. Claus Offe has written extensively on the potential conflict of interests between those in employment, with their legal protections and job security, and the increasing mass of dependent non-employed or underemployed (Offe 1985, 1991), a point also noted by such scholars of the *Versorgensklassen* as Alber and Lepsius. Offe draws attention to the political salience of this issue with reference to the electoral strategies adopted by the major political parties from the late 1970s onward: the Christian Democrats came up with a successful populism based upon 'women, children and families versus male-dominated and employment-centred corporate actors', while the Social Democrats campaigned against the 'two-thirds society' wherein unemployment and poverty was marginalising a substantial minority. In Offe's interpretation, the appeal to benevolence inherent in the latter was no match for the appeal to self-interest in the former (Offe 1991: 145). There is consequently little difficulty in accepting Esping-Andersen's characterisation of Germany.

Turning to the United States, Esping-Andersen's liberal welfare state par excellence, the identification again seems apt. Piven (1991) writes of how, in the post-war era, industrial unions aimed at securing higher payments from the social security system, as well as national health insurance and state action on childcare, housing and other social services. After failing to gain any of these from Congresses dominated by Republicans and Southern Democrats, they turned instead to collective bargaining with employers for such things as health insurance plans and occupational pensions: The result was that, over time, core working-class groups looked less to government for the measures that would guarantee their security and more to the market place (Piven 1991: 253).

American social assistance measures in income support and social services are probably more closely geared to labour force participation than is the case anywhere else in the developed world. For example, as Levitan observed at the beginning of the 1980s, in order to qualify for unemployment relief, the worker in question typically needed to have worked for two of the last five quarters, and in most states to have earned over this period about 30 times the weekly amount of benefit. What this implied was that those on low wages and thus usually at greatest risk of unemployment had to work longer than the better paid in order to be eligible. According to Levitan, these and other restrictions disqualified more than half of all unemployed persons at any one time (Levitan 1980: 44–5). The handful of provisions not subject to such conditions, such as the Medicare and Medicaid programmes and Aid to Families with Dependent Children (AFDC) are targeted at the indigent and are strictly means-tested. Associated with the decidedly limited decommodification of the American system historically, and more than ever in the 1980s and beyond, has been a public ideology emphasising self-reliance and obsessed with work incentives and disincentives. In summary, the United States is the quintessential liberal welfare state.

It is unsurprising that the United States and Germany fit neatly into Esping-Andersen's typology; they are, after all, his preferred examples of their respective regime types. The case of Norway complicates matters a little, not least because of the habit among many of those who write of 'the Scandinavian model' to effectively assume that Norway and Sweden – the latter the archetype of Esping-Andersen's social-democratic variant – are much the same as each other (see for instance, Bryson 1992: 110–19). Indeed, in *The Three Worlds of Welfare Capitalism* itself there are few specific references to Norway (or Denmark or Finland for that matter). Indeed, some critics have taken issue with Norway and neighbouring countries being treated as part of a 'Scandinavian model' of which Sweden is representative (e.g. Ringen 1991).

On the question of how far Norway and Sweden are similar in these terms (and thus whether the typification of Sweden as of the social-democratic type can be applied to Norway as well), the available evidence would indicate that while there are some notable differences between the two, the main distinguishing traits of this sort of welfare state apply in large measure to both countries. Both have large public sectors in terms of both expenditure and employment, as well as substantial employment in health, education and welfare; both display a high degree of universalism and comprehensiveness in their social insurance schemes; both have been characterised by high labour force participation rates, especially among women, and (at least until very recently) low rates of unemployment (see Kuhnle 1986; Olson 1986; Marklund 1988; Nordic Social-Statistical Committee 1990; OECD 1991). Certainly, there are differences between the two countries. For instance, employees' contributions comprise a much greater proportion of social security finances relative to those of their employers in Norway than they do in Sweden (Nordic Social-Statistical Committee 1990: 15). Nevertheless, on balance, the

Norwegian regime of work and welfare can be judged to fit quite satisfactorily under Esping-Andersen's social-democratic rubric.

Thus, we return from the excursus into the specifics of different welfare state capitalisms to the purpose for which this overview has been carried out, namely to look at the effects of these different institutional structures on the relationship between labour force status and attitudes towards welfare state decommodifications. Testing this relationship against social survey data should indicate how far the nature of people's positions within and outside of the labour force matter for their political values in four distinctly different versions of contemporary capitalist society.

The data to be used in the following analyses are taken from the 1990 *Role of Government II* and the 1992 *Social Inequality II* modules of the International Social Survey Programme (ISSP). An overview of the ISSP is given in Davis and Jowell (1989); for some earlier findings from these surveys, see Taylor-Gooby (1995). In order to examine the issues surrounding whether and how a person's labour force status mediates their experiences of living within a particular sort of welfare state regime, we turn to these opinion survey findings on attitudes to inequality, redistribution and the government's role in this. The first of our data, from the 1992 ISSP on *Social Inequality* both reveal some interesting patterns in this regard, and raise questions for further investigation.

Insider/outsider status, egalitarianism and redistribution

There is recent evidence from late capitalist and post-communist countries alike that people form both egalitarian and inegalitarian values about their societies: this has been termed 'split consciousness theory' (Kluegal and Mateju 1995: 209). An illustration of this 'split consciousness' is presented in the first two columns of Table 7.1. The results for the first item have a considerable percentage of people across the four countries supporting equality, if what we mean by that is at least some government-driven equalising of their society. At the same time, from just below two-thirds to three-quarters of people across the four countries support the inegalitarian sentiment that 'inequality is necessary for economic prosperity'. Findings on the latter seem particularly anomalous when contrasts are drawn between the social democracy of Norway (79.4 percent) and the liberal regimes of Australia (63.8 per cent) and the United States (65.3 percent). It is tempting to speculate on these and other equally odd or seemingly contradictory results. Thus for instance we could suggest that the unemployed in Norway display a particularly strong rate of endorsement (86.6 percent) of the need for inequality, given that they too benefit from prosperity through universalistic social policies and contributive unemployment benefits when traded off against existing inequalities. We would go on to argue that under such conditions as pertain in the more unequal societies, support for an inegalitarian ideology that targets prosperity as a competing public good to that of equality (as in the frame of this item) is less likely. Interestingly,

Table 7.1 Percentages saying that they agree or strongly agree that . . .

	Govt should reduce income differences	Income diffs. are necessary for prosperity	Govt should provide jobs for all	Govt should provide a basic income	Taxes on high incomes are too low
Australia					
Full-time worker	48.6	62.7	43.7	58.2	59.1
Part-time worker	52.2	65.4	55.5	63.2	57.7
Unemployed	76.2	78.9	57.6	76.0	77.2
Student	56.4	75.5	58.3	71.2	54.5
Retired	59.5	58.7	52.1	63.5	70.2
Keeping house	57.2	68.7	60.5	68.1	60.9
Total of the above	52.4	63.8	49.3	61.4	60.3
West Germany					
Full-time worker	73.4	72.3	73.3	61.6	87.1
Part-time worker	77.7	80.0	81.6	59.5	77.5
Unemployed	87.9	67.4	82.4	50.6	71.4
Student	75.0	84.7	76.2	55.6	88.2
Retired	75.2	63.5	77.2	39.2	81.0
Keeping house	83.9	76.5	86.5	76.4	88.5
Total of the above	76.4	72.5	77.5	57.3	86.3
Norway					
Full-time worker	65.0	76.1	86.6	81.8	61.4
Part-time worker	82.9	78.4	93.3	92.2	54.1
Unemployed	86.3	86.6	98.5	95.7	84.0
Student	74.7	81.8	89.0	89.4	63.5
Retired	79.0	85.3	91.4	69.3	67.3
Keeping house	74.3	77.2	95.5	90.5	59.7
Total of the above	71.9	79.4	89.5	86.3	63.0
United States					
Full-time worker	44.0	66.7	50.7	35.4	79.2
Part-time worker	59.5	77.8	60.2	44.6	80.8
Unemployed	52.7	61.1	53.5	63.6	85.7
Student	52.8	72.7	68.2	43.2	74.3
Retired	46.8	56.8	50.5	36.8	80.3
Keeping house	59.4	59.1	61.3	48.1	75.7
Total of the above	48.5	65.3	53.8	39.4	79.3

Source: International Social Survey Program, *Social Inequality II*, 1992.

especially historically, lack of support for this alleged prosperity ideology is highest among the retired in both the liberal regimes – 58.7 percent in Australia and 56.8 percent in the United States – and in the conservative regime – 63.5 in West Germany. Perhaps this is to get a little ambitious in the hermeneutic stakes, when more prosaic interpretations are available.

First, there is almost certainly an element of response set in the simultaneous endorsement of pro- and anti-inequality items, respondents not noticing an item's 'change of direction'. Furthermore, the strange irony of the contradictory responses may itself be more apparent than real: it is always possible that the interview subject's understanding of a question or proposal may differ from the researcher's, and an apparent contradiction dissolve with further information (on which see any Survey Methods text). Perhaps most importantly in this regard, one should certainly not assume that a fundamental ideological consistency which the researcher sees as underlying a range of items is equally obvious to the respondent. Thus, with reference to the same data, Miller has noted that 'reducing income differences is not, of course, the same as equalising income' (1995: 78). Miller goes on to point out that there is a tension between support for egalitarian values and support for the state's reduction of income differences. This is borne out by the data for liberal regimes, if not the conservative and social democratic ones. In any case, there is no reason to expect ordinary people's views on inequality or other such political abstractions to be any more consistent than is required by the situations in which they usually find themselves.

Having sounded these notes of caution with respect to any simple, mechanical linkage of economic circumstances and political views, it remains an inescapable conclusion that the data do indeed show life determining consciousness, or at least the two in co-evolution. In Table 7.1, only 52.4 percent of Australians and 48.5 percent of Americans support state intervention to reduce income differences, compared to 76.4 percent of West Germans and 71.9 percent of Norwegians. The stronger support in the BRD and in Norway surely must indicate their histories of strong state welfare intervention including more progressive taxation, labour relations and other income distribution measures. Svallfors (1995: 124) has further argued that the long-standing traditions of peak level wage bargaining such as is the case in Sweden could highlight questioning of wage differences and the need for state intervention. Norway and West Germany have similar long-standing traditions to those of Sweden on wage bargaining and labour legislation. These traditions could also highlight income differences and the need for state action in Norway and West Germany. The social-democratic and conservative regimes show the most support for the egalitarian value that governments should intervene to reduce income differences. This support contrasts markedly with the liberal regimes who show less support for such egalitarian values, presumably reflecting the experience of citizens in liberal welfare regimes with residual and highly targeted state welfare intervention (Esping-Andersen 1990: 26).

To turn to more specific differences by labour force status within each country there are several important findings. The decommodified standing of the unemployed and, to a lesser extent, retirees helps explain the differences across such labour force categories in each country. In Australia, West Germany and Norway the unemployed stand out as disenchanted with the scale of income difference in their countries. This lends support to the argument that the unemployed are politicising in the more extreme positions of Right and Left (more Right than Left) under current labour market and general economic conditions in these countries. Thus, the unemployed occupy an interesting political space in late capitalism in that they have little economic strength because of their lack of labour power and, yet, have the means – most especially the flexible time budgets – to exit the political mainstream and take direct action to resist commodifying processes.

Students are another decommodified category who also display relative strong support for governments to reduce income differences. This is particularly the case in West Germany (75 percent) and in Norway (74.7 percent). Again, interestingly enough, students in the liberal regimes of Australia (56.4 percent) and the United States (52.8 percent) are no more supportive of government reductions than other groups (apart from the unemployed in Australia). Even so, across all regimes students appear to display no extraordinary support relative to other groups on this item and on other items and, thus, their political consciousness on equality is unremarkable. This is certainly contrary to several alternative leftist expectations of the political position and potential of students ranging back to the 1960s. On the evidence, the times have indeed been a-changing since the days of Marcuse's (1968) arguments for the essential potential radicalism of students or even the more recent contentions of post-industrialist theorists such as Gorz (1983) regarding the likely political resistance of students to the commodifying processes of late capitalism.

The question remains open, of course, as to whether strongly expressed support for egalitarian values will translate into delegitimation processes and, thus, heightened potential for social conflict over distribution and redistribution. Strategies of redistribution are arguably directly related to attitudes to equality, but with the added dimension of actual policies and processes that enable equality as an outcome. To test the degree of support for state-based redistribution, three modest strategies are discussed below: provision of jobs for all, basic incomes, and taxation of high-income earners (or a form of progressive taxation) by governments. As a quick glance at the data in the remaining columns of Table 7.1 will attest, there is by no means a consensus of attitudes towards these redistribution proposals within or across the four countries by labour force status.

To focus again on the responses of the unemployed raises further questions about the social and political position of this category in the social structures of late welfare capitalism. Among the post-industrial theorists, the unemployed are central to the abolition of work through a Guaranteed Minimum Income (GMI) or basic income policy. Conversely, underclass theorists see unemployed people, especially the long-term unemployed, as politically passive and as excluded from political life as they are from the labour market (Willets 1992). Neither of these positions fully explains the political consciousness of the unemployed. A more useful view of the unemployed is as a prime instance of those who lose in the labour market-based distribution of resources characteristic of liberal–residual regimes, and perhaps advanced capitalism generally. Unemployed people do favour state intervention and are particularly supportive of government strategies affecting social survival such as increasing access to work or redressing general inequalities. Further, given the flat rate, means-tested non-contributory nature of the unemployment relief system in welfare states like that of Australia these systems present a common interest for those subject to it.

Table 7.1 shows the unemployed across the four countries as having the strongest opinions of all labour force categories on state intervention on employment, basic incomes and a progressive tax. The exceptions to this statement among the unemployed are in lower support for state activity on unemployment in the United States (53.5 percent) and Australia (55.5 percent) and less support for a basic income and taxes on high income in the BRD (56.6 percent and 71.4 percent, respectively). There appears to be no intrinsic comparative logic to these exceptions. Each exception may reflect idiosyncratic aspects of each country's labour market or social security arrangements and, perhaps, the depth of poverty and length of unemployment experienced by the unemployed in each country. Some unemployed West Germans may have already experienced what Leibfried (1993: 140) terms 'a fragile tradition of virtual universalism' from the 1950s to the 1970s and therefore feel that there are adequate state-based arrangements for themselves that have eased their expected temporary exit from the labour market. Experience of this post-war universalism would also explain the lack of support for a basic income among West German retirees (only 39.2 percent) in the view that their experience tells them that the system already adequately provides for the worst off.

A basic income is strongly supported in the social democratic regime of Norway. Immediately, one considers possible explanations: such support may encourage a strategy of workers opting out of the labour market or may, on the other hand, be seen as complementary to already existing universalist and institutional arrangements. In fact, what we have here appears to be an effect of translation: Norwegian survey respondents were apparently asked about a minimum wage. Full-time workers and retirees in the liberal regimes of Australia and the United States show least support for a basic income. This lack of support demonstrates their social position within or as an ex-member of the commodified and market-based resource distribution system. Workers and retirees are the most likely to have been rewarded financially through work and through social wage benefits in the four decades after the second world war. Given the class structure of such countries, those who have unfettered access to the market look upon any possible restriction to their lifestyle – say through more direct taxes to pay for a basic income – as depleting the income benefits and rewards of their work.

We turn next to the retired as one of the decommodified labour force categories whose members conceivably show different class histories and experiences of work to those of the unemployed. Smith (1992) and Alber (1984) agree that the aged have what the former describes as 'a stable historic relationship

145

with legitimate employment' (p. 8) of which, if they are pensioners, their state pension represents recognition or their private pension continuation. Even Van Parijs sees only those on low pensions as part of the target audience of his GMI proposals (1987: 240). In Europe, however, retirement incomes derive largely from earnings-related contributory schemes whereas in Australia the situation is different again, for as with the unemployment benefit, state pensions are flat-rate and thus independent, aside from means-testing, of lifetime earnings. Thus, as with the unemployed, retirees in liberal–residual regimes create a cross-class interest in maintenance and extension of such state activity. This argument and the situation tested so far for the unemployed across the four countries strengthens our claim that market-generated class inequalities are translated by the mediating influence of labour force status into political attitudes.

In light of these theoretical reflections, it is interesting that in Table 7.1 the retired are largely supportive of more humane and, in certain case, limited redistribution policies. Barring their attitudes to basic income in Australia, West Germany and the United States, the retired are among the strongest supporters of government intervention on employment and taxes on high-income earners. The sheer level of support provides an important instance of a cross-class articulation of support for modest redistribution policies (see Matheson 1997 for a comparative account of public support among the aged and other status groups for aged pensions). The United States is the least indicative of a common interest among the retired in support of redistribution (with Australia not far behind).

One explanation for a lack of common interest among the retired in the United States could be the fragmented and highly targeted State and Federal unemployment and aged pensions schemes and the stigma associated with claimants of these schemes. In the United States there is a heavy reliance among low-income retirees on benefits from Social Security payments and from Medicare (the same also applies in Australia). In 1989, Social Security payments provided 'at least half of the income of 62 percent of retirees and it is the only income of 19 percent of single retirees' (DiNitto 1991: 82–5). All US retirees only weakly support the three redistribution strategies proposed in Table 7.1 when compared to their cohort in the three other countries and also when compared to other labour force categories such as students in their own country. This weak support could indicate the stigma associated with claiming state-related income and in-kind benefits and/or the moral stigma in the United States generally against the aged poor.

The problem that emerges in the course of all this lies in the realisation that when we are looking at the relationship between a particular social status – here a labour force status – and attitudes toward public policy, we are not in fact dealing with questions of rational, calculating response as much as we are with the nature of a survey respondent's taken-for-granted lifeworld. That is, it is not enough to ask what one thinks of a particular strategy or policy; rather, it is necessary to examine default orientations toward the possible and desirable role of government in the first place. Fundamentally, what should governments expect of their people, and what should they be able to offer in return?

The need to work and the role of governments

Table 7.2 provides some preliminary indication of the variations by current labour force status within the four countries in the popularity of welfare state interventions. In Australia, the unemployed again stand out as the most commonly in favour of all but one of the seven proposed interventions (price controls being the exception this time), while the margin by which they are ahead of the field is again greatest where the issue is employment, unemployment or income differentials. As for the difference between the full-time employed and the rest, this is if anything more pronounced: on all seven items, the full-time workers have a lower percentage in favour of state involvement than any other category. The results reflect a component of self-interest and a quite substantial component of adherence to the prevailing values of the society. That is, while the retired and the unemployed are strongly in favour of 'a decent standard of living' for their respective groups, there are, regardless of labour force status, substantial differences between support for health care and taking care of the aged on the one hand and support for income redistribution and taking care of the unemployed on the other.

The pro-government stance of the unemployed is a phenomenon common to the United States and Germany also. In the BRD, the unemployed have the greatest percentages in favour on all questions, while in the United States, this is true for every item except health care, but the margins separating those out of work from the other categories of respondent tend to be greater in the latter country. This points to the alienated position of the unemployed in the liberal welfare state, but also hints at the insider/outsider split of the conservative regime. However, most interesting is the finding that the singularity of the unemployed category does not occur in social-democratic Norway. On only two of the issues, full employment and industry policy, are the Norwegian unemployed the labour force category most commonly pro-welfare state. Even considering the most obviously self-interested issue of the living standards of the unemployed, the proportion of the unemployed endorsing this proposition is actually less than the proportion of full-time workers. This lack of an effect of personal unemployment on political attitudes is, as further analysis will confirm, one of the most consistent and striking characteristics of the Norwegian data.

More generally, then, is there an observable split between the 'workers' and the 'non-workers' in each country, in a manner consistent with post-industrial utopian thinking? The short answer is: not really. It has already been observed that the Australian case shows full-time workers to be less interested in state intervention than the other categories of the population, but this is likely to be

Table 7.2 Percentage saying that it should or definitely should be the government's responsibility to . . .

	Provide jobs for all	Control prices	Provide health care	Look after old	Assist industry	Look after un-employed	Reduce income differentials
Australia							
Full-time worker	36.3	78.2	90.7	91.7	81.7	47.2	45.3
Part-time worker	39.1	84.8	92.2	93.4	82.2	50.3	47.4
Unemployed	57.8	82.2	95.6	95.6	86.7	80.0	68.9
Student	45.8	86.9	95.3	93.5	82.2	54.2	57.0
Retired	41.5	81.9	95.5	95.5	82.5	65.2	53.8
Keeping house	45.5	87.4	95.3	94.9	85.2	55.2	54.2
Total of the above	39.7	81.5	92.6	93.2	82.5	52.6	49.2
West Germany							
Full-time worker	70.2	63.7	93.9	92.2	47.6	71.9	57.9
Part-time worker	77.5	70.1	94.8	95.1	47.8	79.7	62.4
Unemployed	91.2	86.0	98.2	96.5	57.9	93.0	77.2
Student	66.7	60.7	96.3	95.6	37.8	89.6	54.8
Retired	69.7	71.0	92.3	93.6	51.0	71.0	58.4
Keeping house	68.9	67.9	90.0	89.0	54.4	73.8	61.3
Total of the above	71.1	67.0	93.3	92.6	49.1	74.3	59.3
Norway							
Full-time worker	76.0	88.8	98.0	98.2	59.4	88.5	65.6
Part-time worker	86.1	96.5	97.4	100.0	68.7	89.6	73.9
Unemployed	92.7	85.4	97.6	92.7	75.6	82.9	73.2
Student	88.6	87.5	95.1	96.2	62.5	82.1	59.2
Retired	86.9	91.0	96.7	98.0	71.8	88.6	73.9
Keeping house	79.3	88.0	96.7	96.7	59.8	87.0	69.6
Total of the above	80.9	89.5	97.3	97.8	63.1	87.5	67.3
United States							
Full-time worker	37.3	71.4	84.5	83.2	63.4	42.1	38.6
Part-time worker	41.4	69.4	83.4	83.4	63.7	53.5	38.9
Unemployed	57.7	80.8	84.6	92.3	84.6	73.1	73.1
Student	47.7	68.2	75.0	72.7	61.4	61.4	47.7
Retired	38.2	70.6	86.5	82.9	61.2	50.6	37.6
Keeping house	45.2	70.6	84.2	79.7	65.5	54.8	42.4
Total of the above	39.9	71.0	84.2	82.5	63.8	48.0	40.1

Source: International Social Survey Programme, *Role of Government II*, 1990.

explainable as a result of the idiosyncratic Australian combination of work-based welfare and a wide-ranging but heavily targeted welfare state. The German distinction between the unemployed and the others does not appear generalisable to the core versus the periphery, at least at this level of analysis. The pattern of responses from retired Germans, for instance, resembles fairly closely that among the full-time employed (with the exception of the retirees being more commonly sympathetic to inflation control than the workers are). The US data give evidence of no clear split of this nature, and the same is true of the results for Norway. Indeed, it may save words to note at this point that there is very little systematic variation in Norwegian attitudes by labour force status at all. It should be remembered, however, that all of the preceding results refer to a simple tabulation of relative frequencies; the picture may change noticeably when controls for other influences are introduced, as we shall see below.

Before leaving the table of percentages, one further point remains outstanding. This involves the relative overall popularity of different areas of state activity from country to country. As was indicated for Australia, the amount of variation from one policy issue to another in many instances dwarfs that associated with any of the breakdowns by social position. Thus the government's responsibility towards the sick and the aged is widely perceived as legitimate in all four countries, these two items being the most consistently agreed with overall, regardless of national context. Beyond this, there is considerable variation from one nation to another in the rank ordering of potential government functions in terms of aggregate support. For example, full employment is (relatively) a concern of middling rank in the two European countries, but least commonly endorsed of all the items in both Australia and the United States.

Various explanations for the variations in support for government functions shown in Table 7.2 are possible. These might turn on the individualising ideology of residual welfare states, wherein it is not perceived to be the state's function to interfere with the labour contract, an explanation which would be consistent with the comparative lack of support in both countries for income redistribution and providing adequate unemployment relief. Alternatively, the dimensions of unemployment as a social problem in Australia and the US may have produced a kind of fatalism such that employment levels are seen as something over which the state has little or no control. Another example, less easily theorised, is the cross-national variation in the popularity of industry policy. While similar proportions of Americans and Norwegians see a role for the state in this area (63.8 and 63.1 percent respectively), less than half of German respondents see this as the government's concern, as opposed to a massive 82.5 percent of the Australians. It is conceivable that the high figure for Australia represents the legacy of protectionism, which was a central element of the policies of successive governments from the late nineteenth century until quite recently. The apparent similarity of the Norwegian and US data in this regard is harder to explain, as is why both are considerably ahead of Germany; national idiosyncrasies in the interpretation of the question once more suggest themselves.

Cross-national differences at the aggregate level follow a similar pattern to those found for 1985–6 by Bean (1991) and Papadakis (1993), who compared the countries in the previous 'Role of Government' round of the ISSP. Bean (1991: 80–2) observes a similar pattern of low support for full employment, unemployment relief and income redistribution in Australia and especially the United States, compared with European countries (and also the lack of support for industry policy in Germany). It would seem that public opinion on these issues was relatively stable in its cross-national structure over the late 1980s. Papadakis uses the same data to argue that while the similarity in attitudes to employment and income distribution in the United States and Australia is consistent with their characterisation by Esping-Andersen as liberal welfare states, high levels of support in Australia for other areas of the welfare state count against the wholesale adoption of this appellation (Papadakis 1993: 253–4).

These international differences in the relative popularity of different forms of welfare state intervention are certainly quite substantial relative to most of the variations by labour force status within countries. Thus, the conceptual hypothesis is supported that cross-national variations in political ideology will be greater than variations by social position within any country. However, when it comes to attempting generalisations about the patterns from country to country, both overall and broken down by labour force position, it is apparent that the effects of the latter cannot be ignored. Thus, for instance, if one were tempted to generalise to the effect that Norway is consistently more pro-welfare state than is Germany, this would be to ignore that unemployed persons in the latter country have on most items at least slightly greater proportions in favour than among their Norwegian counterparts. Similarly, while the proportions in favour of state responsibility tend on the whole to be higher in Australia than the United States, the differences are least among the unemployed and (albeit to a lesser extent) the full-time workers.

At the level of specific attitude items it can be concluded that the two countries with the most similarity in their pattern of variations by policy issue and by labour force status are the United States and Australia. This would be consistent with their common characterisation as liberal regimes. However, as Papadakis noted for the earlier comparative survey, the levels of support for certain key components of the welfare state are considerably higher in absolute terms in Australia than in the United States, thus lending support to the critics of this characterisation. At the other end of the scale, the Norwegian results are notable for the way in which (admittedly with exceptions such as industry policy) the levels of support for state responsibility are high and relatively undifferentiated by labour force status as an indicator of social position. The patterning of the West German results places them in an intermediate position: on the one hand, the political exceptionalism of the unemployed found in Australia and the United States recurs in the BRD; on the other, the levels of support for government involvement in employment and unemployment sets them apart from these. We thus reach the likely limits of this level of analysis.

One task remains for this chapter: to combine the various role of government items into a summary index, and thus pose empirically the question of how much difference labour force status makes *net of other indicators of social standing*. It is to this that we turn next.

The effects of labour force status, net of social class

The multivariate analysis proceeds in two phases. First, a summary index of expressed attitudes to the range of governmental responsibilities for welfare is regressed on the same measure of point-in-time labour force status as before, incorporating only the most perfunctory controls for the age and gender of the respondent. Then, the exercise is repeated, controlling for social class (including present or past occupational class, family income and respondent education level) to see how far effects hitherto ascribed to labour force status might be plausibly attributed to respondents' trajectories through the social space over time, to the different biographies which lie behind status on a given survey day. Unfortunately, due to data limitations for Australia, the second part of the exercise can only be conducted for the other three countries.

Our major criterion variable is a composite index of the seven items in Table 7.2. It thus addresses whether in the respondent's view such things as jobs for all, stable prices, industry assistance, reducing inequality, care for the sick and/or the living standards of the aged and/or the unemployed 'definitely should', 'probably should', 'probably should not' or 'definitely should not' appropriately be considered the responsibilities of governments. As such, it could be seen as an indicator of someone's expressed stance toward the development, diversification or extension of civil government, rather than just its size, growth or cost. Procedurally speaking, 'definitely should' and 'probably should' are scored as $+2$ and $+1$ respectively, with $-2(-1)$ for 'definitely(probably) should not' and zero for any other response at all (e.g. 'don't know'), yielding an aggregate score running, in theory, from -14 to $+14$. Most scores tend to be on the positive side of the ledger, a score of zero indicating a complete ambivalence: either no views are expressed or positives cancel negatives. The assumption that favouring any one of these seven counterbalances opposing any other seems no more absurd than any other weighting, particularly in light of the four-nation comparison. While there are equally no particular grounds to believe that 2:1 is a reasonable ratio for Definitely:Probably, a brief sensitivity analysis not shown here revealed that varying this over a range from 1.1:1 to 4:1 had no real impact on the patterning of the relativities.

The scale, known in an earlier incarnation (Matheson 1993) as one of 'welfare-statism', to the extent that it possesses an explicit theoretical rationale, seeks to gauge expectations as much as preferences, and reflects a notion of development and diversification in the institutionalisation of social policies. Indeed, it is the very range of governmental concern across areas of income support and service provision which self-styled 'liberals' or 'libertarians' tend to disparage as 'state intervention' or worse yet 'The Welfare State' (replete with Scare Capitals). From a quite different perspective, to endorse a greater diversity of state responsibilities could be seen as an endorsement of an increase in social integration and administration, and with them pacification and civilisation. These two alternative readings of the scale scores despite their opposed normative commitments are sufficiently similar in their factual content (if only as measures of the numbers of things one favours and opposes) to justify some sort of claim to social-scientific respectability.

To elucidate the predictor variables briefly, labour force status consists of the same categories as in the earlier tables, expressed as a series of yes/no dummy variables. Age is in years, and gender a dummy variable (female = 1). Incomes were imputed as category midpoints where not given in more detail, and are expressed in thousands of the respective national currencies per year. The figures are gross income before income tax and social security contributions, except in the case of Germany, where only net income data were available. On the scale of precision with which we are dealing, the difference this makes should not be great. Education is in years completed; the limitations of this are recognised, but it is difficult to devise a more consistent basis for a cross-national data analysis.

Occupational social class is defined on the basis of the present or most recent job of the respondent. The classification employed is a collapsed and rather approximate version of the Goldthorpe class schema (Erikson and Goldthorpe 1992). We separately identify the service class, routine non-manuals, farmers and farm workers, and the self-employed, with the remainder comprising a working class of skilled and unskilled manual workers together with unskilled service workers. Class also enters the regression equation as a series of dummies. It is because the Australian survey did not ask for details of the occupational background of those currently out of the labour force that the major part of the regression analysis is confined to Germany, Norway and the United States. Combining this occupational class coding with the labour force dummies and other variables thus gives us a default or comparison category for the fully specified multiple regression equations consisting of a full-time employed working-class male of average age, education and family income: perhaps a bit of a labour aristocrat as so described, but surely the quintessential figure of industrial modernity.

Table 7.3 provides some descriptive details for the variables on the samples to be employed, while the regression coefficients and associated statistics are themselves presented in Table 7.4. Estimates were made using the ordinary least squares regression routine in SPSS®, sample weightings applied where prescribed, and means substituted for missing data in the OLS calculations.[1] As can be seen, the predictive power of the equations is not great, although the adjusted R-Square figures of 10.5 and 10.7 percent for Norway and the United States would have to be judged not too bad by the standards of the literature, especially given the rather amorphous nature of the scale scores and the crudity of many of the other indicators employed here.

The first equation for each country might appear to represent little more than the results of Table 7.2 translated into a multiple-regression idiom, although we do introduce controls for age and gender. These latter two variables may be summarised across the following analyses generally by observing

Table 7.3 Descriptive data for multivariate analysis

	Australia		Germany		Norway		USA	
	Mean	SD	Mean	SD	Mean	SD	Mean	SD
Scale score	4.05	4.66	5.09	4.91	8.41	4.35	3.02	5.79
Full-time worker	0.50	0.50	0.47	0.50	0.54	0.50	0.53	0.50
Part-time worker	0.13	0.33	0.07	0.25	0.07	0.25	0.11	0.32
Unemployed	0.02	0.14	0.02	0.15	0.03	0.17	0.02	0.15
Student	0.05	0.22	0.05	0.22	0.13	0.33	0.04	0.19
Retired	0.17	0.38	0.23	0.42	0.17	0.38	0.14	0.35
Keeping house	0.13	0.34	0.16	0.37	0.06	0.24	0.15	0.36
Education (years)			10.26	2.80	11.19	2.28	12.90	3.03
Family income ('000 pa)			38.34	22.22	269.81	138.45	31.23	19.89
Service class (I, II)			0.25	0.37	0.32	0.42	0.33	0.46
Routine non-manual (IIIa)			0.27	0.38	0.25	0.39	0.24	0.42
Petty bourgeoisie (IVa,IVb)			0.06	0.20	0.04	0.17	0.05	0.21
Farm (IVc,VIIb)			0.04	0.17	0.08	0.24	0.02	0.13
Working class (V,VI,VIIa,IIIb)			0.38	0.49	0.32	0.47	0.36	0.48
Female	0.48	0.50	0.50	0.50	0.47	0.50	0.56	0.50
Age	44.45	15.83	46.49	17.44	41.77	17.22	45.32	18.00
n	2113		2554		1447		1176	

Source: International Social Survey Programme, Role of Government II, 1990.

Table 7.4 OLS regression of composite scale scores on Labour Force Status and selected characteristics, 1990

	Australia		West Germany		Norway		USA	
	I	II	I	II	I	II	I	II
(Constant)	3.760***		5.614***	8.893***	7.978***	13.370***	3.142***	8.322***
Part-time worker	0.297		1.054*	1.108**	0.740	0.451	0.106	-0.187
Unemployed	3.199***		3.032***	2.644***	1.021	0.011	3.501**	1.773
Student	1.313**		-0.397	-0.088	-0.355	-0.466	-0.311	-0.692
Retired	1.552***		1.443***	1.105**	1.720***	0.475	1.781**	0.641
Keeping house	0.971**		0.479	0.164	-0.073	-0.925*	1.066*	-0.088
Education (years)				-0.197***		-0.253***		-0.210***
Family income ('000 pa)				-0.010*		-0.005***		-0.041***
Service Class (I, II)				-1.041**		-1.337***		-2.055***
Routine Non-manual (IIIa)				-0.786**		-1.625***		-1.181*
Petty Bourgeoisie (IVa,IVb)				-1.619**		-2.661***		-2.291**
Farm (IVc,VIIb)				-1.008*		-1.718***		-4.084***
Female	0.599*		0.362	0.408*	0.890***	1.067***	1.263**	1.253**
Age	-0.013		-0.026**	-0.030***	-0.007	-0.007	-0.029*	-0.021*
R	0.169		0.137	0.218	0.185	0.336	0.163	0.342
R square	0.029		0.019	0.048	0.034	0.113	0.026	0.117
Adjusted R square	0.025		0.016	0.043	0.030	0.105	0.021	0.107
Std error of the estimate	4.596		4.872	4.806	4.285	4.115	5.725	5.467
F	8.893***		6.938***	9.746***	7.286***	14.068***	4.538***	11.824***

Source: ISSP Role of Government II, 1990.
Significance level: * p <0.1; ** p <0.01; *** p <0.001.

that, whether statistically significantly or not, women and younger people tend to favour a larger role for the state, regardless of country. Apart from this, the equations (I) are largely recapitulation. Thus in Australia, for instance, the contrast between the state's popularity among the full-time workers versus among the rest again emerges, while everywhere except Norway sees a difference between the employed and the unemployed. Other results are a little more surprising even at this level. For instance, while the contrast between full-timers and the out-of-work in the US sample might have been anticipated from the earlier discussion, would one have expected an effect for the retired, whose only evident difference from the employed in the earlier table was a greater incidence of sympathy for the unemployed in this regard?

The point of the exercise, of course, comes with the addition of the controls for social class, past and present. It is only then that it becomes possible to see how far apparently substantial effects of labour force status at a point diminish when the broader social relations of respondents are considered. In other words, we see how far, e.g. unemployment or retirement merely proxies for a history in the working class. In fact, the effect of these labour force dummies does indeed fade to insignificance both in the United States and in Norway when the class controls are introduced. In both countries, the self-employed are more anti-government than the 'proletariat', but the US shows a greater impact on this of a service class or farm job or background than does the Norwegian sample. While the relative sizes of the coefficients on these dummies are certainly interesting, and may well say something about the organisation of political identities in each country, it is more important to note the main point here, which is that the effects of labour force status decline when controlled for class.

In the *Bundesrepublik*, however, conditioning on class history has no such effect. Even net of class, it remains the case that retired, part-time employed and especially unemployed Germans remain more favourably inclined to the extent of the welfare state. Such results support the claim that German society is characterised by a distinct insider/outsider split between workers and *Arbeitslos*, at least in so far as patterns of question answering are any guide to broader ideological formation. It was suggested above that post-industrial utopian views of a world after employment have something distinctively continental about them; it equally seems no coincidence that the majority of those writing about transfer classes, such as Alber and Lepsius, do so within a German national context. For in the case of Germany as a corporatist welfare state, the material and symbolic division between the core active labour force and the remainder of the population could be expected to be much more pronounced than in Scandinavia or North America. It would be interesting to see whether similar patterns hold in the other continental European nations which, according to Esping-Andersen's arguments, are of a similarly 'conservative' regime type. From another perspective, the results from the 'two-thirds society' of Germany would appear to have serious implications for the arguments of post-industrial utopians. The setting within which Andre Gorz and Philippe van Parijs formulated their ideas on the primacy of the work/non-work divide was also that of continental Europe. Could it not be the case that, while not as applicable to other societies, their arguments and strategies are quite appropriate to the specific sorts of societies of which they were writing? As foreshadowed above, even this restricted version of their claims is difficult to sustain. In the first instance, there is the problem of collective action. Here we see the relevance of Alber's observation that the diversity of place and circumstances characterising the members of the transfer classes reduce their prospects for the formation of organised interest groups. Esping-Andersen is of a similar view, arguing that while fiscal strains could emerge in supporting those outside the core workforce, it is difficult to envisage a situation where 'such a heterogeneous and fragmented surplus population' could take part in collective political action (1991: 164).

Furthermore, what are we saying in distinguishing Norway and the United States on the one hand from Germany and other putatively similar countries on the other? Presumably, their common lack of expressed ideological difference between the fully employed and others when social class is taken into account makes them alike in some way, and yet the United States and Norway would appear to be about as dissimilar as capitalist democracies could be. The resemblance is more apparent than real, and only goes to show how similar patterns can be arrived at by differing routes. Note the means and standard deviations of the attitude index for the two countries as shown in Table 7.3 and the Y-intercepts of their respective (II) equations in Table 7.4. Note for that matter the differences between them in the raw percentage tables. Similarities in the pattern of dispersion should not blind one to major disparities in the overall levels of something from one sample to another, and this is a classic case. When combined with the relative rates of opposition of different non-working-class strata (the service class, the farmers, small business) in the two countries, the historical differences become more noticeable.

Concluding remarks: on choice and necessity

Do those who argue for the inevitability of the 'abolition of work' miss the possibility that the progressive division of the population into employed 'insiders' and non-employed 'outsiders' is not the natural tendency of late capitalism, but instead the result of a policy regime? Esping-Andersen and others have sought to demonstrate that state policies over time are instrumental in developing welfare state regimes and, equally, labour market regimes. Indeed, the comparison of the German situation with those of Scandinavian countries is instructive in this regard. Sweden, Norway and their neighbours sought to deal with the problem of employment in a 'post-industrial' era not by a strategy of excluding the old, the young and the child-carers but by actively encouraging full employment – of everybody. That this violated the tenets of conventional economic wisdom in such ways as expanding public social service employment and tolerating absenteeism was evidently less of a concern than the full employment objective itself. From the point of view of social integration through the welfare state, the attitudinal survey data for Norway tend to support this universalist strategy. The full employment strategy thus plays a significant role in maintaining popular support for a universalist welfare state. Hence the strategy of getting everyone into the labour *market* – only seemingly paradoxically – contributes to the general public's rejection of the idea of leaving everything to the *market mechanism*.

Of course, politics is the art and the science of the possible, and governments may be constrained by more than mere opinion poll findings, as political–economic events of the 1980s and beyond have reliably demonstrated. Furthermore, if comparative opinion surveys teach us anything, it is that what people say – their taken-for-granted worlds, their vocabularies of motive, their discursive frameworks – reflects more than it shapes their lived realities, and these in turn stem from the histories of their social worlds. Structural determinants will always play an important part in constraining or enabling change in social policy development. Hence, while we readily endorse the view that 'politics matters' to social policy development (Castles and Mitchell 1992; Overbye 1997), we would equally insist that this is as much a matter of 'crystalline' politics in the form of existing institutions as it is of 'fluid' politics in the day-to-day life of liberal democracy. Policy-makers choose among options, just as much as do survey respondents, but only after previous history has chosen the menu of offerings. We cannot do just anything we please, and the latter itself is hardly static. After all, it might turn out to be the case that large-scale joblessness on the middle-European model is inevitable in late capitalism and that social-democratic solutions are in retrospect mere stopgaps. In that case, public opinion by then may have adapted itself to policies which currently remain unpalatable to many. Of course, whether we will ever confront such a situation before future developments, technological, geopolitical or otherwise, completely revise the menu is something that only time will tell.

Note

1   Using pairwise rather than mean-substitution treatment of missing data made some significant differences less dramatic, but still significant, and otherwise had little effect.

References

Alber, Jens (1984) Versorgensklassen im Wohlfahrstaat. *Kölner Zeitschrift für Soziologie und Sozialpsychologie*, 36(2): 225–51.

Alber, Jens (1986) Germany, in Peter Flora (ed.) *Growth to Limits. The Western European Welfare States Since World War II* (Vol. 2), Berlin and New York: Walter de Gruyter.

Bauman, Zygmunt (1982) *Memories of Class: the Pre-history and After-life of Class*, London: Routledge and Kegan Paul.

Bean, Clive (1991) Are Australian attitudes to government different? A comparison with five other nations, in Francis G. Castles (ed.) *Australia Compared: People, Policies and Politics*, North Sydney: Allen and Unwin.

Bryson, Lois (1992) *Welfare and the State: Who Benefits?*, New York: St Martin's Press.

Castles, Francis G. and Mitchell, Deborah (1992) Identifying welfare state regimes: the links between politics, instruments and outcomes, *Governance*, 5(1): 1–26.

Cochrane, Allan and Clarke, John (eds) (1993) *Comparing Welfare States: Britain in International Context*, London: Sage Publications.

Davis, James A. and Jowell, Roger (1989) Measuring national differences: an introduction to the International Social Survey Programme (ISSP), in R. Jowell, S. Witherspoon and L. Brook (eds), *British Social Attitudes: Special International Report*, Aldershot: Gower.

DiNitto, Diana M. (1991) *Social Welfare: Politics and Public Policy*, Englewood Cliffs: Prentice-Hall.

Erikson, Robert and Goldthorpe, John H. (1992) *The Constant Flux*, Oxford: Clarendon Press.

Esping-Andersen, Gøsta (1990) *The Three Worlds of Welfare Capitalism*, Cambridge: Polity Press.

Esping-Andersen, Gøsta (1991) Post-industrial cleavage structures: a comparison of evolving patterns of social stratification in Germany, Sweden and the United States, in Francis Fox Piven (ed.) *Labor Parties in Postindustrial Societies*, Cambridge: Polity Press.

Frankel, Boris (1987) *The Post-Industrial Utopians*, Madison: University of Wisconsin Press.

Gershuny, Jonathan (1978) *After Industrial Society? The Emerging Self-Servicing Economy*, London: Macmillan.

Gorz, André (1983) *Farewell to the Working Class*, London: Pluto Press.

Gorz, André (1985) *Paths to Paradise. On the Liberation from Work*, London and Sydney: Pluto Press.

Gorz, André (1989) *Critique of Economic Reason*, London and New York: Verso.

Jones, Catherine (ed.) (1993) *New Perspectives on the Welfare State in Europe*, London: Routledge.

Jones, Barry O. (1983) *Sleepers Wake! Technology and the Future of Work*, 2nd edn, Melbourne: Oxford University Press.

Keane, John (1988) *Democracy and Civil Society*, London and New York: Verso.

Kluegal, James and Mateju, Petr (1995) Egalitarian vs. Inegalitarian Principles of Distributive Justice, in James R. Kluegal, David S. Mason and Bernd Wegener (eds) *Social Justice and Political Change: Public Opinion in Capitalist and Post-Communist States*, New York: A. de Gruyter.

Kuhnle (1986) Norway, in Peter Flora (ed.) *Growth to Limits. The Western European Welfare States Since World War II* (Vol. 1), Berlin and New York: Walter de Gruyter.

Lawson, Bill E. (ed.) (1992) *The Underclass Question*, Philadelphia: Temple University Press.

Leibfried, Stephan (1993) Towards a European Welfare State? On integrating poverty regimes into the European Community, in Catherine Jones (ed) *New Perspectives on the Welfare State in Europe*, London: Routledge.

Lepsius, Rainer (1979) Soziale Ungleichheiten und Klassenstrukturen in der Bundesrepublik Deutschland, in Hans-Ulrich Wehler (ed.) *Klassen in der europäischen Sozialgeschichte*, Göttingen: Vandenhoeck und Ruprecht.

Levitan, Sar A. (1980) *Programs in Aid of the Poor for the 1980s*, 4th edn, Baltimore and London: Johns Hopkins University Press.

Marcuse, Herbert (1968) *One Dimensional Man*, London: Shere Books.

Marklund, Staffan (1988) *Paradise Lost? The Nordic Welfare States and the Recession 1975–85*, Lund: Archiv.

Matheson, George (1997) Universality, Selectivity and Public Attitudes Towards Income Support for the Aged, in Sheila Shaver (ed.) *Universality and Selectivity in Income Support*, Social Policy Research Centre, Reports and Proceedings No. 134, Kensington, Sydney, Australia, pp. 74–102.

Matheson, George (1993) The Decommodified in a Commodified World: a Study of Labour Force Status in the Class Politics of the Welfare State with Particular Reference to Contemporary Australia. Unpublished PhD thesis, Department of Sociology, The University of New England, Armidale, Australia.

Miller, David (1995) Popular beliefs about social justice: a comparative approach, in Stefan Svallfors (ed.) *In the Eye of the Beholder: Opinions on Welfare and Justice in Comparative Perspective*, Stockholm: Bank of Sweden Tercentenary Foundation.

Nordic Social-Statistical Committee (1990) *Social Security in the Nordic Countries: Scope, Expenditures and Financing 1987*, Copenhagen: Nordic Social-Statistical Committee.

OECD (1991) *Labour Force Statistics 1969–1989*, Paris: OECD.

Offe, Claus (1985) in John Keane (ed.) *Disorganised Capitalism. Contemporary Transformations of Work and Politics*, Cambridge: Polity Press.

Offe, Claus (1991) Smooth consolidation in the West German welfare state: structural change, fiscal policies and populist politics, in Francis Fox Piven (ed.) *Labor Parties in Postindustrial Societies*, Cambridge: Polity Press.

Offe, Claus (1994) A non-productivist design for social policies, in John Ferris and Robert Page (eds) *Social Policy in Transition*, Aldershot: Avebury.

Olson, Sven (1986) Sweden, in Peter Flora (ed.), *Growth to Limits. The Western European Welfare States Since World War II* (Vol. 1), Berlin and New York: Walter de Gruyter.

Overbye, Einar (1997) Convergence theory reconsidered: the politics of pensions in Scandinavia and Australia, *Australian Journal of Political Science*, 32(1): 7–27.

Papadakis, Elim (1993) Class interests, class politics and welfare state regime, *British Journal of Sociology*, 44(2) 249–70.

Piven, Francis Fox (1991) Structural constraints and political development: the case of the American Democratic Party, in Francis Fox Piven (ed.) *Labor Parties in Post-industrial Societies*, Cambridge: Polity Press.

Pixley, Jocelyn (1993) *Citizenship and Employment. Investigating Post-industrial Options*, Cambridge: Cambridge University Press.

Ringen, Stein (1991) Do welfare states come in types?, in Peter Saunders and Diana Encel (eds) *Social Policy in Australia: Options for the 1990s*. SPRC Reports and Proceedings No. 96. Kensington: Social Policy Research Centre, University of New South Wales.

Smith, David J. (1992) Defining the underclass, in David J. Smith (ed.) *Understanding the Underclass*, London: Policy Studies Institute.

Svallfors, Stefan (1995) Institutions and the comparative study of beliefs and values about justice, in Stefan Svallfors (ed.) *In the Eye of the Beholder: Opinions on Welfare and Justice in Comparative Perspective*, Umeå: Scandbooks.

Taylor-Gooby, P. (1995) Who wants the welfare state? support for state welfare in European countries, in S. Svallfors (ed.) *In the Eye of the Beholder: Opinions on Welfare and Justice in Comparative Perspective*, Stockholm: Bank of Sweden Tercentenary Foundation.

van Parijs, Philippe (1987) A revolution in class theory, *Politics and Society*, 15(4): 453–82.

van Parijs, Philippe (ed.) (1992) *Arguing for Basic Income*, London and New York: Verso.

Wearing, Michael (1994) The effect of corporatism on public attitudes to welfare, *Journal of Sociology and Social Welfare*, 21(3): 175–99.

Willetts, David (1992) Theories and explanations of the underclass, in David J. Smith (ed.) *Understanding the Underclass*, London: Policy Studies Institute.

Wilson, William Julius (1987) *The Truly Disadvantaged: The Inner City, The Underclass and Public Policy*, Chicago: University of Chicago Press.

8

NEED, CITIZENSHIP
OR MERIT

Public opinion on pension policy in
Australia, Finland and Poland[1]

Pauli Forma and Olli Kangas

Much of the sociological debate on the welfare state has revolved around
different social policy models and their antecedents. As a rule, the models, their
founding figures and driving forces have been based on historical accounts of
the political making of the welfare state: Who favoured selectivism, who instituted universalism, and who was the most eager adherent to income-graduated
benefits. The debate on the welfare state models is not only of historical
interest, but also has important ramifications for present attempts to resolve
the fiscal problems and new challenges that most welfare states are facing.
Different social policy models derived from international comparisons may
serve as a fruitful base-line to which new alternatives in national policy making
can be contrasted.

In rapidly changing circumstances, there is an increasing demand for up-
dated information on acceptable ways to reform national social policy programmes. How will people deal with uncertainties of life? What is the proper
role of the state versus individuals in the guaranteeing safety nets? No wonder,
then, that opinion surveys are living their heyday, and polls on a most varied
array of topics related to the welfare state have become a common feature in the
media. In addition, data from opinion polls are increasingly used also in the
scientific debate on the antecedents of the welfare state. The problem is that the
results are strikingly contradictory: where one survey demonstrates growing
support for the welfare state, another depicts decreasing legitimacy. The polls
seem to be an inexhaustible treasure trove yielding support to almost any
endeavour.

There are various reasons for the discrepancies in findings. First, since the
welfare state is not a single entity but a mixed bag of more or less incompatible
programmes, each of which enjoys a different degree of public support (Ervasti
and Kangas 1995; Sihvo and Uusitalo 1995; Svallfors 1995; Forma 1997),

results may point to different conclusions on the legitimacy and the support base of the welfare state depending on which aspect of social policy is at stake. Second, the focus of questions also plays a certain role. General questions on values or attitudes toward redistribution, questions on people's willingness to spend more money, or questions on specific dimensions of welfare programmes (e.g. flat-rate versus income-related benefits, etc.) may lead into conflicting results on the support base of public policy (see Kangas 1997). Thus, if we are interested in income transfer systems for the elderly – as we are in the present study – survey questions can deal with people's overall eagerness to improve the lot of the elderly, pension expenditure, or the legitimacy of various dimensions of a pension scheme.

As a rule, previous research has focused either on general attitudes towards the welfare state (e.g. 'Government should reduce income differences between citizens') or on public expenditures (e.g. 'Government should spend more/less in pensions'). Although very important and useful, such opinion questions tell us little about the popular support of different institutional solutions to provide pensions and spend more money in pensions. The purpose of the present study is to unpack what is wrapped in more general questions about proper size and scope of governmental activity. We try to find out what are perceived as legitimate ways of organising pension programmes. The difference between our approach and most previous opinion studies is about the same as the difference between studies on social expenditure and studies dealing with social rights. Social expenditures as such do not tell very much about the principles or social rights according to which money is actually distributed (see Palme 1990).

This article will use material from a public opinion survey – the International Survey of Economic Attitudes (ISEA) – conducted at the end of 1994 and in the beginning of 1995. The ISEA provides data on the role of government in welfare and other policy areas. In this chapter we utilise questions on pension policy, one of the most central and challenged aspects of the modern welfare state. In our inquiry we seek to answer: (i) whether there should be legislated basic pensions and whether they should be targeted to the needy only or paid universally to every citizen; and (ii) whether there should also be employment-related pensions and in what way, if any, should they be diversified according to income and contributions paid, and who should run these schemes. In each item we analyse the impact of some important background variables such as gender, class, income, education, age and sector of employment on pension policy opinions. Is there substantial variation in opinions between different categories of people? To what extent are our results compatible with previous accounts on the driving forces of different welfare state models? Is public opinion affected by the national institutional set-ups?

There are previous studies in which the popularity of different aspects of pension policy is analysed (Ervasti and Kangas 1995; Kangas 1995; Zagorski and Carne 1995), but those studies are based mainly on data for individual countries. The problem with surveys on one nation is that we run the risk of generalising specific national patterns to a universal trajectory (see also Svallfors 1995: 70). In a comparative research design it is easier to avoid the fallacy of interpreting national results as universal truths. In this study we compare three nations, Australia, Finland and Poland, each of which represents a different welfare state model[2] and each of which is going through a period of new challenges in their national economies and more or less substantial changes in their pension policies. Therefore, the comparison of these nations may be a fruitful ground to tackle old issues with a new kind of data.

The chapter is arranged as follows: first, we briefly summarise previous studies and formulate a theoretical platform for this study, followed by a description of the database used. Our analysis begins with an examination of the legitimacy of basic pensions followed an analysis of employment-related pensions. Finally, the results from this study will be related to earlier research findings and theories of social policy development.

Driving forces in pension policy

In the discussion of the welfare state models one of the most important aspects is the coverage of social policy. On what grounds are social benefits guaranteed to citizens? No wonder then that the question of who the forerunners of universalism were is one of the most debated issues in sociological/historical accounts of the welfare state. Some scholars have stressed that the universal model has its roots in the goals of the labour movement, which represents the unprivileged classes. Esping-Andersen (1990), for instance, maintains that for the working class, the battle against 'stigmatising' and 'punitive' means-testing was the most important social policy goal in all industrialised countries (see also Esping-Andersen and Korpi 1984, 1987). According to this historical interpretation, we may expect the working class to be against selective pro-grammes and committed to maintaining universalism.

This interpretation of the working class as the most important advocate of universalism has also been challenged. Historical accounts (Hatland 1992; Salminen 1993) show that in many cases labour has preferred means-testing to universal benefits even in Scandinavia – often prized for its universal social policy mode. To explain this strategy in social policy, it has been pointed out that many wage earners belonging to the traditional working class are entitled to means-tested benefits because of their low incomes. Since means-tested systems are funded by tax revenue, fiscal responsibility does not fall on the beneficiaries themselves. Higher-earning middle classes end up defraying the cost of social security for the working class. Upholding means-testing has thus been in the interest of the working class. Based on this line of argument, Baldwin (1990) reinterprets the class basis of universalism, and contends that it benefited the middle class more than any other group to have eligibility restrictions abolished and social benefits extended to all citizens. The reason is simple: employment contracts guaranteed the middle classes occupational pensions proportional to salaries, but because of means-testing these benefits cut them off from the basic pension. As a consequence, the middle classes ended up paying taxes in order to fund a social security benefit that they could not themselves enjoy. This situation led to increasingly vociferous demands from the bourgeois side to do away with means-testing and establish a universal basic pension to be paid to every citizen (see also Salminen 1993; Overbye 1994). If still valid, this interpretation predicts positive links between the middle classes and universalism.

It has also been claimed that in some countries selectivism has been labour's explicit and deliberate socio-political strategy. According to Castles (1989; see also Castles and Shirley 1996), antipodean labour built its welfare policy in the first place on wage control and in the second place in selective welfare programmes. Thus, the Australian experience hints that labour may be an eager proponent of selectivism, not of universalism. Some previous opinion surveys give qualified support to this interpretation: in their study of socio-political strategies of various occupational groups in Finland, Ervasti and Kangas (1995) found that the traditional working class is more in favour of selectivism in pension policy than white-collar workers (see also Kangas 1995).

Basic security is one of the most central aspects of pension policy. Another aspect is income security, i.e. the existence and institutional set-up of employment-related, second-tier pensions. The testimony given by previous historical studies is not unambiguous here either. Especially in the Scandinavian context, income-related pension schemes are often treated as a social democratic creation (Esping-Andersen 1985), and from that point of view one could expect to find firm support for income-related pensions among workers. However, the idea that the working-class movement safeguard earnings-related social security is not unproblematic. In his analysis of pension rights in 18 OECD countries, Palme (1990: 117) found that working-class power mobilisation did not yield significant effects on income-related pensions. Historical studies also give an ambivalent picture. The Swedish Social Democratic movement, for example, vacillated in attitudes toward income-related pensions. As late as in the 1950s a significant fraction of the Social Democrats spoke eagerly in favour of flat-rate benefits: everyone should receive pensions, sickness, and unemployment daily allowances, of the same amount (Therborn 1989: 22–4).

Also, some opinions polls done in that time show that voters of Social Democrats and Communists were, more than voters of other parties, in favour of obligatory insurance schemes with flat rate benefits, whereas Conservative Party voters were the strongest supporters of income-related benefits (Lindqvist 1989: 67). Not until the need to build up political support among the middle classes, and to obtain for the blue-collar workers similar benefits as the white-collar workers had, did income-related social security become part of the social democratic agenda in the late 1950s (for a closer discussion, see Esping-Andersen 1985; Therborn 1989). It was the inspiration of the middle strata and the reaction against the menace from the middle classes that forced the labour movement to adopt income-graduated pension benefits. In some previous analyses the income graduation is attached to 'conservative-corporatist' strategies to differentiate benefits according to status and class (Esping-Andersen 1990). These interpretations thus indirectly emphasize the relative importance of the middle classes. The central role played by the middle class is sometimes spelled out more explicitly. It has been argued that the welfare state is a middle-class creation for the middle classes (Gould 1981: 407; see also Goodin and LeGrand 1987). Most welfare benefits – especially the income-related ones – profit the salaried employees, and the welfare state itself is a very important employer for the middle strata. Therefore, one may anticipate that the middle stratum supports especially those welfare programmes that deliver benefits stratified according to claimant's work history and income.

Not all scholars share this sunny picture of the middle classes sustaining the welfare state. It has been pointed out that the embourgeoisment of society may cause serious challenges for the welfare state. First, the expansion of the welfare state increases the tax burden and as important tax payers the middle strata is first to be hit by heavy taxes. Second, in many theories – as shown above – the origin of the welfare state is attached to working-class campaigns inspired by the ideology of collectivised solidarity. The relative importance of the 'solidaristic' working class declines and is gradually replaced by the well-educated middle stratum that is more individualistic in its social policy orientation. This tendency, in turn, undermines the basis for collective solidarity and welfare-state programmes built on it. Third, because of its strong negotiation power against employers, the middle classes can very well satisfy their need for social protection via the labour market by contracting occupational schemes instead of statutory benefits (Marklund 1982). According to this strand of theory, the expansion of the middle strata will increase the importance of occupational schemes, and as a consequence the popular legitimacy of statutory programmes will gradually be eroded. Most opinion surveys support this more gloomy picture: middle classes and the better-offs are the most willing to cut down almost all kinds of public expenditure (Sihvo and Uusitalo 1995; Svallfors 1995; Forma 1997). Indeed, the better-offs seem to hate the welfare state (Nordlund and Coughlin 1996).

All interpretations presented above derive their explanatory power more or less explicitly from class analysis and the class structure of society. The point of departure is that when a group of people lives and works in similar circumstances and/or under similar risks, the group gradually forms a common awareness. This mutual awareness and the common set of incentives to act are then mirrored in class-based social policy strategies. However, it has been claimed that in post-modern societies both those risks of life and structural cleavages that previously gave impetus to distinctive social classes are replaced by new forms of social stratification. Therefore, the traditional class analysis is increasingly outdated and in need of thorough modification (for closer discussion, see Barnes 1995; Lee and Turner 1996). This brand of interpretation predicts that social classes have lost their explanatory power in opinion surveys. Testing of these hypotheses would imply access to longitudinal data. Unfortunately, our data are for only one point in time and do not provide sufficient basis for assessing trends. However, some preliminary hypotheses can be tested. In our case, providing that the post-modern theory of classless society is true, we cannot expect to find substantial differences between socio-economic groups in their opinions of the welfare state. Other factors such as gender, age, sector of employment, etc. should be more important.

All institutions, including social policy, do have important feed-back effects (Pierson 1993). The present set-up of the welfare state creates a platform from which new solutions are discussed and from which citizens evaluate alternative policy models. These ideas form a theoretical underpinning in most studies assessing public support for either the total welfare state or some parts of it (Korpi 1980; Hasenfeld and Rafferty 1989; Kangas 1995; Svallfors 1995; Forma 1997). Korpi (1980), for example, argues that in the institutional welfare state guaranteeing universal benefits to all citizens there is no room for substantial 'welfare backlash', whereas selective social policy generates a cleavage between the better-off majority and the clients of targeted social policy programmes. The idea can be extrapolated further. If the institutional welfare state unites different sections of society, it may simultaneously reduce the salience of class conflicts and minimise all class-based differences ranging from the level of living to opinions of social policy (Lee and Turner 1996: 6). In addition to this hypothesis of disappearing class differences, we can expect that the present institutions affect the public opinion that is contaminated by some kind of 'institutionalised nationalism'. The present ways of doing things in respondents' own countries are supposed to get stronger support than other forms of social policy solutions.[3] We can then expect to find a stronger support for means-testing in Australia than in Finland and Poland, while the principle of universalism should be pronounced in Finland. Because of the great transformation from communism to capitalism, the Polish situation is a bit more complex. It can be anticipated that the new situation of Eastern Europe in the 1990s bifurcates into two legitimacy profiles: those whose interests were relatively well satisfied during the old regime – i.e. workers – give their support to the statutory programmes, while those whose interests were blocked are more enthusiastic to the emerging new capitalist rule and support marketising and voluntary insurance arrangements instead of statutory schemes (see Deacon 1992; Evans 1996).

Data and methods

In our analyses of public opinion on pension policy we will utilise material derived from the International Survey of Economic Attitudes (ISEA) that provides ample data on the role of government in welfare and other policy areas in Australia, Finland and Poland. In the present chapter we limit our analyses

166

to opinions on pension policy in the three nations. We have several batteries of questions on: (i) basic security/first-tier pensions; (ii) pensions quarantining income security/second-tier superannuation or employment-related pensions; and (iii) the administration of the superannuation scheme. (The exact questions will be presented later in this chapter.)

The ISEA surveys were conducted in late 1994 and early 1995. In Australia, the survey was executed by the National Social Science Survey, Research School of Social Sciences, the Australian National University, Canberra. The sample was compiled from the Electorate Statistics by the Australian Bureau of Statistics. Since the ISEA was a part of constantly rotating opinion surveys it is difficult to define the exact response rate for the ISEA wave. Analyses presented in this study are based on those 1,378 valid responses received by the end of 1994 (for a closer description, see Zagorski and Carne 1995). Australian data are slightly biased to middle-aged respondents and male, while data on the sector of employment and political variables are close to the distributions among the total population (see Appendix 8.1).

The Finnish survey was also conducted as a postal survey by the Department of Social Policy, University of Turku. The Finnish sample ($n = 3,100$), derived from the Central Population Register, represents the total population aged 18 to 70 years. The effective response rate was 56 per cent, which amounted to 1,737 questionnaires returned (for a closer description, see Ervasti 1995). In a similar vein as in the Australian case, males are over-represented in Finnish data. The same goes for the Social Democrats and Conservatives, whereas the age and socio-economic compositions of the data base are more or less identical with population data (Appendix 8.1).

In Poland, the survey was based on personal interviews conducted by the governmental Centre for Public Opinion Research (Centrum Badania Opinii Spolecznej, CBOS) in collaboration with the Institute of Political Studies, Polish Academy of Sciences. A total of 2,127 persons over 17 years of age were interviewed, giving a response rate of 94 per cent. Contrary to the other national data-sets, in Polish data there is a slight female bias, while the age structure and political background variables correspond satisfactorily to the population statistics (Appendix 8.1).

Since most of the sociological discourse has dealt with the class basis of this or that welfare state model, the respondents' class position is also in this study an important background factor that will be used when examining the determinants of attitudes. However, in international comparisons there are some problems in making class categorisation comparable between nations. We try to overcome these problems by transforming the respondents' occupations (coded according to the International Standard Classification of Occupation, ISCO) into a common class schema. Following Svallfors (1997) we utilise a six-class model devised by Erikson and Goldthorpe (1992) and divide the respondents into: (i) self-employed including farmers; (ii) unskilled manual workers; (iii) skilled manual workers; (iv) routine non-manuals; (v) service class

II pertaining to the lower-level controllers and administrators; and (vi) service class I representing the higher-level controllers and administrators (Svallfors 1997, Appendix 2). However, we had some problems with the classification of the Australian occupation structure, and that is why our variable of the Australian class structure is not completely comparable with the Polish and Finnish ones.

Each country has its own specific educational systems. Therefore, it is hard to compound cross-nationally homogeneous variables of the level of education. In this chapter the variable called education is compiled on the basis of a question on the respondent's highest grade of school (*What is the highest grade of school you have completed?*). Although the grades of school are named differently and the grades require a different number of years to complete, it is possible to construct an indicator that is not fully comparable, but is satisfactory for our purposes. The school grades vary from 'no further education', i.e. the person in question has completed primary school (or in some cases less), to the university degree (bachelors, masters and doctors). Between these two extremes there are vocational education and various college diplomas. Thus, we operate by a four-degree scale of education: (i) no further education (grade I, in regression models shown later); (ii) vocational education (grade II); (iii) college (grade III); and (iv) university degree (grade IV).

The classification of political parties into one continuum is a hard task, even within a single country. The problem is more severe in international comparisons – not least in dealing with the rich flora of newly instituted Polish parties. With some force we squeezed the large number of parties in Poland into six categories: Democratic Union, Peasant Party, Democratic Left, Social Democrats, Labour Union and 'others'. In the Australian context we used the scale of four categories: National Party, Liberal Party, Labour Party and 'others'. The Finnish party system was reduced into five major groupings: National Coalition, the Center Party, Social Democrats, Left-wing League and 'others'. In all countries this classification to some extent also represents the political spectrum from Right to Left (with the exception of 'others'). One should remember that the parties classified to be the 'most' rightist parties in their countries are not equivalents with similarly classified parties in other countries. The same also goes for the other political groups. Therefore, we cannot directly compare parties across nations.

In each pension policy item, our starting point is a tabular inspection of frequency distributions. This scrutiny of the distributions will possibly reveal certain differences in attitudes between social classes, but the bivariate presentation neither indicates nor explains what the factors are that are bound up with the position of being a worker, a self-employed person or a white-collar worker, or what are the determinants of the differences found. On the grounds of previous studies, such additional explanatory background factors as education, age, income, gender, sector of employment (public/private) and political affiliation are included in regression models assessing the relative importance of these factors. In regression models the categories not included in the equations form a baseline against which the impacts of the other categories are evaluated (de Vaus 1991: 222). The model is interpreted in relation to the constant, which is an estimate of the opinions of a person who belongs to a group left out of the analysis. The dummies excluded from our models are as follows: male, age 40–49 years, vocational education (grade II), second income quartile, votes for Social Democrats, and works in the private sector.

In order to pick up the impacts of the national contexts, we merged the three national data-sets into one larger database and by utilising country dummies in that pooled data we try to capture nation-specific effects. In the subsequent regression models, Finland is used as a 'Scandinavian' yardstick by which attitudes in the two other countries are measured.

By choosing the contrast groups differently, e.g. by selecting extreme groups as benchmarks, we would have received more significant results, but since we tried to form a theoretically meaningful benchmark we ended up with the present selection of omitted categories. The baseline for our analysis is a social democratic male worker implicitly regarded as the primus motor in welfare state developments, the regression coefficients indicate the deviance from that 'ideal type'.

Because of national variations in compiling the sample, differences in response rates, and because of some problems in constructing comparable variables – as discussed above – we must be careful not to over-interpret results. For the very same reasons, one should not to focus too much on small differences in gross percentages that may be biased by research designs. Instead, it is more fruitful and reliable to try to find general patterns and to unravel how different categories of people contrast with each other in the three countries.

Marginalism, selectivity or universalism?

In all industrialised countries, people seek shelter against the uncertainties of life. There are numerous ways to safeguard oneself against risks and, therefore, the institutional forms of social protection vary considerably between nations. Individuals may to varying degrees rely on the family and kinship, they may contract insurance policies in private insurance companies, or the state may play an important role in delivering income support. In the ISEA, the battery of questions on basic pensions was constructed to represent three different solutions to provide income support for the elderly: (i) the 'marginal' solution; (ii) means-tested/selective benefits; and (iii) universal basic pensions. The items were worded as follows:

What do you think of these government policies for *providing income for retired people*:
(a) No government old age pensions[4], people save for themselves.
(b) A government old age pension paid from taxes given *only to poor people*.

(c) A government old age pension paid from taxes given to *everyone* over 65.

The respondents could react to these three statements on a scale of seven degrees: (1) the best policy; (2) very good; (3) good; (4) neither good nor bad; (5) bad; (6) very bad; (7) terrible. In Table 8.1 we present the proportion of those respondents that have chosen some of the positive alternatives (from 1 to 3).

As can be seen in Table 8.1, in all three countries there is an overwhelming scepticism against the marginal pension policy model ('no government old age pension'), the Finns and Poles being more ambiguous about the option than the Australians. The distribution of opinions displayed according to the respondents' class position reveal some differences between classes in all countries. In Australia and Poland, the most eager proponents of marginalism are found among the upper white-collar workers (Service I), whereas the Finnish upper strata are more in favour of statutory programmes. In all countries the self-employed also have some adherence to self-help. Although the variance in opinions between status groups is significant, one should not overstate the differences. All classes are more or less unanimously rejecting the pure self-help model, and some kind of statutory involvement in quarantining basic income security for the elderly is the most legitimate option.

As a rule, the involvement of the state in guaranteeing basic income support for the elderly has taken two main forms: means-tested benefits targeted at the needy, and universal benefits payable to everyone over the legislated pension age (Palme 1990). In our sample of countries, Australia and Poland have followed the former route, while Finland has instituted a universal national (people's) pension. As stated above, we can expect at least some correspondence between the institutional settings of the welfare state and the legitimacy. Hypothetically, we can expect to find the strongest support for means-testing in Australia, while the Finns should be the firmest defenders of universalism. The hypotheses get qualified support. Australia leads in the overall legitimacy of selective benefits, whereas universal pensions are the most popular ones in Finland (Table 8.1).

A cross-tabulation of attitudes on selectivism by class position reveals some stratification-based patterns. In Australia and Poland, the salaried employees (service I–II) and unskilled workers are somewhat more approving of means-testing, while in Finland the workers regard selectivism as good policy more often than the other groups do – the result is in accordance with previous Finnish studies on attitudes toward means-testing (Ervasti and Kangas 1995; Kangas 1995). However, it must be remembered that the majority of the respondents in all countries regard selective pensions as bad policy. In addition, differences between occupational hierarchies are not statistically significant in any country, which indicates that means-testing is not a clear-cut class issue in the public opinion.

Table 8.1 Attitudes on pension policy in Australia, Finland and Poland; the share of positive responses (%). (Values within parentheses are p-values)

	No government pensions at all	Means-tested government pensions	Universal government pensions
Total			
Australia	15.6	34.2	51.7
Finland	6.0	29.5	76.3
Poland	7.5	24.7	50.7
Australia	(0.007)	(0.061)	(0.075)
Service I	17.9	38.7	48.3
Service II	15.9	40.3	48.8
Routine non-manual	13.7	32.6	49.8
Skilled	16.4	33.9	55.8
Unskilled	12.3	37.5	52.6
Self-employed	20.5	26.9	62.4
Finland	(0.018)	(0.669)	(0.131)
Service I	4.7	24.6	76.2
Service II	6.9	27.1	73.0
Routine non-manual	3.7	27.6	77.2
Skilled	7.8	35.6	74.8
Unskilled	3.6	30.5	77.9
Self-employed	10.9	32.9	80.4
Poland	(0.001)	(0.130)	(0.000)
Service I	14.3	29.9	25.8
Service II	6.8	25.4	45.9
Routine non-manual	7.4	22.7	47.3
Skilled	7.1	24.8	53.5
Unskilled	5.7	25.2	55.7
Self-employed	8.2	22.7	58.3

In Finland, a substantial majority, and a slight majority in Australia and Poland, are in favour of universal old-age support. In Australia and Finland, universalism is not a class issue, either. Especially in Finland, universal pensions are strongly and rather equally supported by all occupational groups, indicating that this aspect of pension policy is a more or less settled question. In Poland, universalism is more of a class-related issue than in the two other countries. The Polish results seem to lend qualified support to those theories prizing the working class for promoting universal social policy, while such a conclusion is not warranted when it comes to the Australian and Finnish cases. In Australia, there are some minor class-based differences that are interesting in the light of the previous theoretical discussion. In Australia, respondents belonging to the working class are among the firmest supporters of universalism, a result that contrasts with historical accounts of the strategies of organised labour (Castles 1989; Castles and Shirley 1996). This discrepancy indicates that labour as a social actor may to some extent pursue different strategies than its grass-roots constituencies individually do. But as said above, differences between classes are small, and we must therefore be careful not to take conclusions based on Table 8.1 too far.

In order to control for the fact that socio-economic groups differ from each other in terms of age, gender, sector of employment, political affiliation, etc. we utilise a regression model to assess the relative importance of various background factors. Results from regressions are summarised in Table 8.2. In analyses, the original dependent variables were changed in such a way that a negative sign indicates a more sceptical attitude to the issue in question, and correspondingly, a positive sign refers to a more positive attitude than that of the base category. A lower value of the constant term hints at a more negative overall response pattern (the most negative attitude = 1 and the most positive attitude = 7).

There are three ways to read and interpret Table 8.2. First, we can read figures column-wise and concentrate on national coefficients. In this approach, we study differences between various categories of people within a country. Second, we can inspect coefficients row-wise, nation by nation and compare differences in figures between the three nations. Third, in the pooled data-set we are mostly interested whether differences between nations are significant or not, and if the national dummies are more important than the other background variables. Because of problems in constructing the background variables, the most reliable way to proceed is first to analyse differences between categories within a country, and then compare these differences with the corresponding differences in the other nations. If we assume, say, that strategies of various classes are the same across nations, the coefficients for different class categories should be in the same direction in each country. For example, if we suppose that men – our reference category, left out from the table – are more hostile against *marginalism* (no government age pensions at all) than women, coefficients for females should be significantly positive in all countries. As can be seen in Table 8.1 this is not exactly the case. Differences not only in the gender variable but also in the other variables are small, and especially in the Finnish settings the whole model performs very poorly. In the pooled data, country dummy variables for Australia and Poland are significant and positive, which indicates that the marginal social policy option is more popular in these two countries than in Finland.

In the case of *selectivism/means-tested benefits*, the coefficients for gender are similar across nations. In all the countries women are more hostile than men to this form of social policy, but only in Australia is the coefficient significant, which indicates that the question of marginalism and selectivism is not a universal gender issue. In Australia, willingness to support selective pensions decreases in older age brackets, while the Finnish pattern depicts a U-form, the youngest and the oldest defending most eagerly selectivism. In Poland, the differences between age groups are smaller. The class variable behaves quite similarly in all countries, the upper strata and the self-employed opposing

Table 8.2 Multiple regression analysis of attitudes on pension policy in Australia, Finland and Poland

	No government pensions at all				Means-tested government pensions				Universal government pensions			
	Australia	Finland	Poland	All	Australia	Finland	Poland	All	Australia	Finland	Poland	All
Australia	—	—	—	0.88^c	—	—	—	0.28^a	—	—	—	-1.55^c
Poland	—	—	—	0.67^c	—	—	—	0.08	—	—	—	-1.23^c
Gender												
Woman	0.04	-0.09	-0.20	-0.08	-0.57^b	-0.17	-0.14	-0.24^a	0.33	-0.15	0.15	-0.00
Age												
-29	0.37	0.06	0.11	0.16	0.21	0.23	-0.09	0.14	0.14	-0.36	0.19	-0.38^c
30-39 years	0.21	0.03	-0.03	0.10	0.21	0.03	-0.18	-0.02	-0.41	-0.23	0.05	-0.15
50-59 years	-0.75^b	-0.12	-0.04	-0.28^a	-0.08	0.10	-0.26	2.14	0.62^a	0.02	0.69^a	0.25^a
60- years	0.42	0.25	0.24	0.26	-0.14	0.92^c	-0.11	0.63^b	0.69	-0.88^c	-0.09	0.01
Level of education												
I	-0.27	0.07	-5.54	0.01	0.27	-0.12	-0.13	-0.13	-0.12	0.22	0.74^b	0.08
III	-0.14	0.08	-0.04	0.01	0.23	-0.05	0.00	0.02	0.45	-0.03	0.06	-0.11
IV	-0.65	0.31	0.77^a	0.17	0.83^a	-0.11	0.50	0.23	-0.01	-0.14	-0.15	-0.23
Sector												
Public	-0.03	-0.02	0.16	-0.01	-0.40	0.17	-0.20	0.00	0.27	0.22	-5.11	0.11
Class												
Service I	-0.41	0.22	-0.43	0.04	-0.25	-0.19	-0.33	-0.31	-0.25	-0.16	-0.01	-0.11
Service II	-0.68	0.21	-0.02	0.17	-0.48	-0.07	-0.07	-0.21	0.22	-0.12	0.32	-0.05
Routine non-manual	-0.32	0.22	-0.07	0.16	-0.18	-0.07	-0.28	-0.20	-0.08	-0.10	0.30	-0.16
Unskilled worker	-0.01	-0.05	0.03	-0.01	-0.46	0.12	-0.03	-0.01	0.77	0.07	0.18	0.02
Self-employed	0.35	0.05	-0.43	0.26	-0.76	-0.72	-0.36	-0.33	0.57	-0.01	-0.08	-0.33
Income quartile												
I	-0.26	0.01	-0.02	0.02	0.39	0.18	-0.15	0.28	-0.64	-0.14	-0.57	0.10
III	0.12	0.02	0.25	0.12	0.41	-0.01	-0.07	0.14	0.30	-0.44^a	-0.28	-0.09
IV	0.69^a	-0.02	0.53	0.29^a	0.74^a	-0.08	0.04	0.19	-0.70^a	-0.32	-0.17	-0.23^a
Party												
National/Nat Coal/Dem Uni	0.66	0.12	0.39		-0.26	-0.11	0.74		-1.10^a	0.51^b	-0.23	
Liberal/Center/Peasant	0.69^b	0.12	0.26		0.24	-0.01	0.43		-0.05	0.59^b	0.75	
Left League/Dem Left		-0.13	0.59			0.00	0.23			-0.03	0.25	
Labour Union			1.02				-0.10				0.61	
Other	0.17	0.16	0.33		0.77	-0.20	0.12		-0.04	0.36	0.23	
Constant:	2.88^c	1.64^c	1.93^b	1.68^c	3.36^c	3.57^c	3.71^c	3.53^c	4.53^c	5.59^c	3.65^c	4.55^c
Variance explained R²:	0.13	0.03	0.10	0.10	0.12	0.05	0.07	0.03	0.12	0.05	0.15	0.29

Levels of significance: ^{a}, p ≤0.05; ^{b}, p ≤0.01; ^{c}, p ≤0.001.

means-testing more than the benchmark category of skilled workers. As can be seen in the table, selectivism is not an intense political issue. In no country do the political variables become significant.

The subject of forerunners of the *universal social policy* is one of the most eagerly debated issues in sociological accounts of the welfare state. Especially the party affiliation has been focused on in this debate (Salminen 1993). As can be seen in Table 8.2, universalism is indeed to some extent a political question, but in a rather interesting way. In Australia, the right-wing parties show the greatest aversion to universalism, whereas in Finland the voters for the leftist parties are more sceptical to universalism than the bourgeois parties. These results indicate that national settings may affect policy preferences and strategies chosen by social actors in such a way that results derived from national studies may not necessarily be extrapolated to other settings. Institutional contexts matter, as displayed by the highly significant country dummies indicating that the overall support for universalism is significantly larger in the Finland than in the two other countries (see also Papadakis and Bean 1993). Nevertheless, the undeniable conclusion is that the traditional models applied in many previous studies perform very poorly in our analyses to explain variations in opinions of the proper way to guarantee basic pension security for citizens.

Statutory superannuation or not?

In all three countries debates about the existence and form of superannuation are high on the political agenda. In Australia, the legislated superannuation was instituted as late as 1992 and still is developing and trying to find its legitimacy. The Finnish employment-related pensions (legislated in 1961) are facing severe challenges because of the skyrocketing unemployment rate in the 1990s (the Finnish unemployment rose from 3.5 per cent in 1989 to 17 per cent in 1995). In Poland, the old pension system instituted during the communist period is in need of more or less thorough modification and adaptation to market economy.

In this section we examine whether statutory superannuation is perceived as legitimate or not. The questions measuring the public opinion on a legitimate superannuation scheme inquired first (A) if there should be some kind of employment-related pension system or not. Then, we were interested in the administrational form of pension programmes (B). In (A), the respondents could choose one of the three, and in (B) one of the four alternatives.

(A) Aside from a government pension, do you think it is a good idea for people to join a superannuation[5] scheme during their working years:
    (1) No, not a good idea.
    (2) People should join only if they want to.
    (3) People should be required by law to join.

(B) Should superannuation schemes be run by the government, private companies or what?
(1) Government should run them itself.
(2) Private companies – like banks and insurance companies – should run them under strict government supervision.
(3) Private companies should run them under broad government guidelines.
(4) Private companies should run them entirely on their own.

As can be seen in Table 8.3, the majority of the respondents in Australia and Finland want to institute a compulsory (legislated) superannuation scheme, while the Poles would build up superannuation on a voluntary basis. In

Table 8.3 Attitudes on superannuation in Australia, Finland and Poland. The share of positive responses (%). (Values within parentheses are p-values)

	Should there be superannuation?		Opinions on administration of superannuation fund			
	Yes voluntary	Yes compulsory	Government should run itself	Private companies under strict supervision	Private companies with broad guidelines[a]	Private companies entirely on their own
Total						
Australia	29.9	68.0	15.4	55.9	27.2	1.5
Finland	37.2	56.6	35.5	53.0	10.6	1.0
Poland	62.8	22.0	69.6	22.7	—	7.8
Australia	(0.000)		(0.218)			
Service I	18.2	79.9	20.4	56.5	23.1	0.0
Service II	26.8	73.2	13.4	56.8	29.3	3.7
Routine non-manual	28.8	69.7	12.3	57.7	27.6	1.6
Skilled	39.2	55.8	15.9	56.6	24.8	2.7
Unskilled	28.6	69.6	24.1	42.6	33.3	0.0
Self-employed	45.2	51.6	16.7	56.7	25.6	1.1
Finland	(0.016)		(0.000)			
Service I	34.9	60.6	23.2	61.0	15.9	0.0
Service II	34.0	59.3	29.4	60.2	9.2	1.2
Routine non-manual	36.7	57.7	34.0	50.7	12.6	2.8
Skilled	34.2	61.0	48.8	45.0	5.4	0.8
Unskilled	37.4	54.8	42.4	46.2	11.1	0.4
Self-employed	52.0	41.4	40.2	53.7	4.9	1.2
Poland	(0.000)		(0.000)			
Service I	76.7	16.4	47.8	38.8	—	13.4
Service II	68.0	23.1	55.6	31.2	—	13.2
Routine non-manual	64.3	22.9	69.6	22.2	—	8.2
Skilled	63.0	20.2	73.7	20.6	—	5.7
Unskilled	56.7	25.1	77.1	17.4	—	5.5
Self-employed	57.2	20.7	76.0	18.5	—	5.5

Notes: [a] This alternative was not given in Poland.

Australia, the salaried employees more than the other occupational groups are in favour of legislated superannuation schemes; the skilled workers are least willing to implement such a scheme. In Finland, differences between various groups of employees are very small, the only deviant group being the self-employed, who want to develop pensions on a voluntary basis. In Poland, the overall support for an obligatory scheme is strikingly low in all population categories, and the highest stratum in particular prefers voluntary schemes.

Despite the fact that the Poles are more against obligatory superannuation than the Australians and Finns, they insist on governmental *administration* of the pension scheme. In the two other countries, the public opinion prefers a scheme carried through private insurance institutions that are controlled by the state. Interestingly enough, the Australian and Finnish opinions mirror the existing administrational form of employment-related pensions. In Finland and Poland there is a significant class bias in opinions. The two blue-collar groups are the most significant supporters of governmental administration. In Australia, there are no substantial differences in opinions between occupational groups.

Regression models in Table 8.4 reinforce the above-presented results on class-based support for the existence of superannuation schemes. In the Australian case, the significant coefficients for various class variables indicate that super-annuation is to some extent a class issue, but in a bit surprising way. Both the higher white-collar employees and the unskilled workers are the most eager supporters of a statutory pension scheme, whereas in Finland and Poland the coefficients for the class variables are not significant if the other background variables are controlled for. Instead of being a question related to the occu-pational hierarchy, the employment-related pensions seem to be an obvious political issue in these two latter countries. Also, the age of the respondents plays a certain role in Australia and Finland: the youngest are the most sceptical and the oldest most positive about statutory superannuation.

Benefit diversification

In most industrialised countries superannuation benefits are somehow related to the claimant's previous work history and income. Here, we evaluate the legitimacy of a number of alternative criteria for relating pension to the claimant's work career. In this study we were interested in the public support for five different distributional criteria: a flat-rate principle, graduation accord-ing to the number of years worked, benefits related to previous income, benefits related to contributions paid, and the existence of maximum benefits or pension ceilings. The battery of questions measuring the support base of these principles was as follows:

Should superannuation benefits be:
    (1) The same for all regardless of how much they have paid in?

Table 8.4 Multiple regression analysis on superannuation in Australia, Finland and Poland

	Should there be superannuation?				Government-run superannuation funds			
	Australia	Finland	Poland	All	Australia	Finland	Poland	All
Australia				0.11[b]				-0.17[c]
Poland				-0.37[c]				0.18[c]
Gender								
Woman	-0.08	0.03	0.04	0.02	0.03	-0.04	0.02	0.00
Age								
-29	-0.06	-0.25[c]	-0.16	-0.22[c]	0.07	-0.09	0.12	-0.02
30–39 years	0.01	-0.10[a]	0.07	-0.03	0.03	0.01	0.00	3.01
50–59 years	0.17[a]	0.11	0.29[b]	0.17[c]	0.13[a]	0.01	0.19	0.07
60– years	0.33[a]	0.22[b]	-0.01	0.24[c]	0.05	-0.06	0.36	0.00
Level of education								
I	0.08	-0.08	-0.01	-0.00	-0.16[a]	0.14[b]	0.25[b]	0.05
III	0.07	-0.01	0.10	0.03	-0.09	-0.05	-0.03	-0.03
IV	0.07	-0.05	-0.13	-0.05	-0.12	-0.09	-0.11	-0.11[a]
Sector								
Public	-0.13[a]	0.04	-0.01	0.01	0.05	0.13[b]	0.03	0.07[a]
Class								
Service I	0.34[b]	0.03	0.01	0.04	-0.11	-0.11	0.07	-0.09
Service II	0.12	0.00	0.01	-0.00	-0.12	-0.15[a]	0.14	-0.13[b]
Routine non-manual	0.31[b]	-0.01	0.03	0.01	-0.17[a]	-0.11	0.20	-0.12[b]
Unskilled worker	0.56[b]	-0.04	0.18[a]	0.04	0.21	-0.12	0.05	-0.08
Self-employed	-0.09	0.10	-0.20	-0.22a	-0.19	-0.65	0.11	-0.15
Income quartile								
I	-0.05	0.01	0.04	-0.04	-0.12	0.05	-0.05	-0.04
III	0.01	0.00	-0.02	-0.01	-0.06	0.07	-0.08	-0.03
IV	0.10	0.04	0.03	0.05	-0.09	0.03	0.02	-0.04
Party								
National/Nat Coal/Dem Uni	0.05	-0.14[a]	-0.21		0.06	-0.07	-0.00	
Liberal/Center/Peasant	-0.03	-0.15[a]	-0.27[a]		-0.04	-0.01	0.21	
Left League/Dem Left		0.03	-0.32[b]			0.09	-0.02	
Labour Union			-0.29[a]				0.01	
Other	0.03	-0.13[a]	-0.27[a]		-0.08	0.03	0.11	
Constant:	2.40[c]	2.72[c]	2.39[c]	2.56[c]	0.40[c]	0.38[c]	0.24	0.43[c]
Variance explained R²:	0.15	0.12	0.15	0.21	0.10	0.09	0.13	0.11

Levels of significance: [a] p ≤0.05; [b] p ≤0.01; [c] p ≤0.001

(2) Bigger for people who worked and paid in most of their life, and smaller for those who worked only a few years?

(3) Bigger for people who had high incomes when they worked, and smaller for the poorly paid?

(4) All in all, should benefits depend on how much people paid in to superannuation throughout their working life?

(5) Should there be a ceiling on benefits, a maximum that anyone can get regardless of how much they contributed?

In each item (1–5) respondents could choose between five alternatives: (1) yes, definitely; (2) yes, probably; (3) mixed feelings; yes and no; (4) no, probably not; and (5) no, definitely not.

The public support for all these alternatives is depicted in Table 8.5. The flat-rate principle is not especially popular. In Australia and Poland only one-tenth

Table 8.5 The determination of benefit level in superannuation in Australia, Finland and Poland. The share of positive responses (%). (Values within parentheses are p-values)

| | Flat-rate | Benefits diversified according to | | | |
		Working years	Income	Contri-butions	Pension ceiling
Total					
Australia	11.0	84.2	49.9	83.7	40.1
Finland	31.9	83.1	45.0	72.5	84.9
Poland	12.1	94.0	68.1	80.2	59.7
Australia	(0.000)	(0.019)	(0.000)	(0.081)	(0.007)
Service I	8.6	86.2	64.4	86.1	44.1
Service II	7.4	89.0	65.9	92.7	40.3
Routine non-manual	10.9	85.1	47.2	83.3	35.0
Skilled	14.6	77.6	38.2	80.0	43.5
Unskilled	23.6	76.8	29.7	72.2	31.5
Self-employed	5.5	85.7	49.5	84.6	36.3
Finland	(0.000)	(0.044)	(0.000)	(0.018)	(0.004)
Service I	12.7	87.8	65.7	83.7	80.6
Service II	22.9	86.2	51.6	74.6	84.6
Routine non-manual	31.6	83.5	46.4	69.4	85.0
Skilled	43.3	81.4	36.8	71.3	87.5
Unskilled	42.5	77.6	33.5	69.2	86.9
Self-employed	34.2	82.0	41.1	67.9	82.9
Poland	(0.000)	(0.000)	(0.000)	(0.000)	(0.000)
Service I	2.8	96.3	78.5	88.7	38.3
Service II	9.5	95.0	70.3	80.7	51.5
Routine non-manual	13.8	93.2	58.8	79.0	62.9
Skilled	12.4	94.2	68.4	79.9	60.7
Unskilled	14.5	94.3	68.5	76.1	63.5
Self-employed	15.3	91.4	69.8	82.1	71.5

of the respondents would have the same benefits for all regardless of income and work history. Finland deviates from the other countries in its greater inclination to support equal benefits. In all countries, the legitimate pension scheme rewards work and contributions paid. Also benefit-graduation according to income gets substantial support. Interestingly enough, the general tendency in all countries is that the length of the work career and contributions paid are perceived morally as more legitimate bases for benefit graduation than income.[6]

Most countries with income-related benefits have instituted some maximum benefits (see Palme 1990). But as can be seen in Table 8.5, such maximums are not that popular in Australia, where the majority of the respondents are in fact against pension ceilings, whereas in Finland the overwhelming majority would institute maximums. The latter result is interesting if we bear in mind that Finland is the only OECD country without maximum limits to legislated pension benefits (Palme 1990). All in all, the results shown in Table 8.5 indicate that in Finland there is more hesitancy toward stratified benefits and a stronger commitment to equal provisions than in the other two countries.

In order to reduce the number of regression equations and to improve the reliability of the measurement, we constructed a 'Diversity' index that consists of the three questions of benefit graduation and the question of flat-rate benefits. The values of the original questions were changed in such a way that higher values indicate stronger support for stratified pensions and lower values support for the flat-rate principle. The scale thus varies between the minimum value of 5 and the maximum value of 20. Cronbach alpha measuring the reliability of the overall index is 0.70 for Australia and Finland and somewhat lower (0.57) for Poland. According to alpha, the question of pension ceiling forms its own opinion dimension, and therefore we run separate analyses for these two dimensions of stratified benefits.

According to results displayed in Table 8.6, the regression models perform a bit better than in explaining attitudes to basic security, especially so in the Finnish case. In Australia and Finland the upper strata, self-employed and high income earners more than the reference categories support the diversification in pensions. Moreover, in these two countries the diversified benefits are supported by the voters of right-wing parties, when the various background characteristics of the respondents are controlled for. By and large, the results on diversification are applicable, in a reversed order, also to the question of pension ceiling. It is supported by the traditional working class and opposed by the upper strata and the voters for the bourgeois parties – something that indicates that the grass-root members of the working class are not the most eager proponents of income-related benefits, instead they seem to be more inclined towards the Beveridgean approach guaranteeing basic security that could possibly be complemented by individually obtained insurance policies.

We assumed that national settings create a sufficient support base for that kind of policy applied in a country in question. The hypothesis got qualified support in the case of basic pensions. The Finns were the most eager proponents

Table 8.6 Multiple regression analysis on attitudes on benefit diversification in Australia, Finland and Poland.

	Diversification				Pension ceiling			
	Australia	Finland	Poland	All	Australia	Finland	Poland	All
Australia				0.14[c]				-1.55[c]
Poland				1.22[c]				-1.24[c]
Gender								
Woman	-0.54	-0.43	-0.34	-0.50[c]	-0.32	0.03	0.44[a]	-0.01
Age								
-29	-0.24	-0.09	-0.94[a]	-0.25	-0.49	-0.56[c]	0.80[a]	-0.37[c]
30–39 years	-0.10	-0.13	-0.25	-0.10	-0.15	-0.15	0.17	-0.15
50–59 years	0.44	0.07	-0.40	-0.10	0.42[a]	0.11	0.69[a]	0.25[a]
60– years	0.13	0.57	-0.40	0.44	0.79[a]	0.16	0.41	0.00
Level of education								
I	0.51	-0.20	-0.19	0.13	-2.84	0.02	0.48	0.08
III	0.25	0.70[a]	-0.17	0.51[b]	-0.02	-0.26[a]	-0.37	-0.11
IV	0.44	0.86[a]	0.72	0.72[b]	0.07	-0.46[b]	-0.22	-0.23
Sector								
Public	0.31	-0.09	0.18	0.02	0.05	0.11	0.23	0.11
Class								
Service I	0.47	0.48	-0.06	0.52	-0.14	-0.04	0.00	-0.10
Service II	0.64	0.19	-0.07	0.50[a]	-0.51	0.06	0.56	-0.04
Routine non-manual	1.28[b]	0.61	-0.00	0.91[c]	-0.42	-0.07	0.34	-0.14
Unskilled worker	-0.17	-0.12	-0.37	-0.09	0.54	0.03	0.33	0.03
Self-employed	1.26	2.43	-0.88	0.74	-0.81[a]	0.20	0.71	-0.32
Income quartile								
I	0.12	0.06	-0.49	0.14	0.09	0.27[a]	0.02	0.10
III	-0.05	0.06	-0.30	0.08	-0.12	0.02	-0.01	-0.09
IV	1.22[b]	0.51	-0.08	0.74[c]	-0.40	0.08	-0.40	-0.24[a]
Party								
National/Nat Coal/Dem Uni	0.41	0.91[b]	-0.27		-0.33	-0.32[b]	-0.13	
Liberal/Center/Peasant	0.77[b]	0.26	-0.78		-0.18	0.17	-0.27	
Left League/Dem Left		-0.74	-0.21			0.04	-0.80	
Labour Union			-0.60				-0.46	
Other	1.26	-0.01	-0.41		0.61	-0.03	-0.50	
Constant:	9.73[c]	10.21[c]	13.05[c]	10.26[c]	3.32[c]	4.57[c]	2.68[c]	4.56[c]
Variance explained R^2:	0.15	0.13	0.11	0.11	0.14	0.11	0.15	0.29

Levels of significance: [a], $p \leq 0.05$; [b], $p \leq 0.01$; [c], $p \leq 0.001$

of universalism and the Australians favoured selectivism according to the national set-ups of the pension schemes. When it comes to the benefit diversification, contextual country dummies are again highly significant, but now they contrast to our hypothesis. In Finland, the superannuation scheme is totally income-graded without any ceilings, but despite this the Finns are the most sceptical to benefit diversification and the most eager to adopt pension ceilings (see also Table 8.5) – an indication that Graubard (1986) calls the Nordic 'passion' for equality?[7]

Discussion

Class and political backgrounds of various social policy models have been a source of almost endless disputes among social scientists. The aim of this chapter was to analyse old issues of the support base of different social policy models by utilising a new kind of comparative data on public opinion toward the welfare state in Australia, Finland and Poland. Instead of asking general questions of attitudes to the welfare state or more specific questions on social spending, we were more interested in the popular support for different institutional solutions to guarantee basic income and employment-related pensions for the elderly. We proceeded from asking whether there should be statutory basic pensions or not and, if the answer is affirmative, should the benefits be means-tested or paid universally to everyone over the pension age. We then continued with questions on superannuation: whether there should be employment-related pensions at all and, if the answer is positive, in which way should the benefits be diversified and who should be responsible for running the scheme(s).

The results show that in all three countries there is a substantial scepticism against such a marginal pension policy model where there are no basic pensions at all and where the individuals themselves save for their old age. This kind of marginalism was more popular in 'liberal' Australia than in 'corporatist' Poland, or in 'universal' Finland, and Australia leads in the support for selectivism, while universal benefits are most popular in Finland. However, again it must be pointed out that universal basic pensions in all three countries are far more popular than selective benefits or the marginal self-help model. The majority of the Australians and the Finns will complement basic pensions by compulsory superannuation, organised through private insurance companies, while the Poles are in favour of voluntary superannuation administered by the government. When it comes to benefit diversification, pensions diversified according to the claimant's work history and contributions paid rather than income are regarded as more legitimate. Presumably, the results indicate that in all countries studied, people consider that hard work is morally more valuable as a basis for pensions than high income.

Our results display that the national contexts make a difference: country dummies were in most cases highly significant. There seems to be some correspondence between the national welfare state models and popular opinion when it comes to the construction of basic pension security. Countries behave 'as they should': Australians are the most eager proponents of selective benefits, whereas the Finns lead in the support for universal benefits. The correspondence between opinions and national pension programmes is broken in superannuation schemes. The Finns seem to be hostile to their totally income-graduated pensions, whereas benefit diversification is much more popular among the Australians and the Poles. Despite this 'anomaly', we can conclude that the national settings make a big difference in opinions. The support of pension regimes among different strata varies depending on which country we are speaking about. Therefore, we should be careful not to draw too eagerly universal conclusions from national results.

The overall impression on our regression models basing on the 'traditional' explanatory factors (gender, class and political affiliation) of the welfare state expansion was that they do perform poorly in explaining variation in basic security – something that could be taken as a support for a claim that we must replace those traditional background variables by new 'post-modern' ones. It may be that class-related variables are losing ground, but before we take farewell from those variables, we must deal with two problems that may contaminate our results. First, in order to provide a proper answer to the question of the erosion of class variables, we should have data for a longer period of time. Since our data are cross-sectional, we cannot satisfactorily handle the issue. Second, our results show that opinions on basic security are more consensual among social classes and political parties than opinions on superannuation. Obviously, the constitution of basic security is the smallest common denominator: it is the moral task of the welfare state to organise at least basic income support for citizens (Goodin 1988: 15–21). When moving beyond this obligation the moral consensus begins to fade away, and questions attached to superannuation are issues that more clearly divide socio-economic groups and political parties.

The expansion of the middle classes has been a never-ending source of inspiration among social scientists discussing the potential to sustain the welfare state. The embourgeoisment of society has often been sketched as a threat against the existing social policy programmes. However, the discussion has been somewhat diffuse and carried out without specifying which aspects of the welfare state are especially endangered. Our results indicate that if a pension scheme contains elements of diversification, it is likely to win legitimacy among the salaried employees, but simultaneously runs the risk of diminishing legitimacy among the traditional working class that seems to be more in favour of basic security and flat-rate benefits.

When interpreting our results a few words of warning are needed. First, researchers often tend to extrapolate the results of a poll far beyond the reasonable limits of their study. Let us assume that we would have asked in this survey – as has been done in various opinion surveys on social policies – whether social spending should be down-sized. The results in all likelihood would have shown that white-collar workers are more in favour of cuts than blue-collar workers. The researcher would have concluded that white-collar workers form a threat against the welfare state. But if opinion questions ask specifically, say, about the very ways to distribute social entitlements or about relinquishing income-relatedness, it will appear that the middle class is more likely to defend universalism and income-related benefits, i.e. the big 'institutional' welfare state, than is the working class. All in all, these cursory examples indicate that it is important to remember whether an opinion survey has enquired about general attitudes to social policies or about views on specific issues such as cuts in welfare expense, determining rights to benefits, organisatory models of social benefits, or the use of social benefits. People might respond to these questions in fairly incongruous ways, and it would be an interesting research task to try to analyse more systematically the effects of different wordings.

Second, historical accounts of the making of the welfare state document intensive political fights between interest groups and political camps. Against this testimony it is somewhat surprising that the respondents' class position and political preferences – despite in some cases being significant – explain rather little in our regression models. Does this imply that the importance of politics and class has eroded? Not necessarily. We know extremely little, if anything, about grass-roots opinion in the past. In other words, we do not have sufficient data to establish a reliable picture of what laymen/women or members of particular socio-economic groups or voters of different political parties thought of various socio-political issues – the same goes also for gender analyses. Most historical data available deal with the elite discourse, and from this discourse researchers have tried to reconstruct the mass opinion and 'class interest' of this or that group.

Here, we easily confuse two different analytical levels in our inquiry. First, some previous studies (for example Baldwin 1990) have tried to trace the class basis of social policy reforms by studying risks and who would have benefited from the reforms. Here, the analysis operates at the grass-roots level – that also is the analytical level of opinion surveys. Second, the majority of historical accounts of the welfare state are based on strategies of various collective actors such as trade unions and political parties. Now, the focus is on the acting elites. We must be careful not to equate these analytical levels too easily. The 'will' of the masses does not necessarily coincide with the actions taken by elites. By confusing these analytical levels we easily interpret historical developments as too monolithic, and coincidence as a problem-free expression of class or gender interest. To put the criticism to its extreme: only individuals have interests, and since classes or groups of people are comprised of individuals, there is always a wide array of conflicting interests among those groups, as indicated by opinion surveys. In collective decision-making these interests are more or less successfully melted down and transformed into more or less coherent actions that, for their part, are data for historical analyses of the welfare state. This mediation of interests in the making of social policy would be an another interesting task for future research.

Appendix 8.1 Representativeness of the data-bases.

ISEA Data and the Australian population

	ISEA	*Population*
Gender		
Female	45.3	50.4
Male	54.7	49.6
Total	100.0	100.0
Age (years)		
20–29	14.8	21.0
30–39	21.9	23.7
40–49	26.2	20.4
50–59	15.6	14.1
60–69	14.0	10.6
70–79	6.5	7.2
80–	1.0	3.0
Total	100.0	100.0
Sector of employment		
Private	72.8	72.4
Public	27.2	27.5
Total	100.0	99.9
Political parties		
Liberal	37.9	36.8
Labour	44.9	44.8
National	5.2	7.2
Democrats	3.1	3.6
Other	8.9	7.4
Total	100.0	99.8

Sources: Australian Bureau of Statistics (ABS): Australian Demographic Statistics 1996, 17, 34, 85, 134.

ISEA Data and the Finnish population

	ISEA	Population
Gender		
Female	47.7	51.5
Male	52.3	48.5
Total	100.0	100.0
Age (years)		
18–24	11.9	12.1
25–34	19.5	20.7
35–44	20.8	22.4
45–54	21.8	19.3
55–64	14.7	14.1
65–74	11.2	11.4
Total	100.0	100.0
Socioeconomic status		
Workers	36.5	37.0
Farmer	5.2	6.8
Other self-employed	3.8	7.4
Lower white collar worker	35.2	31.8
Upper white collar worker	19.3	17.0
Total	100.0	100.0
Political parties		
National Coalition/Conservative	26.5	20.0
Centre Party	23.5	25.7
The Green	8.3	7.1
Social Democrats	29.8	22.9
Left League	6.3	10.4
Other	5.7	13.8
Total	100.0	100.0

Sources: Forma 1995, 53.

ISEA Data and the Polish Population

	ISEA	*Population*
Gender		
Female	54.9	51.3
Male	45.1	48.7
Total	100.0	100.0
Age (years)		
18–24	8.7	14.4
25–34	16.6	18.9
35–44	24.4	23.2
45–54	15.5	14.9
55–64	16.0	13.5
65–74	18.9	15.2
Total	100.1	100.1
Political parties		
Democratic Left Alliance (SLD)	19.8	20.4
Polish Peasants' Party (PSL)	20.0	15.4
Democratic Union (UD)	12.4	10.6
Labour Union (UP)	7.6	7.3
Catholic Electoral Committee 'Fatherland'	4.1	6.4
Confederation of Independent Poland (KNP)	3.3	5.1
Non-Party Bloc for the Support of Reforms (BBWR)	4.3	5.4
German Minority	0.5	0.6
Other parties	28.0	28.2
Total	100.0	100.0

Sources: Central Statistical Office: Statistical Yearbook of Demography 1995, 58, 67; Central Statistical Office 1994, Vol. 13 (2), p. 181.

Notes

1 Earlier versions of the article have been presented in Canberra at the International Sociological Association Research Committee 19 meeting, August 1996 and in Essex at the European Sociological Association's Conference, August 1997. We wish to thank all participants of those meetings, especially Toni Makkai, Stefan Svallfors, Peter Taylor-Gooby, Hannu Uusitalo, and Krzysztof Zagorski, for constructive comments.

2 In Australia, government age pensions have been means-tested. Although the pension is selective, about 70 per cent of Australians over the pension age receive either a full or reduced age pension (Borowski 1991: 31). A law of employment-based superannuation was instituted in 1992. The new scheme is mandatory, but privately managed and organised through private insurance carriers. In Finland, there is a basic 'national pension' scheme consisting of a universal basic amount and an income-tested supplement that is tested against other pension income (private or legislated earnings-related benefits). In addition to this basic pension, there is an earnings-related second-tier pension system that covers the whole working

population (see Kangas and Palme 1992). In Poland there are two separate pension systems. One is a compulsory work/earnings-related system guaranteeing super-annuation to those who have been in work (there are some privileged groups such as miners, officers, teachers, etc.). The other one is for those elderly who have not accumulated their work-related pensions (SSPTW 1995). Thus, the Polish system is similar to those Central European 'corporatist' schemes, Australia represents the 'means-tested model', and Finland belongs to the Nordic 'universal' social policy model.

3   This hypothesis gets support if we look at the discussion of various welfare state models where nationalism lurks behind the seemingly scientific 'the good, the bad and the ugly' debate on the best social policy models. The Scandinavians are prone to equate the Scandinavian model and the most advanced welfare state. The Central-Europeans, irritated by this Scandocentrism, are proving that the actual level of welfare in Continental Europe is at least as high, or even higher, than in Scandinavia. The Antipodeans, for their part, are inclined to show how effectively the welfare states relying on means-testing improve the lot of the miserable human being.

4   'Age pension' pertains to the Australian survey. In the Finnish and Polish surveys the term was replaced by national equivalents.

5   'Superannuation' is an Australian term for the second-tier pensions. In the Finnish and Polish questionnaires, the term was replaced by its national equivalencies.

6   In the ISEA the wording of the question of the income-graduated benefits obviously affects the results. For example, in some previous Finnish studies a corresponding question was simply worded as follows: *'Employment-related pensions should be related to previous earnings'*. The question yielded much stronger support (74 per cent) for benefits stratified according to income (see Ervasti and Kangas 1995: 359). The result indicates that a slight modification in the wording of the question may appeal to different sides of human motivation and thereby have important effects on results (Kangas 1997).

7   In his cross-national attitude study, Svallfors (1997) found this to be true to some extent for Sweden and Norway where 54 per cent and 60 per cent, respectively agreed with the statement that it is the responsibility of the government to reduce income differences. In Finland, as many as 77 per cent consider that the most important task of the government is to narrow down the income differentials (author's calculations from the Finnish ISEA survey). The corresponding figures for such 'liberal' countries as Australia (43 per cent), and the United States are lower (43 per cent and 38 per cent, respectively).

References

Australian Bureau of Statistics (1996) *Australian Demographic Statistics 1996*. Census Edition.

Baldwin, Peter (1990) *The Politics of Social Solidarity*, Cambridge: Cambridge University Press.

Barnes, Barry (1995) *The Elements of Social Theory*, London: UCL Press.

Borowski, Allan (1991) 'The economics and politics of retirement incomes policy in Australia', *International Social Security Review*, 44(1/2): 27–40.

Castles, Francis (1989) 'Social Protection by Other Means: Australia's Strategy of Coping With External Vulnerability', pp. 16–55 in Francis Castles (ed.) *The Comparative History of Public Policy*, Cambridge: Polity Press.

Castles, Francis and Shirley, Ian (1996) 'Labour and Social Policy: Gravediggers of Refurbishers of the Welfare State', pp. 88–106 in Francis Castles, Rolf Gerritsen and Jack Vowles (eds) *The Great Experiment: Labour Parties and Public Policy Trans-formation in Australia and New Zealand*, Sydney: Allen and Unwin.

Central Statistical Office (1995) *Statistical Yearbook of Demography 1995*, Warsaw.

Central Statistical Office (1994) *Electoral Studies*, 13(2).

Deacon, Bob (1992) 'East European Welfare: Past, Present and Future in Comparative Context', pp. 1–30 in Bob Deacon *et al.* (eds) *The New Eastern Europe: Social Policy Past, Present and Future*, London: Sage.

DeVaus, David (1991) *Surveys in Social Research*, London: Allen and Unwin.

Erikson, Robert and Goldthorpe, John (1992) *The Constant Flux. A Study of Class Mobility in Industrial Societies*, Oxford: Clarendon Press.

Ervasti, Heikki (1995) 'Bringing the Family Back in? Attitudes towards the role of the family in the care for the elderly and children', *Yearbook of Population Research in Finland*, **XXXII**: 80–95.

Ervasti, Heikki and Kangas, Olli (1995) 'Class bases of universal social policy: pension policy attitudes in Finland', *European Journal of Political Research*, 277(2): 347–67.

Esping-Andersen, Gøsta (1985) *Politics against Markets: the Social Democratic Road to Power*, New Jersey: Princeton University Press.

Esping-Andersen, Gøsta (1990) *The Three Worlds of Welfare Capitalism*, Cambridge: Cambridge University Press.

Esping-Andersen, Gøsta and Korpi, Walter (1984) 'Social Policy as Class Politics in Post-War Capitalism', pp. 179–208 in John Goldthorpe (ed.) *Order and Conflict in Contemporary Capitalism*, Oxford: Clarendon Press.

Esping-Andersen, Gøsta and Korpi, Walter (1987) 'From Poor Relief to Institutional Welfare States', pp. 39–74 in Robert Erikson, Erik-Jorgen Hansen, Stein Ringen and Hannu Uusitalo (eds) *The Scandinavian Model*, New York: M. E. Sharpe.

Evans, Geoffery (1996) 'Social class and interest formation in post-communist societies', pp. 225–44 in David Lee and Bryan S. Turner (eds), *Conflicts about Class: Debating Inequality in late Industrialism*, London and New York: Longman.

Forma, Pauli (1995) Hyvinvointimallien kannatus Suomessa. Tutkimus intressien välittymisestä. (Support for the welfare state models: a study of the mediation of interests) Unpublished Master Thesis. University of Turku: Department of Social Policy.

Forma, Pauli (1997) 'The Rational Legitimacy of the Welfare State: Popular Support for Ten Income Transfer Schemes in Finland', *Policy and Politics*, 25(3): 235–49.

Goodin, Robert (1988) *Reasons for Welfare: The Political Theory of the Welfare State*, Princeton, NJ: Princeton University Press.

Goodin, Robert and LeGrand, Julian (eds) (1987) *Not Only the Poor. The Middle Classes and the Welfare State*, London: Allen and Unwin.

Gould, Arthur (1981) 'The Salaried Middle Class and the Corporatist Welfare State', *Policy and Politics*, 9(4): 401–18.

Graubard, S. M. (1986) *Norden – the Passion for Equality?*, Oslo: Norwegian University Press.

Hatland, Aksel (1992) *Till dem som trenger det mest?*, Oslo: Universitetsforlaget.

Hasenfeld, Yehskel and Rafferty, Jane E. (1989) 'The Determinants of Public Attitudes Toward the Welfare State', *Social Forces*, 67(4): 1027–48.

Kangas, Olli (1995) 'Attitudes on Means-Tested Social Benefits in Finland', *Acta Sociologica*, 38(4): 299–310.

Kangas, Olli (1997) 'Self-Interest and the Common Good: The Impact of Norms, Selfishness and Context in Social Policy Opinion', *Journal of Socio-Economics*, 26(5): 475–94.

Kangas, Olli and Palme, Joakim (1992) 'The Private-Public Mix in Pension Policy', pp. 199-237 in Jon Eivind Kolberg (ed.) *The Study of Welfare Regimes*, New York: M. E. Sharpe.

Korpi, Walter (1980) 'Social Policy and Distributional Conflict in the Capitalist Democracies', *West European Politics*, 3(3): 294–316.

Lee, David, J. and Turner, Bryan S. (eds) (1996) *Conflicts about Class: Debating Inequality in late Industrialism*, London and New York: Longman.

Lindqvist, Rafael (1989) Konflikt och kompromiss vid den almänna sjukförsäkringens tillkomst, *Arkiv*, 41–42: 52–81.

Marklund, Staffan (1982) *Klass, stat och socialpolitik*, Lund: Arkiv.

Nordlund, Anders and Coughlin, Richard, M. (1996) Who hates the welfare state – evidence from Sweden. A paper presented at the 8th International Conference on Socio-economics, Geneva, Switzerland, July 12–14, 1996.

Overbye, Einar (1994) 'Convergence in Policy Outcomes: Social Security Systems in Perspective', *Journal of Public Policy*, 14(2): 147–74.

Palme, Joakim (1990) *Pension Rights in Welfare Capitalism. The Development of Old-Age Pensions in 18 OECD Countries 1930 to 1985*, Stockholm: Swedish Institute for Social Research.

Papadakis, Elim and Bean, Clive (1993) 'Popular Support for The Welfare State: A Comparison Between Institutional Regimes', *Journal of Public Policy*, 13(3): 227–54.

Pierson, Paul (1993) 'When Effect becomes Cause: Policy Feedback and Political Change', *World Politics*, 45(July): 595–628.

Salminen, Kari (1993) *Pension Schemes in the Making*, Helsinki: The Central Pension Security Institute.

Sihvo, Tuire and Uusitalo, Hannu (1995) 'Economic Crises and Support for the Welfare State in Finland 1975–1993', *Acta Sociologica*, 38(3): 251–62.

SSPTW, Social Security Programs Throughout the World 1995, U.S. Social Security Administration Office of Research and Statistics, Washington, DC: U.S. Government Printing Office.

Svallfors, Stefan (1995) 'The End of Class Politics? Structural Cleavages and Attitudes to Swedish Welfare Policies', *Acta Sociologica*, 36(1): 53–74.

Svallfors, Stefan (1997) 'Worlds of Welfare and Attitudes to Redistribution: A Comparison of Eight Western Nations', *European Sociological Review*, 13(3): 283–304.

Therborn, Göran (1989) Arbetarrörelsen och välfärdsstaten, *Arkiv*, 41–42: 3–51.

Zagorski, Krzysztof and Carne, Sarah (1995) Australian Public Opinion on Superannuation 1994. Working Paper Series 1/1995. The University of Melbourne: Institute of Applied Economics and Social Research.

9

EGALITARIANISM, PERCEPTION OF CONFLICTS AND SUPPORT FOR TRANSFORMATION IN POLAND[1]

Krzysztof Zagórski

Economic transformation, which constitutes one crucial element of the transition from state-socialism to free-market democracy in Central–East Europe, can be described in terms of reducing the role of government in the economy and dismantling the system of central planning as well as predominantly public (or rather government) ownership.

This chapter is based on the obvious conviction that public opinion, however differentiated, fragmented or even atomised it may be, constitutes a crucial element in the democratic political system, especially a democratic system in the making or undergoing radical transformation. Each democratic system requires two kinds of public social consensus. The first concerns the most general rules of democratic political game. Since this chapter is not about the theory of democracy, only one such rule will be emphasised here. It relates to conflicts of interests. The institutionalisation of conflicts constitutes the very essence of a democratic political system, while the attempt to eradicate them is typical of authoritarian systems (Lipset 1985; Dahrendorf 1988; Przeworski 1992). The fact that losing parties are not doomed to have their interests suppressed forever, since they hope to win the next time or to gain something through political bargaining, contributes to the legitimisation of the democratic system. Such a system is based on a widely accepted notion that the conflict of interests is legitimate and on a rejection of the authoritarian idea that only one set of interests represents the common good, so the articulation of other interests, not to mention the fight for them, should be banned or grossly limited.

One of the shocks suffered by the societies under transition toward parliamentary democracy was caused by a sudden appearance of conflicts on the political scene, once the superficial uniformity of communism had fragmented and the curtain had been pulled aside. Having no experience of normal democratic political life, the public had a tendency to perceive open political conflicts as a sign of selfishness on the part of the politicians and a lack of broad, altruistic approach in politics. Such feelings, if persisting, may reduce the social legitimacy of the transformation as a whole. To allow democracy to develop, the idea of legitimised conflicts has to be accepted both by the political players and by the public as a whole. Democracy cannot exist without public support of its rules and this support is linked to attitudes toward social conflicts.

Some level of public acceptance of particular economic and political goals constitutes the second kind of social consent necessary for the democratic system in general and, especially, for democratic transformation. Such a conviction is behind the question posed by Offe (1991), namely 'is a transition to free-market capitalist democracy possible by democratic means?'. If most of the particular goals of the transformation are rejected by the public, transformation through democratic means is impossible. People will vote out political forces whose goals and policies are grossly and permanently incompatible with public opinion. The usual ephemerality of consensus on particular goals, especially in times of change, was very well understood by Balcerowicz (1995), the architect of the Polish 'shock therapy' or the 'big bang', as he prefers to say. Balcerowicz has claimed that effective transformation is impossible without the public being ready to accept the 'bitter medicine', and that the consent to take such a medicine is relatively short-lasting. Because of that, various reformist policies have to be implemented as soon and as quick as possible in order not to be democratically rejected.

Public attitudes and opinions have to be analysed not only because it is morally right to take them into account in democratic political life, but also because they may cripple the democracy or, at least, hamper attempts to reform the economy and the state.

Two attitudinal predispositions seem to influence support for transformation in general and for its particular aspects. Theoretical considerations (Hirschman 1981; Offe 1991) and empirical analyses (Zagórski 1994) suggest that decline in egalitarian attitudes is one of the very important preconditions of transformation (as well as of other radical economic change), since the latter usually increases inequality, at least at its initial stage. The hope for improvement in one's own material situation is, on the other hand, a significant determinant of inegalitarian attitude. It influences the support for transformation both directly and indirectly, through reducing egalitarian tendencies. Expectations are more important in this respect than evaluations of the actual situation.

Such attitudinal interrelations were apparent at the initial stage of transition in Poland and other countries (Zagórski 1994; Mishler and Rose 1996). However, as Hirschman and Offe suggest, the role of hope should diminish and the role of evaluation of actual changes should gain importance with time. We claim that this marks the end of the period called by Balcerowicz 'extraordinary', in which the reformists can count on the support of the public irrespective of growing inequality and relative or even absolute deterioration in the material living conditions of many social groups.

One of the aims of this chapter is to see whether the decline of support for transformation in Poland is associated with changing relations between this support and inegalitarian attitudes on one hand and expectations for the future as well as evaluations of current material conditions on the other.

Our first hypothesis is that the support for transformation is still strongly affected by egalitarian vs. inegalitarian attitudes. However, after several years of transformation, we expect attitudes toward inequality to be influenced to a greater extent by evaluations of actual changes than by expectations for the future, which were more important at the beginning of the transformation processes.

The second hypothesis stems from game theory, more particularly from the distinction between zero-sum and positive-sum games (Schelling 1980).[2] This hypothesis has two levels. On the first level, we claim that people who see their society as conflict-ridden have a tendency to take an egalitarian stance, and to expect the government to execute various redistributive, protectionist and generally interventionist policies. Thus, they are not strong supporters of transformation to democratic market capitalism. On the second level, we claim that this is true only if the conflicts, and the world in general, are perceived in terms of zero-sum rather than positive-sum games. We expect those who believe that if one gets rich the other inevitably has to get poorer, and that each conflict has to end with a winner and a loser to have egalitarian attitudes and to disapprove the transformation to market democracy. That may be not neces-sarily so for those who see the world in positive-sum terms, who understand that many conflicts may be solved in a way which benefits both opponents. Thus, egalitarian and etatist (anti-liberal) attitudes are not necessarily stimulated by the perception of the world as conflict ridden but by the interaction of such a perception and a conviction that conflicts inevitably create winners and losers.

Dahrendorf (1988) has stressed that the positive-sum game approach to reality is associated with pro-development attitudes. While rejecting extensive redistributive policies as unnecessary because everybody gains something or will gain in a near future, it facilitates economic growth. In opposition to that, the zero-sum approach stimulates redistributive policies and hampers growth. Dahrendorf has formulated the so called Martinez Paradox: 'from growth with-out redistribution to redistribution without growth'. Martinez was a minister of foreign trade in the Ortega's Nicaragua government. For Balcerowicz or Klaus, irrespective of the differences between Polish and Czech approaches to eco-nomic transformation, the paradox may take a reverse form: 'from redistribution without growth to growth without redistribution'. Such extreme formulations usually oversimplify real problems. In this case, however, the problem of the relation between redistribution and poverty is far from spurious or unimportant.

Changes in support for transformation and economic attitudes in Poland

Surveys conducted in Central–East European countries suggest that reformist policies enjoyed the strongest public support at very early stages of economic and political transformations, when they were most painful. This support has shrunk at more advanced stages. Two complementary explanations of this phenomenon are possible. The first pays attention to the negative side-effects of transformation. They were not clearly foreseen by the public who expected a rapid improvement in all spheres of social and economic life, once the old system is replaced by the new one. These unforeseen negative side-effects cause shock and a withdrawal of the support for transformation. The journalistic description of the so-called 'shock therapy' as 'more shock than therapy' is quite adequate in many cases, since people often suffer the shock irrespective of how good the therapy is. Even if the medicine works, they see negative side-effects and either disregard or simply do not see the positive results.

The second explanation claims that support for transformation may diminish when the negative conditions which justified the reforms in the past disappear (Przeworski 1996). Paradoxically, the more successful the transformation is, the less reason for its continuation may be seen by the public. Since the public is no longer affected by old miseries but faces new negative consequences of the reforms, support for the continuation of transformation policies may diminish and the nostalgia for the old system may emerge.

A successful continuation of the reforms despite weak public support eliminates or reduces some of their negative side-effects, which are usually most acute at the beginning of transformation, when the painful destruction of the old system predominates over construction of the new one. When the elements of the new system consolidate, its negative features begin to disappear or to be counterbalanced by the positive ones. More and more people feel the positive effects of transformation and regain hope for a better future. That should lead to growing support for the transformation in general and for particular reformist policies. Of course, such a sequence is possible only when the reforms are not halted or significantly slowed down before the new system begins to function and the new economic as well as political changes are brought at least to a partial fruition. In other words, the 'point of no return' has to be reached (Frentzel-Zagórska 1993). Some correctional policies may also contribute to the economic improvement and thus to the growing legitimacy of transformation, though it would be difficult to say whether the determined continuation of reformist policies or the correction of their misconceived and most painful elements are more important for the economy and for the public opinion.

It seems that the processes in Poland took the route described above (Figure 9.1). The public strongly supported the transformation right after the demise of the old communist regime. About 40 per cent of the population were of the opinion in 1991 that the transformation has brought people more benefit than harm, while only about 25 per cent had the opposite feeling. The rest took the neutral opinion that there is as much benefit as harm. Subsequently, 'bitter medicine' has resulted in 'shock therapy'. Many people faced negative side-effects of radical reforms despite general improvement in the economic conditions of the country. That has resulted in a fall in positive evaluations of

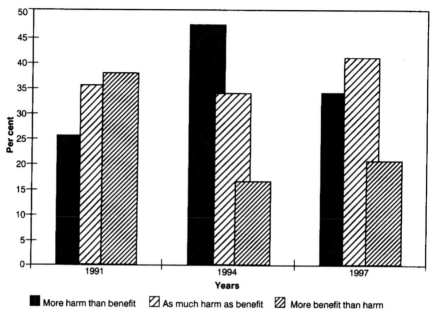

Figure 9.1 Public opinion about transformation bringing people more benefit or harm. Poland, 1991–7.

transformation from about 40 to only about 15 per cent in 1994, while the number of negative evaluations exceeded 45 per cent. Such a change in public evaluation of transformation has contributed to the electoral victory of ex-communists, repackaged as social-democrats, in the 1993 parliamentary elections. Despite the fears based on their electoral campaign and their political roots, the new coalition government of the ex-communist Democratic Left Alliance (SLD) and the pre-transformation communist ally the Polish Peasant Party (PSL) has neither reversed (with some non-crucial exceptions) nor halted the reforms, though it has evidently slowed them down. However, even a limited continuation of former radical reforms has further improved the general economic conditions of the country as well as the material living conditions of many people. That has resulted in a decline in negative evaluation by almost 10 percentage points and a parallel increase in positive valuations of transformation by about 5 percentage points between 1994 and 1997. The number of ambivalent evaluations has also somewhat risen. The 1991 and 1994 surveys were conducted in the autumn, while the 1997 survey took place in January and February, so the actual time difference between the two last surveys was not three but less than 2½ years. Thus, during both 1991–4 and 1994–7, substantial but contrary changes in public evaluation of transformation were observed.

If the evaluation of transformation is carried out through an ordinal five-point scale recoded into 0 to 100 points, with 50 points indicating the neutral opinion and values below and above it indicating negative and positive evaluations respectively, the mean of such a scale has changed between 1994 and 1997 from 41.53 to 46.01 (Table 9.1). Despite the improvement, it still has a negative value.

This moderate rise of support for transformation is associated with a remarkable rise in subjective well-being. The answers for four questions are analysed here. The first question concerns evaluation of the present material situation of the respondents compared to the situation right before transformation. The second concerns the expectation for improvement or deterioration of this situation in 3 years' time. Two remaining parallel questions concern the present and future material situation of Polish society as a whole. The answers constitute five-point scales recoded from −100 (the most negative) to +100 (the most positive), with 0 indicating a neutral point of no changes perceived or expected.

On the average, people see their own situation and the situation of the Polish society as worse than by the end of the 1980s decade. However, there is a remarkable improvement in these evaluations between 1994 and 1997. Even if we divide the values by two in order to make them comparable to the measure of support for transformation, the improvement in evaluations of changes in living conditions will be much bigger than the improvement in evaluations of transformation. The expectations for future material living conditions were always optimistic in Poland and they have further improved between 1994

Table 9.1 Changes in economic attitudes, perception of social conflicts, egalitarianism and support for transformation, 1994–7.

Variable names	Means, 1994	Means, 1997
Evaluation of transformation	41.53	46.01
Egalitarianism	78.55	79.26
Functional inegalitarianism	66.36	69.41
Perceived intensity of social conflicts	55.24	54.28
Perception of conflicts in zero-sum terms	n.a.	66.59
Perception of conflicts in positive-sum terms	n.a.	65.79
Evaluation of personal material living conditions as compared to the end of 1980s	−33.51	−18.03
Expectation of improvement in personal material living conditions in 3 years' time	6.97	17.03
Evaluation of material living conditions in Poland as a whole, as compared to the end of 1980s	−44.30	−27.45
Expectation of improvement in material living conditions in Poland in 3 years' time	5.19	16.36
Support for public ownership of institutions in health service, education and welfare	79.65	76.95
Support for price control by government	69.65	64.62
Support for subsidies by government	68.88	68.97
Support for direct involvement of government in fighting unemployment	68.78	70.42

Note: Description of the variables is given in Appendix 9.1.

and 1997. All of these changes are much faster than the changes in public attitudes to transformation. This difference suggests that the latter are influenced both by material considerations and, perhaps to a greater extent, by various political and social factors.

Neither the intensity of egalitarian vs. inegalitarian attitudes, nor the perceived intensity of social conflicts have changed significantly in Poland between 1994 and 1997. The same may be said about the attitudes to specific aspects of etatism. There is a slight, if not negligible, decline in support for public ownership of health, education and welfare institutions and for price control by the government. However, there is no decline in support for government subsidies to the economy and there is a negligible increase in support for active role of the government in fighting unemployment.

Correlates and determinants of egalitarian attitudes and perception of conflict

The differences in intensity of changes of various attitudes and evaluations pose the question of the interrelations between these variables. As in other surveys in many different countries (Kluegel and Smith 1986; Mueller 1993; Svallfors 1993; Zaborowski 1994; Zagórski 1994; Kluegel et al. 1995) two separate attitudinal dimensions of 'egalitarianism' (or 'critical egalitarianism') and 'inegalitarianism' (or 'affirmative legitimisation of inequality' or 'functional inegalitarianism') have been empirically defined in Poland. The first consists of the belief that there is too much undesired inequality which should be reduced. The second consists of the belief that inequalities are necessary for economic progress, general well-being and individual motivation for work. Instead of constituting two opposite poles of the same attitudinal dimension, critical egalitarianism and functional inegalitarianism constitute two relatively independent dimensions. Consistent with expectations, the correlation between them is negative but, surprisingly, quite low. Many people think that inequality is good for the economy, and at the same time they say that it is too big and should be reduced. Such an inconsistency is the extreme form of attitude fragmentation. The inconsistencies are often found in the attitudes to various other subjects (possible examples concern the opinions about taxation and government spending or about reduction of government power and demand for its more effective regulatory functions). Two separate attitudinal scales of support for neo-corporatism and for the liberal type of industrial relations have been also defined in Australia, Finland and Poland (Zagórski 1998). The present study reveals that perceptions of the world in terms of zero-sum and positive-sum games also do not create one bi-polar attitudinal dimension, but should be measured by two separate scales.

The correlations between egalitarian attitudes, subjective well-being and perceptions of social conflicts are consistent with the hypotheses (Table 9.2). Both in 1994 and in 1997, correlation coefficients between egalitarianism and

Table 9.2 Correlates of egalitarian attitudes, 1994–7. (Pearson's 'r')

Correlates	Egalitarianism 1994 Correlates 1994	Egalitarianism 1997 – Correlates 1997	Egalitarianism 1994 – Correlates 1997	Egalitarianism 1997 – Correlates 1994
Subjective improvement of personal material conditions since the end of 1980s	−0.28**	−0.22**	−0.18**	−0.23**
Predicted improvement in personal material conditions in 3 years	−0.18**	−0.14**	−0.12**	−0.12**
Subjective improvement of material conditions in Poland as a whole since the end of 1980s	−0.22**	−0.22**	−0.13**	−0.16**
Predicted improvement in material conditions in Poland as a whole in 3 years time	−0.12**	−0.14**	−0.10**	−0.12**
Perceived intensity of social conflicts	0.28**	0.22**	0.14**	0.12**
Perception of conflicts as zero-sum games	n.a.	0.28**	0.17**	n.a.
Perception of conflicts as positive-sum games	n.a.	0.14**	0.06*	n.a.

**, Significant at 0.01 level; *, Significant at 0.05 level; n.a. = not available.

positive evaluation of past changes in material living conditions of both individual respondents and the Polish society as a whole are significantly negative, and quite high as compared to most correlations found in other attitudinal surveys.

Political scientists have established a general regularity that voting behaviour and political attitudes are influenced to a greater degree by assessments and predictions of the economic situation of the country that by assessments and predictions of one's own situation (Lewis-Beck 1991). Egalitarian attitudes, however, are related equally strongly to private and public material concern in 1997, while in 1994 their correlations were even stronger with individual than with public concern.

As predicted, there are relatively strong positive correlations between egalitarianism and perception of social conflicts as well as perception of these conflicts as a zero-sum game. Surprisingly, perception of conflicts as a positive-sum game is also positively correlated with egalitarianism, albeit – consistent with expectations – this correlation is twice as weak. Most of the correlations discussed above tend to lose strength between 1994 and 1997.

It may be reasonably assumed that evaluations and expectations of changes in material living conditions as well as perceptions of social conflicts, especially of a zero-sum type, influence the intensity of egalitarian (or inegalitarian) attitudes. However, it is also possible that causality runs in the opposite direction, and that egalitarianism leads to a perception of society as ridden by zero-sum conflicts. Moreover, it cannot be excluded that egalitarianism, being a more general attitude, influences evaluations and expectations of living conditions rather than vice versa. The panel data from the 1994 and 1997 Polish surveys allow causality to be investigated over time. Cross-lagged panel correlation analysis will be applied to this effect (Campbell and Stanley 1966; Orpen 1978; Cramer 1995).

Cross-lagged correlation analysis is based on the assumption that if the correlation between attitude 'x' in time 't' with attitude 'y' in time 't+1' is stronger than the correlation between attitude 'x' in time 't+1' and the attitude 'y' in time 't', the causal sequence goes in time from 'x' to 'y' rather than in the opposite direction. The correlations presented in Table 9.2 suggest that positive evaluations of past improvement in material conditions of both the individuals and the society as a whole reduce egalitarian attitudes over time. No such conclusion can be reached, however, about the relation between expectations for the future and egalitarianism, since the cross-lagged correlations are very similar. The same lack of causal time sequence concerns egalitarianism and perception of the intensity of conflicts.

The correlations between opinions about material situation, social conflicts and functional inegalitarianism are statistically significant (with few exceptions) but much lower than the correlations with egalitarianism. Of course, the latter have the opposite sign to the former. However, no causality in time can be established (Table 9.3).

Unlike an egalitarian attitude and similar to functional inegalitarianism, the perception of social conflicts is very weakly, albeit significantly correlated with evaluations and expectations of changes in material living conditions. The more satisfied are people with past changes and the more optimistic they are about the future living conditions, the less conflict they see in the society. Though weak, the correlations suggest a causal time sequence from opinions about material living conditions to perceived intensity of social conflicts (Table 9.4).

One can expect that perception of the world in zero-sum terms not only influences various attitudes, but that it also increases the tendency to see much conflict. That is actually true. The correlation of the intensity of perceived conflicts with the tendency to see them as zero-sum games is twice as strong as its correlation with the tendency to see them as positive-sum games.

The majority of correlations discussed above, though statistically significant, are quite low. In such circumstances regression models should be estimated in order to determine whether the results remain valid when net impacts rather than gross correlations are examined. This has been done only for 1997.

Several Polish surveys suggested that in the time of transformation the level of education is the most important determinant of economic and political attitudes among socio-demographic characteristics. The effect exerted on attitudes by various class-related socio-occupational variables is either very weak or wiped out in multi-variat analysis, when controlled for education

Table 9.3 Correlates of functional inegalitarianism, 1994–7. (Pearson's 'r')

Correlates	Functional inegalitarianism 1994 Correlates 1994	Functional inegalitarianism 1997 – Correlates 1997	Functional inegalitarianism 1994 – Correlates 1997	Functional inegalitarianism 1997 – Correlates 1994
Subjective improvement of personal material conditions since the end of 1980s	0.18**	0.13**	0.09*	0.11**
Predicted improvement in personal material conditions in 3 years	0.17**	0.09**	0.06*	0.08*
Subjective improvement of material conditions in Poland as a whole since the end of 1980s	0.20**	0.09**	0.09**	0.06*
Predicted improvement in material conditions in Poland as a whole in 3 years' time	0.10**	0.09**	0.07**	0.05
Perceived intensity of social conflicts	0.00	0.01	−0.01	−0.02
Perception of conflicts as zero-sum games	n.a	0.05	−0.12	n.a.
Perception of conflicts as positive-sum games	n.a.	0.20**	0.05	n.a.

**, Significant at 0.01 level; *, Significant at 0.05 level; n.a. = not available.

(Zaborowski 1991; Sokolowska and Tyszka 1992; Frentzel-Zagórska and Zagórski 1993).

Education and income are the only characteristics of social position that significantly influence egalitarian attitudes (Table 9.5). Despite the significant negative correlations of all four subjective well-being variables with egalitarian attitude, only the evaluation of the material situation in Poland as a whole as compared to pre-transformation period, retains a statistically significant negative effect on egalitarianism, when other variables are controlled. Consistent with expectation, only the interaction between perceived intensity of social conflicts and the perception of these conflicts in zero-sum terms increases egalitarian attitudes.

To sum up, egalitarianism is reduced by high education and income as well as by a positive evaluation of the present material living conditions of the nation, while it is strengthened by belief in the existence of intense social conflicts seen as zero-sum rather than positive-sum games.

Functional inegalitarianism seems to be completely independent from all socio-demographic and class-related characteristics as well as from measures of subjective well-being, both concerning the individuals and the nation as a whole. When all other variables are kept controlled, only self-identification on the left–right scale increases inegalitarian feelings. Those who locate themselves

Table 9.4 Correlates of perceived intensity of social conflicts, 1994–7. (Pearson's 'r')

Correlates	Intensity of conflicts 1994 Correlates 1994	Intensity of conflicts 1997 Correlates 1997	Intensity of conflicts 1994 Correlates 1997	Intensity of conflicts 1997 Correlates 1994
Subjective improvement of personal material conditions since the end of 1980s	−0.14**	−0.06*	−0.05	−0.07*
Predicted improvement in personal material conditions in 3 years	−0.10**	−0.07*	−0.04	−0.07*
Subjective improvement of material conditions in Poland as a whole since the end of 1980s	−0.12**	−0.10**	−0.02	−0.06*
Predicted improvement in material conditions in Poland as a whole in 3 years' time	−0.09**	−0.12**	−0.07*	−0.05
Egalitarianism	0.28**	0.22**	0.12**	0.14**
Functional inegalitarianism	−0.01	0.1	−0.02	−0.01
Perception of conflicts as zero-sum games	n.a.	0.13**	0.09**	n.a.
Perception of conflicts as positive-sum games	n.a.	0.07*	0.08**	n.a.

**, Significant at 0.01 level; *, Significant at 0.05 level; n.a. = not available.

on the right tend to be more inegalitarian. Thus, functional inegalitarianism seems to constitute a relatively autonomous psychological predisposition linked to rightist political inclination.

Correlates and determinants of economic attitudes

Correlations between all the variables discussed so far and economic attitudes are consistent with theoretical expectations (Tables 9.6–9.9).

The more positive expectations and evaluations of material living conditions, the weaker public acceptance of such statist attitudes as: (i) acceptance of government ownership of institutions of education, welfare and health service; (ii) demand for government subsidies in various branches of economy; (iii) demand for the government to take an active role in fighting unemployment; and (iv) demand for price control by the government.

Contrary to what has been established a long time ago for voting and political attitudes, especially party preferences, there is no great difference between the impacts exerted on economic attitudes by individual and nation-oriented subjective well-being indicators. The influences exerted on economic attitudes by evaluations of current individual and national living conditions at present, as compared to the past, are stronger than the influences exerted by

Table 9.5 Determinants of egalitarian-inegalitarian attitudes and intensity of perceived conflicts, 1977. Regression coefficients (Standardised in parentheses).

Independent variables	Dependent variables		
	Egalitarianism	Functional inegalitarianism	Intensity of perceived conflicts
Gender (male = 1, female = 0)	−1.4	1.57	−1.63
	(−0.04)	(0.04)	(−0.04)
Age (years)	0.04	0.06	0.00
	(0.03)	(0.05)	(0.00)
Education (years)	−1.00**	0.30	0.30
	(0.15)	(0.05)	(0.05)
Business owner outside agriculture	−5.29*	1.84	5.38
	(−0.07)	(−0.03)	(0.07)
Private farmer	−3.86	0.65	3.93
	(−0.08)	(0.01)	(0.07)
Employee in private sector	0.71	−1.96	2.84
	(0.02)	(−0.05)	(0.06)
Employment status (full time = 2, part time = 1, no gainful employment = 0)	1.50	−0.62	−1.32
	(0.07)	(−0.03)	(−0.06)
Income (ln zl per month)	−5.10**	2.17	−2.14
	(−0.16)	(0.08)	(−0.07)
Wealth	−0.11	0.05	0.03
	(−0.06)	(0.03)	(0.01)
Subjective improvement of personal material conditions since the end of 1980s	−0.02	0.02	−0.01
	(−0.06)	(0.07)	(−0.04)
Prediction of improvement in personal material conditions in 3 years' time	−0.02	0.01	0.00
	(−0.04)	(0.02)	(0.00)
Subjective improvement in material conditions in Poland as a whole since the end of 1980s	−0.04*	0.01	−0.02
	(−0.11)	(0.02)	(−0.04)
Prediction of improvement in material conditions in Poland as a whole in 3 years time	−0.01	0.01	−0.05*
	(−0.02)	(0.01)	(−0.10)
Self identification on left–right scale (right)	−0.78	1.55*	−0.25
	(−0.04)	(0.08)	(−0.01)
Perceived intensity of social conflicts (0 to 100)	−0.02	−0.01	—
	(−0.02)	(−0.01)	—
Perception of conflicts as zero-sum game	—	—	0.05
	—	—	(0.04)
Perception of conflicts as positive sum game	—	—	0.06
	—	—	(0.05)
Perceived intensity of social conflicts × perception of conflicts as zero-sum game/100	0.24**	0.02	—
	(0.22)	(0.03)	—
Egalitarianism	—	—	0.17**
	—	—	(0.17)
Functional inegalitarianism	—	—	0.03
	—	—	(0.02)
'Yes syndrome' (response set, 0 to 44)	0.33**	0.32**	0.08
	(0.12)	(0.13)	(0.03)
Constant	101.51	36.09	41.51
Adjusted R^2	0.21	0.04	0.05

Table 9.6 Correlates of support for government ownership of education, health and welfare institutions, 1994–7. (Pearson's 'r')

Correlates	Acceptance of government ownership 1994 – Correlates 1994	Acceptance of government ownership 1997 – Correlates 1997	Acceptance of government ownership 1994 – Correlates 1997	Acceptance of government ownership 1997 – Correlates 1994
Subjective improvement of personal material conditions since the end of 1980s	−0.27**	−0.17**	−0.17**	−0.21**
Predicted improvement in personal material conditions in 3 years	−0.22**	−0.11**	−0.13**	−0.12**
Subjective improvement of material conditions in Poland as a whole since the end of 1980s	−0.22**	−0.16**	−0.13**	−0.15**
Predicted improvement in material conditions in Poland as a whole in 3 years' time	−0.25**	−0.09**	−0.12**	−0.13**
Egalitarianism	0.38**	0.38**	0.28**	0.26**
Functional inegalitarianism	−0.15**	−0.09**	−0.08**	−0.17**
Perceived intensity of social conflicts	0.13**	0.13**	0.09**	0.05*
Perception of conflicts as zero-sum games	n.a.	0.25**	0.09**	n.a.
Perception of conflicts as positive-sum games	n.a.	0.09**	0.02	n.a.

**, significant at 0.01 level; *, significant at 0.05 level; n.a. = not available.

expectations of changes in these conditions in the future. Egalitarian attitudes reinforce etatist attitudes, while functionalist inegalitarianism reduces them significantly. However, the impact of egalitarianism is twice as strong as the impact of inegalitarianism.

Perceived intensity of social conflict reinforces statist economic attitudes. However, a much stronger effect is exerted by the perception of conflicts in terms of a zero-sum game, while the perception of conflicts in positive-sum game is very weakly correlated with economic attitudes. These correlations may be interpreted in terms of causal influences, since cross-lagged panel analysis suggests that to be true in the majority of cases.

Two types of regression models were computed to examine further the relationships under discussion. The first one (Table 9.10) includes such independent variables as socio-demographic characteristics, subjective well-being variables, measures of egalitarianism and inegalitarianism and, finally, the opinions about the intensity and nature of social conflicts. The second (Table 9.11) (includes all the independent variables from the first models and additionally the measures of the economic attitudes which are not used as the independent variable in a given model.

Table 9.7 Correlates of support for active role of government in fighting unemployment, 1994–7. (Pearson's 'r')

Correlates	Government should fight unemployment 1994 – Correlates 1994	Government should fight unemployment 1997 – Correlates 1997	Government should fight unemployment 1994 – Correlates 1997	Government should fight unemployment 1997 – Correlates 1994
Subjective improvement of personal material conditions since the end of 1980s	–0.16**	–0.08**	–0.10**	–0.10**
Predicted improvement in personal material conditions in 3 years	–0.04	–0.04	–0.02	–0.03
Subjective improvement of material conditions in Poland as a whole since the end of 1980s	–0.10**	–0.07**	–0.06**	–0.05**
Predicted improvement in material conditions in Poland as a whole in 3 years' time	–0.04	0.02	0.02	–0.01
Egalitarianism	0.28**	0.25**	0.17**	0.17**
Functional inegalitarianism	0.08**	0.12**	–0.01	0.01
Perceived intensity of social conflicts	0.14**	0.13**	0.06*	0.08**
Perception of conflicts as zero-sum games	n.a.	0.20**	0.10**	n.a.
Perception of conflicts as positive-sum games	n.a.	0.12**	0.04	n.a.

**, significant at 0.01 level; *, significant at 0.05 level; n.a. = not available.

Gender and age have almost no effect on economic attitudes, similar to their insignificant effect on egalitarianism and perception of conflicts. The only exception is that women and older people have a weaker tendency to support government subsidies in economy. Education is the most important social position-related determinant of economic attitudes. The higher the level of education, the lower the tendency to support subsidies, government ownership of social service institutions and control of prices. The relation between education and demand for government fighting unemployment is also negative, though the regression coefficient is statistically insignificant.

Wealthy and high-earning people do not support government-owned education, health and welfare institutions. Wealth (though not income) has also a negative effect on support for subsidies, while income (though not wealth) reduces the demand for price control. Business ownership, employment status and economic sector of employment exert no net impact on economic attitudes whatsoever. Despite statistically significant negative correlations between specific economic attitudes and subjective living conditions, the latter have no net effect on the former, when all other variables are controlled. Self-identification on the left–right scale has a significant net impact on attitudes to

Table 9.8 Correlates of support for government subsidies in economy, 1994–7. (Pearson's 'r')

Correlates	Support for subsidies 1994 – Correlates 1994	Support for subsidies 1997 – Correlates 1997	Support for subsidies 1994 – Correlates 1997	Support for subsidies 1997 – Correlates 1994
Subjective improvement of personal material conditions since the end of 1980s	−0.20**	−0.14**	−0.14**	−0.17**
Predicted improvement in personal material conditions in 3 years	−0.10**	−0.06*	−0.11**	−0.11**
Subjective improvement of material conditions in Poland as a whole since the end of 1980s	−0.14**	−0.14**	−0.11**	−0.12**
Predicted improvement in material conditions in Poland as a whole in 3 years' time	−0.12**	−0.06*	−0.08**	−0.08**
Egalitarianism	0.36**	0.36**	0.26**	0.30**
Functional inegalitarianism	−0.12**	−0.03	−0.06*	−0.07**
Perceived intensity of social conflicts	0.20**	0.15**	0.10**	0.14**
Perception of conflicts as zero-sum games	n.a.	0.22**	0.14**	n.a.
Perception of conflicts as positive-sum games	n.a.	0.09**	0.05	n.a.

**, significant at 0.01 level; *, significant at 0.05 level; n.a. = not available.

government provision of social and welfare services and to price control. The 'rightists' are against such functions of the state. Egalitarianism substantially increases all four etatist attitudes, while the functionalist inegalitarianism, measured as a separate predisposition, exerts less clear effect.

The perceived intensity of social conflicts, when the conflicts are seen as zero-sum games, strengthens three out of four etatist attitudes, namely support for involvement of the government in health, education and welfare, price control and the fight against unemployment. The perceived intensity of social conflicts net of a zero-sum perception of the world has no significant net effect on economic attitudes. It may be even said that it insignificantly reduces etatist attitudes.

The idea behind the inclusion of economic attitudes among independent variables in the second type of regression model was to check whether all four attitudes reinforce each other and can be treated as belonging to a more general attitudinal etatist syndrome. The analysis proves that to be true, since most of the influences are statistically significant and some of them are quite strong. Moreover, the inclusion of other specific economic attitudes as independent variables wipes out all effects of socio-demographic (income and wealth included) variables but does not wipe out the effect of egalitarianism. It suggests that

Table 9.9 Correlates of support for price control by government, 1994–7. (Pearson's 'r')

Correlates	Support for price control 1994 – Correlates 1994	Support for price control 1997 – Correlates 1997	Support for price control 1994 – Correlates 1997	Support for price control 1997 – Correlates 1994
Subjective improvement of personal material conditions since the end of 1980s	−0.24**	−0.16**	−0.15**	−0.24**
Predicted improvement in personal material conditions in 3 years	−0.19**	−0.13*	−0.13**	−0.18**
Subjective improvement of material conditions in Poland as a whole since the end of 1980s	−0.15**	−0.17**	−0.14**	−0.18**
Predicted improvement in material conditions in Poland as a whole in 3 years' time	−0.19**	−0.13**	−0.19**	−0.18**
Egalitarianism	0.37**	0.40**	0.30**	0.30**
Functional inegalitarianism	−0.14**	−0.11**	−0.11**	−0.18**
Perceived intensity of social conflicts	0.15**	0.13**	0.11**	0.10**
Perception of conflicts as zero-sum games	n.a.	0.24**	0.16**	n.a.
Perception of conflicts as positive-sum games	n.a.	0.05*	0.01	n.a.

**, significant at 0.01 level; *, significant at 0.05 level; n.a. = not available.

economic attitudes are mostly reinforced by each other and constitute an ideological syndrome, quite loosely related to the people's characteristics. It may be assumed that education and material situation, both objective and subjective, influence opinions about the desired economic system indirectly, through egalitarian attitudes.

Correlates and determinants of support for transformation

Correlation coefficients show that the positive evaluation of transformation depends very much on subjective well-being (Table 9.12). Evaluation of present material living conditions as compared to the past seem to be more important in this respect than expectations for future changes, while there are no substantial differences between concern for individual interests and for the nation as a whole.

Evaluation of the transformation is also negatively influenced by egalitarian attitudes and by perceptions of intensive social conflicts, especially of a zero-sum nature. At the same time, it is positively influenced by functional inegalitarianism and by perception of social conflicts in positive-sum terms. Negative influences are stronger than positive ones. It is also possible to interpret the correlation in causal terms, since cross-lagged panel analysis

Table 9.10 Determinants of attitudes to government ownership of social service institutions and fighting unemployment, 1997. Regression coefficients (standardised in parentheses)

Independent variables	Government's social and welfare institutions		Government to fight unemployment	
	Model 1	Model 2	Model 1	Model 2
Gender (male = 1, female = 0)	−0.41	0.64	−0.21	0.83
	(−0.01)	(0.02)	(−0.01)	(0.03)
Age (years)	0.03	0.01	−0.01	0.01
	(0.02)	(0.01)	(−0.01)	(−0.01)
Education (years)	−1.15**	−0.60	−0.47	0.10
	(−0.18)	(−0.09)	(−0.10)	(−0.02)
Business owner outside agriculture	0.84	1.89	1.28	1.82
	(0.01)	(0.03)	(0.02)	(0.03)
Private farmer	0.88	0.51	2.13	2.28
	(0.02)	(0.01)	(0.06)	(0.06)
Employee in private sector	0.33	0.36	−0.63	−0.71
	(0.01)	(0.01)	(−0.02)	(−0.02)
Employment status (full time = 2, part time = 1, no gainful employment = 0)	−0.31	−0.03	−0.77	−0.53
	(−0.01)	(0.00)	(−0.05)	(−0.03)
Income (ln zl per month)	−2.93*	−1.55	−1.04	−0.32
	(−0.09)	(−0.05)	(−0.05)	(−0.01)
Wealth (accumulated possession of goods)	−0.19*	−0.13	−0.06	0.00
	(−0.10)	(−0.07)	(−0.04)	(0.00)
Subjective improvement of personal material conditions since the end of 1980s	0.00	0.00	0.00	0.00
	(0.00)	(0.00)	(0.01)	(0.00)
Prediction of improvement in personal material conditions in 3 years' time	0.00	0.00	−0.07	−0.01
	(0.00)	(0.00)	(−0.03)	(−0.03)
Subjective improvement in material conditions in Poland as a whole since the end of 1980s	−0.02	−0.01	0.01	0.00
	(−0.06)	(−0.03)	(0.02)	(0.00)
Prediction of improvement in material conditions in Poland as a whole in 3 years' time	−0.01	0.00	0.03	0.03
	(−0.01)	(0.01)	(0.07)	(0.08)
Self identification on left–right scale (far left = 1, to far right = 5)	−1.94**	−1.39*	0.94	1.06
	(−0.09)	(−0.07)	(0.06)	(0.07)
Egalitarianism	0.20**	0.08*	0.13**	0.06
	(0.21)	(0.09)	(0.18)	(0.08)
Functional inegalitarianism	−0.05	−0.04	0.10**	0.10**
	(−0.05)	(−0.03)	(0.13)	(0.13)
Perceived intensity of social conflicts (0 to 100)	−0.12*	−0.09	−0.03	−0.01
	(−0.12)	(−0.09)	(−0.04)	(−0.01)
Perceived intensity of social conflicts × perception of conflicts as zero-sum game/100	0.21**	0.14*	0.10*	0.05
	(0.20)	(0.14)	(0.13)	(0.06)
Support for government ownership of social and welfare institutions	—	—	—	0.05
	—	—	—	(0.06)
Support for active role of government in fighting unemployment	—	0.13**	—	—
	—	(0.13)	—	—
Support for government subsidising the economy	—	0.07	—	0.24**
	—	(0.05)	—	(0.33)
Support for price control	—	0.28**	—	0.04
	—	(0.34)	—	(0.06)
'Yes syndrome'	0.18	0.10	0.17*	0.12
	(0.07)	(0.04)	(0.09)	(0.06)
Constant	96.11	58.38	56.60	30.49
Adjusted R²	0.25	0.38	0.13	0.24

**, significant at 0.01 level; *, significant at 0.05 level.

Table 9.11 Determinants of attitudes to subsidies and price control, 1997. Regression coefficients (standardised in parentheses)

Independent variables	Subsidise economy		Control prices	
	Model 1	Model 2	Model 1	Model 2
Gender (male = 1, female = 0)	−3.96*	−3.51*	−1.84	−0.74
	(−0.10)	(−0.09)	(−0.04)	(−0.01)
Age (years)	−0.10	−0.12*	0.11	0.12
	(−0.08)	(−0.10)	(0.07)	(0.08)
Education (years)	−1.12**	−0.55*	−1.33**	−0.56
	(−0.18)	(−0.09)	(−0.17)	(−0.07)
Business owner outside agriculture	−1.91	−2.00	−3.18	−3.19
	(−0.03)	(−0.03)	(−0.04)	(−0.04)
Private farmer	−1.10	−2.17	1.25	0.94
	(−0.02)	(−0.04)	(0.02)	(0.01)
Employee in private sector	0.27	0.49	−0.09	−0.23
	(0.01)	(0.01)	(−0.00)	(−0.01)
Employment status (full time = 2, part time = 1, no gainful employment = 0)	−0.85	−0.45	−0.40	−0.01
	(−0.04)	(−0.02)	(−0.02)	(0.00)
Income (ln zl per month)	−1.88	−0.44	−3.74*	−2.02
	(−0.06)	(−0.01)	(−0.10)	(−0.05)
Wealth (accumulated possession of goods)	−0.17*	−0.10	−0.10	0.02
	(−0.09)	(−0.05)	(−0.05)	(0.01)
Subjective improvement of personal material conditions since the end of 1980s	−0.01	0.00	0.01	0.01
	(−0.02)	(−0.01)	(0.01)	(0.01)
Prediction of improvement in personal material conditions in 3 years' time	0.01	0.01	0.01	0.01
	(0.02)	(0.02)	(0.02)	(0.02)
Subjective improvement in material conditions in Poland as a whole since the end of 1980s	−0.01	0.00	−0.02	−0.01
	(−0.04)	(−0.01)	(−0.05)	(−0.02)
Prediction of improvement in material conditions in Poland as a whole in 3 years' time	0.00	0.00	−0.03	−0.03
	(0.00)	(0.00)	(−0.05)	(−0.06)
Self identification on left–right scale (far left = 1, to far right = 5)	0.22	0.50	−2.27*	−1.61
	(0.01)	(0.02)	(−0.09)	(−0.06)
Egalitarianism	0.22**	0.10*	0.28**	0.14**
	(0.23)	(0.10)	(0.23)	(0.12)
Functional inegalitarianism	0.02	0.00	0.08	−0.07
	(0.02)	(0.00)	(−0.06)	(−0.06)
Perceived intensity of social conflicts (0 to 100)	0.03	0.00	−0.09	−0.03
	(0.04)	(0.00)	(−0.07)	(−0.02)
Perceived intensity of social conflicts × perception of conflicts as zero-sum game/100	−0.01	0.04	0.16*	0.03
	(−0.04)	(0.04)	(0.12)	(0.02)
Support for government ownership of social and welfare institutions	—	0.14**	—	0.41**
		(0.14)		(0.33)
Support for active role of government in fighting unemployment	—	0.39**	—	0.23**
		(0.28)		(0.18)
Support for government subsidising the economy	—	—	—	0.08
				(0.05)
Support for price control	—	0.17**	—	—
	—	(0.20)	—	—
'Yes syndrome'	0.13	0.00	0.20	0.08
	(0.05)	(0.00)	(0.06)	(0.03)
Constant	76.53	27.36	83.95	22.24
Adjusted R²	0.19	0.35	0.25	0.40

**, significant at 0.01 level; *, significant at 0.05 level.

Table 9.12 Correlates of positive evaluation of transformation, 1994–7. (Pearson's 'r')

Correlates	Evaluation of trans- formation 1994 – Correlates 1994	Evaluation of trans- formation 1997 – Correlates 1997	Evaluation of trans- formation 1994 – Correlates 1997	Evaluation of trans- formation 1997 – Correlates 1994
Subjective improvement of personal material conditions since the end of 1980s	0.47**	0.32**	0.17**	0.30**
Predicted improvement in personal material conditions in 3 years	0.33**	0.21*	0.13**	0.20**
Subjective improvement of material conditions in Poland as a whole since the end of 1980s	0.48**	0.38**	0.19**	0.29**
Predicted improvement in material conditions in Poland as a whole in 3 years' time	0.40**	0.26**	0.16**	0.24**
Egalitarianism	–0.30**	–0.24**	–0.17**	–0.15**
Functional inegalitarianism	0.19**	0.17**	0.03	0.14**
Perceived intensity of social conflicts	–0.18**	–0.10**	–0.09**	–0.06**
Perception of conflicts as zero-sum games	n.a.	–0.12**	–0.14**	n.a.
Perception of conflicts as positive-sum games	n.a.	0.06*	0.01	n.a.

**, significant at 0.01 level; *, significant at 0.05 level; n.a. = not available.

suggests a casual sequence in time. Regression models show that socio-demographic and class-related characteristics of the individuals, income and wealth included, have no effect on evaluation of transformation whatsoever. This evaluation depends only on other subjective variables.

Out of four subjective well-being variables, three have substantial positive net effect on the evaluation of transformation (Table 9.13). Prediction of future improvement in one's own material living condition is the only subjective well-being indicator whose influence is statistically insignificant. The influences exerted by both indicators of nationally oriented subjective well-being are stronger than the influence of evaluation of personal living conditions. Evaluation of transformation is positively influenced by left–right self-identification and by egalitarian versus functional inegalitarian attitudes. However, the effects of perceptions of social conflict, apparent in correlational analysis, is wiped out in multi-variate regression models.

The second model shows that the evaluation of transformation does not depend on the intensity of etatist economic attitudes. One could expect that such characteristics as education and income would exert at least an indirect effect on general support for transformation, if the direct effect is wiped out by subjective variables. The obvious 'suspect' for being a vessel of such an indirect

Table 9.13 Determinants of positive evaluation of transformation, 1997. Regression coefficients (standardised in parentheses)

Independent variables	Model 1	Model 2
Gender (male = 1, female = 0)	0.61	0.31
	(0.01)	(0.01)
Age (years)	−0.06	−0.06
	(−0.05)	(−0.05)
Education (years)	0.19	−0.01
	(0.03)	(0.00)
Business owner outside agriculture (0–1)	0.65	0.52
	(0.01)	(0.01)
Private farmer (0–1)	−3.15	−3.00
	(−0.06)	(−0.06)
Employee in private sector (0–1)	−1.65	−1.64
	(−0.04)	(−0.04)
Employment status (full time = 2, part time = 1,	−0.85	−0.96
no gainful employment = 0)	(−0.04)	(−0.05)
Income (ln zl per month)	−0.07	−0.55
	(−0.00)	(−0.02)
Wealth (accumulated possession of goods)	0.12	0.10
	(0.07)	(0.05)
Subjective improvement of personal material conditions	0.03*	0.03*
since the end of 1980s (−100 to +100)	(0.10)	(0.10)
Prediction of improvement in personal material conditions	0.01	0.01
in 3 years' time (−100 to +100)	(0.01)	(0.01)
Subjective improvement in material conditions in Poland	0.07**	0.07**
as a whole since the end of 1980s (−100 to +100)	(0.22)	(0.22)
Prediction of improvement in material conditions in Poland	0.06**	0.06**
as a whole in 3 years' time (−100 to +100)	(0.12)	(0.12)
Self identification on left–right scale	3.24**	3.07**
(far left = 1, to far right = 5)	(0.16)	(0.15)
Egalitarian attitude (0 to 100)	−0.08*	−0.04
	(−0.08)	(−0.04)
Functional inegalitarianism (0 to 100)	0.11*	0.11*
	(0.10)	(0.10)
Perceived intensity of social conflicts (0 to 100)	0.02	0.00
	(0.02)	(0.00)
Perceived intensity of social conflicts × perception of	−0.06	−0.03
conflicts as zero-sum game (interactive, 0 to 100)	(−0.06)	(0.03)
Support for government ownership of social and	—	−0.06
welfare institutions (0 to 100)	—	(−0.06)
Support for government subsidising the	—	−0.05
economy (0 to 100)	—	(−0.05)
Support for active role of government in fighting	—	−0.04
unemployment (0 to 100)	—	(−0.03)
Support for price control (0 to 100)	—	−0.04
	—	(−0.05)
'Yes syndrome' (response set, 0 to 44)	−0.05	−0.02
	(−0.02)	(−0.01)
Constant	40.18	55.82
Adjusted R^2	0.24	0.24

Note: Pairwise deletion of missing cases.

effect is egalitarianism, which actually performs this role in reinforcing specific economic attitudes. However, the support for transformation is significantly reinforced by functional inegalitarianism but not weakened by egalitarianism. Since inegalitarianism does not depend on any socio-demographic characteristics (Table 9.5), no expected indirect effect is found.

Conclusions

General support for transformation does not depend on opinions about particular aspects of economic system, even if described in liberal versus etatist terms. It also does not depend on the socio-demographic characteristics of the individuals. However, it depends very much on such general socio-political attitudes as inegalitarianism and rightist political self-identification.

The perception of social conflicts has no direct effect on the attitude to transformation, though it exerts a significant indirect effect. It increases egalitarian tendencies which, in turn, reduce the support for transformation, at least when specific economic attitudes are not controlled. That concerns first of all a combination of perception of strong conflicts with the assertion that the conflicts must result in the creation of losers and winners, in other words with seeing conflicts as zero-sum games. The acceptance of the fact that conflicts may be resolved in a way beneficial to both parties grossly, if not completely, reduces the negative effect of the perceived intensity of conflict.

Support for transformation depends very much on the evaluation of present material living conditions and expectations of changes in this respect. As in the case of egalitarian attitudes and perception of social conflicts, it depends more on subjective material conditions of the nation as a whole than opinions about the individual's own conditions. Our analysis has not concerned the process of shaping subjective evaluations and expectations of material living conditions, i.e. subjective well-being. Other analyses from Poland and other countries (Headey 1993; Zagórski 1997) confirm the obvious assumption that subjective well-being is greatly, although not completely, determined by objectively measured material conditions. Thus, our conclusion about the lack of a significant effect of material conditions on support for transformation should be qualified. Such an effect is exerted indirectly, through subjective well-being which actually exerts a very strong impact on pro-transformation attitude.

The 'extraordinary' initial period of transformation was characterised by greater impacts of economic hopes and expectations than evaluations of present material living conditions exerted on various attitudes, especially on support for political and economic changes in general. Nowadays, either the perceptions of both present and future conditions are equally important or the present time is more important than the future as determinant of general socio-political attitudes, such as egalitarianism, tendency to see the world as conflict ridden and evaluation of transformation.

As it has already been stressed, perception of society as ridden by strong social conflicts which create winners and losers has a strong effect on egalitarian attitude and, thus, indirectly affects support for transformation. Though it has no direct effect on this support, it significantly reinforces etatist attitudes to different, specific aspects of economy.

Opinions about various forms of state interventionism are very stable. They do not change as quickly as the level of general support for transformation or perceptions of well-being of both individual families and the nation as a whole. Contrary to more general inclinations, they also do not depend on subjective well-being. To be more precise, subjective well-being influences the attitudes to specific aspects of state interventionism only indirectly, through egalitarian attitudes and through perception of strong social conflicts, especially of a zero-sum nature. Thus, significant correlations are wiped out in regression models, when egalitarianism and perception of conflicts are kept controlled. Specific pro-etatist or anti-etatist policies may have little impact on generalised pro-transformation public attitudes, though they may have more direct influence on voting behaviour and support for particular parties, provided that the policies are explicitly formulated in political programmes. So far, this does not take place in Poland.

To sum-up, support for transformation depends very much on changing subjective well-being and on general political–ideological stances, such as attitudes to inequality and self-identification on a left–right continuum, though not on opinions about specific aspects of economic life, particularly about various forms of state-interventionism. The political if not ideological character of the evaluation of transformation in general is further manifested by the fact that concern with public subjective well-being (expectations and evaluations of material conditions of the nation as a whole), is a more important determinant than private concern with family's well-being. However, political and economic programmes and promises may have a diminishing effect on pro-transformation attitudes, while the ability to 'deliver the goods' may be more important now than in the recent past, since the evaluation of actual material conditions seems nowadays to influence attitudes more strongly than hopes for the future. That perhaps marks the end of the initial period of transformation, at least as defined by people's subjective reactions.

Appendix 9.1 Variables

Demographic and socio-economic characteristics

Gender is coded as a dummy variable: $1 =$ male, $0 =$ female.

Age is specified in years.

Education is originally characterised by five levels, complete and incomplete each. That makes 10 categories which are recoded into numbers of years typically needed for reaching a given level.

Socio-occupational groups (business owner outside agriculture, private farmer and employee in private sector) are dummy variables. The group of employees in public sector is left as a reference category. Socio-occupational groups concern current occupations of those who work and the last occupations of those outside the active workforce.

Employment status: 2 = full-time employed, 1 = part-time employed, 0 = not working.

Income: sum of earnings (wages, salaries and own business or profits), pensions, stipends and other welfare benefits, interest on savings and earnings from the stock exchange, if appropriate.

Wealth: measured as the arithmetic mean of 'relative values' of 10 household goods in respondent family's possession: washing machine, refrigerator, microwave oven, dishwasher, colour TV, CD player, video, telephone, car and summer-house. The value of zero is assigned to a given object if it is not possessed by the respondent's household. All possessed goods (objects) are given the values reversely proportionate to the percentages of respondents possessing them in the whole population. Thus, if 85 per cent of respondents declare that they possess a given object, this object's value is set as 15. If only 10 per cent of respondents possess a given object, its value is set as 90, etc. The scale theoretically can range from 0 to 100, though practically its maximum depends on the possession of respective goods in the population as a whole. The assumption behind such a measure is that the fewer respondents possess a given kind of object, the more discretionary possession of such objects is and/or the objects are less affordable. In both cases, rich families are supposed to have more such objects than poor families, so the object is a better indicator of family's wealth. The earlier study, not presented here for the lack of space, indicated that this measure of wealth correlates much better with income, subjective evaluations of living conditions and with some attitudinal variables than the estimated monetary value of accumulated household's possessions (Zagórski, forthcoming).

Positive evaluation of transformation

The questions differ between 1994 and 1997, though their meaning remains the same. The 1994 question reads: 'Do changes that took place in Poland during last 5 years bring people more benefit or more harm?'. The 1997 question reads: 'Has a new social order of democracy and capitalism brought people more benefit or harm?'. The wording differs because a new question was added in 1997 about evaluation of 'post-communist' coalition government, which held the power in the 1993–7 period. In both surveys, the answers were recoded into five-level scale: 100 = only benefit; 75 = more benefit than harm; 50 = as much benefit as harm; 25 = more harm than benefit; 0 = only harm.

Egalitarianism–inegalitarianism

As in many other surveys (e.g. Mueller 1993; Svallfors 1993; Kluegel *et al.* 1995), factor analysis has resulted in two separate scales of egalitarian and inegalitarian attitudes. The egalitarian attitude scale consists of four items: 'Generally speaking, do you agree that: (1) Earning differences are too big in Poland. (2) The government should reduce the differences between people with high incomes and those with low incomes. (3) There is too much inequality between rich and poor. (4) The reduction of inequality between rich and poor should be one of the most important goals during the forthcoming 10 years in Poland'. The functional inegalitarianism scale consists also of four items: '(1) Large differences in income are necessary for Poland's prosperity. (2) For Polish economy to grow, it is necessary to let energetic entrepreneurs to earn a lot. (3) For future prosperity, it is necessary to pay high salaries to those who do the best work. (4) Income inequality is necessary for economic progress'. Original answers are recoded as: 100 = Definitely yes; 75 = Rather yes; 50 = Yes and no; 25 = Rather no; 0 = Definitely no. Each scale is an arithmetic mean of the four constituting items.

Perception of social conflicts

The composite scale of the *intensity of perceived social conflicts* is constructed as a mean of the following items: 'In all countries, there are differences or even conflicts between different social groups. In your opinion, how much conflict is now in Poland between . . . (1) Rich and poor. (2) The working class and the middle class. (3) People at the top of the society and those at the bottom. (4) Managers and workers. (5) Those who govern and those who are governed'. The answers are recoded as: 100 = Very strong conflict; 66.6 = Strong conflict; 33.3 = Not strong conflict; 0 = No conflict.

The questions about *perception of social conflicts as 'zero-sum' or 'positive sum games'* were asked in the 1997 survey only. Factor analysis resulted in two separate scales rather than in one bi-polar scale. *The 'zero-sum game' scale* consists of the items: 'Do you agree with the following opinions about social life? (1) In economy, somebody's gain always means somebody else's loss. (2) Victory in politics is always somebody's defeat. (3) When one gets rich the others get poorer'. *The 'positive-sum game' scale* consists of the items: '(1) It is possible to end political conflicts in such a way that the both opposite parties win. (2) In business, there are not necessarily winners and losers. (3) Arguments and quarrels often end badly for all participants but their skilful resolution may also be beneficial to all'. The answers are recoded and the mean values are computed the same way as in the scales of egalitarianism and inegalitarianism.

The scales of economic attitudes

Each scale, previously defined by factor analysis, is computed as the arithmetic mean of a small number of items recoded as: 100 = definitely yes; 75 = rather yes; 50 = yes and no; 25 = rather no; 0 = definitely no.

The items for *the scale of support for government subsidies* are: 'In order to keep prices low, should the government subsidise: (1) Production of electricity. (2) Basic food products. (3) Housing construction. (4) Health service. (5) Banks and insurance companies?'.

The scale of support for price control consists of five items: 'Should the prices for . . . be regulated by the government or set by the free market? (1) Electricity. (2) Basic food products. (3) Housing. (4) Banking and insurance services'. The scale is computed as above.

The scale of supporting the government's active role in fighting unemployment consists of the items: 'The government can influence the economy in different ways. In your opinion, should it: (1) Support declining industries to save the jobs. (2) Invest to create new jobs. (3) Subsidise unprofitable state enterprises to keep the employment high. (4) Give unemployed people loans to open their own businesses. (5) Organise training for unemployed. (10) Repay private companies part of the cost of creating new jobs, e.g. by tax reduction'.

The scale of support for control of prices by the government consists of four items: 'Should there be high custom tariffs and other limits on imports of cheap goods from abroad in order to protect Polish jobs and industry, even though it means lack of competition and may result in higher prices? (1) On food to protect Polish farmers. (2) Clothing and shoes to protect Polish industry. (3) Cars to protect automobile manufacturers. (4) 'Heavy industry' products, such as steel, machinery etc.?' The original answers are recoded as: 100 = High tariffs and other restrictions; 66.6 = Moderate tariffs and restrictions; 33.3 = Low tariffs and restrictions; 0 = No tariffs and restrictions. The scale is computed as a mean.

Support for public ownership of social and welfare service institutions

This is a scale computed as an arithmetic mean of six items: 'Which of the following institutions should be government-owned and which should be private? (1) Hospitals; (2) Doctor and dentist surgeries; (3) Schools; (4) Universities; (5) Child day care; (6) Old-age care'. The scores for each item are: 100 – All government-owned, 75 = Majority government-owned, 50 = Half–half, 25 = Majority private, 0 = All private. The scale is computed as a mean.

Left–right political self-identification

Single item scale ranging from 1 to 5: 'Would you define your political opinions as leftist or rightist? Where would you place yourself on a following continuum from the left to the right? 1 = Far left; 2 = Left; 3 = Centre; 4 = Right; 5 = Far right'.

Yes syndrome (response set)

The fact that people often express egalitarian and inegalitarian attitudes and perceive the conflicts as 'zero-sum' and 'positive-sum games' at the same time leads to the suspicion that this may partly result from a general tendency to give positive rather than negative answers, when it is difficult to decide which answer is right. If true, that would increase correlation and regression co-efficients. In order to eliminate the tendency to give positive answers and to obtain regression coefficients net of such a tendency, the measure of the 'yes syndrome' is included in regression models. The measure is the number of positive answers for 44 very different questions in the survey, excluding the questions used to construct the variables in the model.

If regression coefficients of one attitudinal scale on the other remains statistically significant after inclusion of 'yes syndrome' variable in the model, the positive relation between the respective attitudinal scales is not caused by a general tendency to give positive answers for all questions. In other words, the strength of this relation is measured net of such a tendency.

Notes

1 The Polish data analysed in this paper are from the 1994 and 1997 International Surveys of Economic Attitudes. The principal researchers (in alphabetical order) are: M. D. R. Evans, J. Frentzel-Zagórska, J. Kelley and K. Zagórski. They represent the Research School of Social Sciences at the Australian National University and the Institute of Political Sciences, Polish Academy of Sciences. The questionnaire and the analyses were partly designed during K. Zagórski's work in the Institute of Applied Economic and Social Research, the University of Melbourne, in collaboration with D. Harding. The 1994 Polish survey was co-sponsored by the International Survey of Economic Attitudes, the Australian National University and the Department of Social Policy, the University of Turku, Finland. The 1997 Polish survey was co-sponsored by the Foundation of Social Security, Warsaw; the Research Support Scheme, Prague and the Institute of Political Studies, Polish Academy of Sciences, Warsaw. Both Polish surveys were conducted by the Public Opinion Research Centre, Warsaw. The 1997 survey was conducted as a panel to the 1994 survey.
2 The author is grateful to D. Harding from the University of Melbourne for his very fruitful suggestion that the distinction between zero-sum and positive-sum conflicts may be important for attitude formation.

References

Balcerowicz, L. (1995) 'Understanding Postcommunist Transitions', *Journal of Democracy* 5(4). Published also in Polish as Chapter 8 in L. Balcerowicz (1997) *Socjalizm – Kapitalizm – Transformacja*, Warsaw: PWN.

Campbell, D. T. and Stanley, J. C. (1966) *Experimental and Quasi-experimental Designs for Research*, Chicago: Rand McNally.

Cramer, D. (1995) 'Life and Job Satisfaction: A Two-Wave Panel Study', *The Journal of Psychology*, 129(3): 261–7.

Dahrendorf, R. (1988) *The Modern Social Conflict*, London: Weidenfeld and Nicholson.

Frentzel-Zagórska, J. (1993) 'The Road to a Democratic Political System in Post-communist Eastern Europe', pp. 165–94 in J. Frentzel-Zagórska (ed.) *From a One-party State to Democracy: Transition in Eastern Europe*, Amsterdam: Atlanta: Rodopi.

Frentzel-Zagórska, J. and Zagórski, K. (1991) 'Polish Public Opinion on Privatisation and State Interventionism', *Europe-Asia Studies*, 45(4): 705–28.

Headey, B. (1993) 'An Economic Model of Subjective Well-Being: Integrating Economic and Psychological Theories', *Social Indicators Research*, 28: 97–116.

Hirschman, A. O. (1981) *Essays in Tresspassing: Economics in Politics and Beyond*, Cambridge: Cambridge University Press.

Kluegel, J. R., Mason, D. S. and Wegener, B. (eds) (1995) *Social Justice and Political Change*, New York: Aldine de Gruyter.

Kluegel, J. R. and Smith, E. R. (1986) *Beliefs About Inequality: Americans' Views of What Is and What Ought to Be*, New York: Aldine de Gruyter.

Lewis-Beck, M. S., 1991, *Economics and Elections: The Major Western Democracies,* Ann Arbor: The University of Michigan Press.

Lipset, S. M. (1985) *Consensus and Conflict*, New Brunswick, Oxford: Transaction Books.

Mishler, W. and Rose, R. (1996) 'Trajectories of Fear and Hope: Support for Demo-cracy in Post-Communist Europe', *Comparative Political Studies*, 28(4): 553–81.

Mueller, W. (1993) 'Social Structure Perception and Evaluation of Social Inequality and Party Preference', in D. Krebs and P. Schmidt (eds) *New Directions in Attitude Measurement*, Berlin: Walter de Gruyter.

Offe, C. (1991) 'Capitalism by Democratic Design? Democratic Theory Facing the Triple Transition in East Central Europe', *Social Research*, 58(4): 865–92.

Orpen, C. (1978) 'Work and Nonwork Satisfaction: A Causal Correlational Analysis', *The Journal of Applied Psychology*, 63: 530–2.

Przeworski, A. (1992) *The Democracy and the Market*, Cambridge: Cambridge University Press.

Przeworski, A. (1996) 'Public Support for Economic Reform in Poland', *Comparative Political Studies*, 29(5): 520–43.

Schelling, T. C. (1980) *The Strategy of Conflict*, Cambridge, MA: Harvard University Press.

Sokolowska, J. and Tyszka, T. (1992) 'Zmiany preferencji spoleczno-ekonomicznych spoleczeństwa polskiego w latach 1990–1991', *Studia Socjologiczne*, 3-4:126–7 (171–89).

Svallfors, S. (1993) 'Dimensions of Inequality: A Comparison of Attitudes in Sweden and Britain', *European Sociological Review*, 9(3).

Zaborowski, W. (1991) 'Aprobata reform politycznych a sympatie proegalitarne', in A. Marszalek (ed.), *Przelom i wyzwanie: Pamietniki VIII Ogólnopolskiego Zjazdu Socjologicznego*, Warszawa-Toruń: PTS.

Zaborowski, W. (1994) 'Beliefs About Inequality: Changing Income Hierarchy in Poland', in M. Alestalo, E. Allardt, A. Rychard and W. Wesolowski (eds) *The Transformation of Europe: Social Conditions and Consequences*, Warsaw: IFiS Publishers.

Zagórski, K. (1994) 'Hope Factor, Inequality and Legitimacy of Systemic Transformation: the Case of Poland', *Communist and Post-communist Studies*, 27(4): 357–76.

Zagórski, K. (1997) 'Education, Economic Status and Life Cycle of Subjective Well-Being. Paper presented at semi-annual meeting of the Research Committee Social Stratification and Mobility of the International Sociological Association, Tel-Aviv, 18–28 May, 1997.

Zagórski, K. (1998) 'Transformation, Reforms and Attitudes to Neo-corporatism in Poland, Finland and Australia', pp 111-140 in E. Wnuk-Lipinski (ed) *Values and Radical Social Change: Comparing Polish and South-African Experience*, Warsaw: ISP PAN.

10

AND WHAT IF THE STATE
FADES AWAY?

The civilising process and the state[1]

Zsuzsa Ferge

> By . . . declaring government intervention the ultimate evil,
> laissez-faire ideology has effectively banished income and wealth
> redistribution. . . . Wealth does accumulate in the hands of its
> owners, and if there is no mechanism for redistribution, the
> inequities can become intolerable.
>
> George Soros

> The armour of civilised conduct would crumble very rapidly if,
> through a change in society, the degree of insecurity that existed
> earlier were to break in upon us again, and if danger became as
> incalculable as it once was. Corresponding fears would burst the
> limits set to them today.
>
> Norbert Elias

A distinguishing characteristic of the European variant of capitalism lies in the
role played by the state. Governments are expected to intervene in the free play
of market forces, not only to provide a safe environment for capital but also
to protect the interests of citizens and particularly of minorities who are
unsuccessful in a free market. The latter is achieved through employment
regulation, social security, health care and equal opportunities – in fact
the whole panoply of measures and policies which make up the modern
welfare state.

State welfare has achieved its most developed form in Western Europe. Now
– after the collapse of 'state socialism' and the strengthening of globalisation –
democratic welfare capitalism is increasingly under threat from the more liberal
variant of capitalism as it has developed in the Unites States. The 'minimal
state' is high on the agenda of the globalists, but this objective is highly
questionable.

This chapter takes a step back from the analysis of contemporary attitude
data to consider the development of modern society. It relies on Elias' analysis

of *The Civilizing Process* (1982). The object is to identify what the core values of European civilisation are and what role the state plays in sustaining them. This provides the basis for an understanding of what Europe – East and West – will lose, if it is the liberal market variant of capitalism that becomes dominant in this sub-region of the world system. This is what is at stake in the debate about state retrenchment.

What is meant by civilisation?

Civilisation has many different meanings, and may be interpreted in a relatively neutral, or a strongly value-loaded way. So let me start by summarising – without giving any definition – what I mean and what I do not mean by the concept.[2]

The sense in which I use the concept originates in the work of Norbert Elias and of those who have followed up his work (de Swaan in the first place). In their sense, civilisation applies essentially to the processes having taken place in Western Europe from about the fifteenth or sixteenth century on, accompanying the development of capitalism, technical modernisation, urbanisation and basic socio-political changes in the fabric of society. The civilising process described by Elias encompasses changes from the most common-place behaviours to elaborate standards, norms, forms of communication. It affects mental functions, morals and sensibilities, the whole affective household. The second half at least of the above period coincides with the well-known process of individualisation. It has been hence accompanied by the changing role of the family and by the increasing need of the individual for privacy (Ariès and Duby 1987). The altering economic and political circumstances have been accompanied also by changes in interpersonal relationships such as the decrease of social distances between groups of different rank, then between genders, generations, 'superiors' and 'inferiors' within organisations, and between governments and their subjects (de Swaan 1990: 150–1). The core element of the whole process is probably *the pacification of everyday life* which has become possible when the state had monopolised violence. This step has freed man from the constant fear of being attacked by others, and the constant necessity of being alert for a counterattack.

It is suggested by the theory that attitudes transmitted through generations end up by being built into the personality, leading to 'the formation of a more complex and secure "super-ego" agency' (Elias 1982: 248)[3] replacing outside by inside constraints. The most frequently mentioned 'civilised' personality traits are, in Elias' work, increasing 'self-restraint in some or in all respects; a more firmly regulated behaviour . . . which is bound up with greater foresight, . . . a greater refinement of manners and which is studded with more elaborate taboos' (Elias and Scotson 1994: 152), and the submission of sudden impulses to the requirements of a more long-term view.

I would like to add to this inventory a few considerations. Some of them just underscore elements included in the above approach. Some may complete it in ways which may or may not coincide with the line of thought of Elias. My intention is not to criticise or to appraise the oeuvre of Elias. I just build upon it and use it as a means to get closer to the problem I grapple with, the impact of the withdrawal of the state from some of its former functions upon human coexistence in complex, modern societies.

First, what is most essential for me is that civilisation is about social coexistence: how to live together in a society. In that sense, all relatively durable societies[4] have 'worked out' a civilisation,[5] consisting of many elements from codes of behaviour and communication to moral norms, and to instruments of coercion to enforce these codes and norms. Society recognises itself through these codes and norms. This implies that 'civilisation' is very closely connected to social integration on the one hand, and to the formation of social identities on the other. From this perspective it is clearly ill-advised to make value judgements about civilisations. It is impossible to decide whether the Peruvian, the Chinese or the modern West-European civilisation is 'better' or 'more developed'.

Second, in the hierarchically organised societies analysed by Elias the values, codes, norms, elements of 'culture' which ultimately become the general social norms seem to evolve in the upper, most powerful strata. It should be repeatedly emphasised that the upper strata are not absolutely autonomous in this 'travail'. The interaction among the various parts of society has probably always had an impact on the end-products – even though we do not know enough about these interactions and mutual influences. Because of the relations of domination, though, the results *appear* usually indeed as the product of the higher strata. (The recently emerging pervasive and apparent domination of the so-called 'mass culture' would require either a different explanation, or, rather, a more complex elaboration of the above explanation.)

Third, it is suggested in the work of Elias that the civilising process has 'happened' by and large spontaneously among the upper classes he is mostly concerned with. It is not analysed in detail how the process has spread through society so as to 'colonize socially inferior outsider groups' (Fletcher 1997: 42), or to yield 'we-identities' in larger communities. Hence, one may gather the impression from his work that if the civilising process has affected larger segments of society, this has happened mainly through a slow *trickling down* process. However, the idea of a spontaneously trickling down stream is probably misleading. The elements of civilisation accepted by those at the top (and presented as their own product) have always been conditioned by their own circumstances and relationships. Since these conditions of the 'bottom', or of all the milieus below the top have been different from those on the top, the process of adaptation was probably not very easy. The 'lower' strata may not have been well prepared – materially as well as spiritually – to adopt the new 'habitus'. The examples to illustrate this point may be very trivial indeed. If 'civilised' manners required the use of forks, knives and spoons, one had to be able to get (to buy or to fabricate) those instrument. One also had to become convinced that the non-utilisation of these instruments puts one among the less-well-civilised, ultimately among the barbarians, who do not really belong to the given society. In other words, there may or may not have existed a fit between the new habitus emerging at the top and the conditions of the 'others'. Habitus as the logic or sense of practice (sense pratique) is the precondition of practices which are in line with the requirements of the given conditions (Bourdieu 1972). It can function 'adequately' if the social actor possesses 'the minimum economic and cultural capital necessary actually to perceive and seize' the requirements of the given situation (Bourdieu and Wacquant 1992: 124). And these capacities and dispositions which help to cope or to follow 'adequate' or 'rational' practices, or just to behave adequately in any given situation (applying for the most modest job, negotiating with public agencies about backward payment of bills, and so forth) have to be acquired somehow. But because of the conditions and the capitals shaping the 'adequate' habitus on the top are so far apart from those at the bottom, the automatic trickling down or imitation may in many cases be impossible.

Fourth, another reading of the above problem suggests that the elements of civilisation are the products of a 'travail' using resources, and they themselves are resources. In unequal societies the resources and the access to resources (for instance literacy and the access to literacy) are unequally distributed. I am unwilling and unable to judge whether the civilisation process makes people and societies better or worse. I suggest, though, that being 'more' civilised *within any given society* is (more often than not) an advantage. It means, among other things, that one knows better the 'rules of the game', that one is better prepared to live according to the accepted dominant norms of this society, and hence to exploit the opportunities offered by it, to cope with its reality and to adjust to its changing realities. If this is true, then one aspect of the process may indeed be assessed in value terms. If being 'more civilised' helps to survive in a given society, then it is a crucial question to what extent does the civilising process reach all the members of this society. Those who are not reached by the major elements of the civilising process, or those who are left with a thin 'coating', or left out altogether, have little chance to succeed in the given society, whatever the stakes of success are. The components of the civilising process are indeed constituent parts of the social or cultural capital. If they are unequally spread, the inequalities in physical and social life chances may become very great.[6] If things are just left to themselves, the gaps between the expected 'civilised', and the real behaviour will usually increase, and may become a source of tensions, of social exclusion, and so forth. My conclusion from this is that either some minimum capital has to be made accessible, or some efforts should be exerted to shape the conditions so as to bridge, at least to some extent, the above gaps.

Fifth, just because of the absence of a spontaneous trickling down process, and the interests of those at the top to 'spread' at least some elements of civilisation, there have always been different *civilising agents*. In Europe for instance, churches and schools have always endorsed a civilising mission (i.e. of spreading codes, norms, etc.). They have been joined in modern or modernising Europe by other institutions, for instance by old and new fraternities and associations, particularly trade unions (Kalb 1997), by factories, but also by the army or the police. Perhaps the first great attempt to build a civilising 'milieu' around production was New Lanark as conceived by Robert Owen at the end of the eighteenth century. (The village built for the workers included all the civilising institutions known at the time including dance classes for the daughters of the workers, self-disciplining devises built into the production process, rules for buying grocery using limited credit, and so forth. The only institution banned from the scene was the pub.) The civilising functions of the firm gained momentum from the middle of the nineteenth century in England (an example being the small town of Saltaire near Bradford, built by the industrialist Sir Rufus Salt), and spread all over Europe (for the Netherlands, see Kalb 1997). Much more research seems to be needed to understand the impact of, and the *competition between* the various civilising agents.

Sixth, the norms, codes, etc. which have been spread (or probably more often than not enforced) throughout society may not have covered everything understood as 'civilisation'. The agenda of the civilising agents may not have been very clear, but probably those elements were prominent on it which were deemed by the more powerful as 'necessary' for everybody. Hence it may well be that – because in unequal societies the top has by definition more resources than the bottom, because the specialists of the symbolic tend to be closer to the top than to the bottom, and because of the will to retain significant distinctions had always been strong – the top have retained, or developed later, more and more intricate, and refined patterns than those 'forced down' on society at large.

Seventh, the above considerations already suggest that the civilising process was never smooth. It may have coincided with the interests of those 'to be civilised', and then some of its elements may have been assimilated or imitated spontaneously. More often than not, though, some form of coercion had to be used to enforce the new or different codes, norms, etc. The history of the civilisation process must be therefore written also as the history of the resistance against, or the fight with, the civilising agents. (This is also part of the story of the interaction between the various parts of society mentioned above.)

Eighth, Elias was essentially concerned with the control and monopolisation of physical violence. It seems to me though that – at least in the European civilisation process – a crucial thread is the change in the respective role and weight of *physical and symbolic violence*. For a long time many agents had been able to rely mainly upon real (physical) violence, or to combine symbolic and physical coercion. In the schools of traditional societies the main educational goals (which may have belonged either to the open, or to the hidden agenda) were obedience and submission to authority. In order to achieve these goals, the most cruel methods of physical punishment and of mental pressure were widely accepted. In some of the modern civilising agencies, the police for instance, physical violence has retained much of its role for long.

The assimilation of norms, or the strengthening of the 'super-ego' is seen as successful when outside constraints are replaced by inside ones. It is doubtful, though, whether physical violence can successfully promote this process, whether indeed our social 'nature' may be changed by sheer physical coercion. If not, then a shift from physical to symbolic constraints may enhance the efficacy of the whole process. As a matter of fact, the legitimacy of physical violence has been questioned in the last decades even in institutions where it had been seen for long as legitimate – from the family through schools to the police[7]. (Whether the open and even punishable repudiation of physical violence has indeed been implemented in the various institutions is subject to doubt, or at least it depends on the public control of the operation of the given institution.) The shift from open to subtle violence may have had different reasons, and may have been rationalised altogether differently from that suggested above. In any case, symbolic violence has had to become so effective as to be able to disguise its real nature, to become soft violence, to make forget that it *is* violence. In fact, modern 'pedagogy' operating in various institutions from schools to prisons apparently endeavours to limit the use of physical violence, while the instruments of symbolic violence are becoming ever more sophisticated and refined. The role of, and the interplay between, these two forms of violence may perhaps help also to understand some characteristics of the modern totalitarian states, and some of the differences between its Nazi and Bolshevik variants.

And lastly, the suggestion of Elias quoted in the motto has to be taken seriously. The process of civilisation is a process of 'longue durée'. Several generations may be needed to make the process of 'absorption' through socialisation effective. However, the process is not necessarily cumulative and continuous in one direction (unilinear). Revolutions, wars, grave natural or social calamities and crises, then in an unprecedented way Fascism and Bolshevism all entailed various anti-civilised or de-civilising effects.[8] The onset of a new decivilising process cannot be excluded on the level of (some) nation-states, or on the global level. Its impact may be felt even if it does not go the whole way. It may start with *those elements crumbling first which were last to be built up,* without the necessary time to become consolidated. Obviously, in crisis situations outside forms may be the first to be shed – in an air-raid shelter one does not dress up for dinner. But if conditions are changing so that physical survival is threatened, the 'super-ego' may also crumble. (It is not an extreme example that with disproportionately increasing energy prices many formerly 'honest' families start to steal electricity.) It is a likely hypothesis that the deeper the roots of the super-ego, the more difficult it is to 'get rid' of it. This may render 'overcivilised' people defenceless in the face of such phenomena of de-civilisation as, for instance, the increase of the level of open violence.

Another, inter-related likelihood is that those will be the first victims of de-civilisation who had been the last ones reached by the civilising process.

In short, civilisation is understood here as a historical process assisting and promoting social coexistence within continuously changing complex modern societies. *The process may have been more or less violent; it has always been socially structured; and it is historically reversible.*

Processes influencing 'modern' civilisation

All established societies have had a civilisation, but these have differed depending on economic, political and other conditions. In the past centuries there evolved processes which conditioned the 'modern' civilising process in particular ways. Out of them I shall mention only three. They influenced not only the contents of what is meant by modern civilisation as an ideal, but also the activity of the agents involved in spreading it, and the outcome of their operation. A crucial element in this story is the changing role of the state.

Increasing social density and complexity

One relevant and (from Durkheim to de Swaan) often analysed thread is the increasing *density* in many realms of society in the last centuries, and hence the increasing *complexity* of social relations. These developments are connected through various feedback mechanisms to the evolution of the capitalist economy, to growing productivity, the improving availability of goods over spreading geographic areas, and the perfection of technologies in many areas of life.

Population growth followed as mortality rates dropped and life expectancy lengthened. The story is familiar. Still, we rarely meditate about the significance of some of the figures involved. Let us just have a look on Europe. What can it signify that the number of its residents grew – albeit in an uneven way because of losses due to wars, migration, epidemics – from 40 to 150 million between 1000 and 1800, and then to 270 million in 1850, and 530 million in 1950? The density may be particularly strongly felt in towns. The ratio of those living in towns of over 100,000 people grew, between 1850 and 1980, for instance in France from 5 per cent to 28 per cent, in Denmark from 9 per cent to 38 per cent, in England from 2 per cent to 71 per cent, and even in Hungary from 1 per cent to 29 per cent (Handbuch, vol. 4: 56; vol. 5: 12, 42; vol. 6: 12, 18, 54). How can so many people live side-by-side?

Meanwhile, the increasing differentiation and specialisation in all fields (the emerging 'organic solidarity' in Durkheim's theory) required the multiplication of more or less autonomous institutions and organisations. The growing complexity of market relations gave rise to a network of ever more dense contractual relations as well as of lengthening networks of communication, based on roads, transport and the media. The process is still continuing in our days when the trajectories of movement on the earth and in the air slowly fill up the space, and the mass of electronic information cram in the ether. The growing number of people had become inter-related by relationships of a widening variety. The situation thus created has been described by historical sociology as 'the extension and intensification of the "chains of human inter-dependence" in the course of time, as the *generalisation of interdependency*' (de Swaan 1988: 2). What concerns us here is that as the number of the relationships with others and the types of the contacts have been multiplying, the likelihood of frictions, of spontaneous or deliberate disturbances affecting these networks, and of damages caused thereby, has been steadily increasing. The threat represented by these disturbances to normal social coexistence, or to civilisation in the above sense is easy to grasp.

Differentiation and exclusion – the dangerous and endangered poor

Another aspect of this history is the changing social nature of poverty. The historical, structural, socio-psychological and causal questions of poverty since the earliest times and particularly since the Middle Ages, as well as the relationships and societal responses to the challenges of poverty are treated by many eminent scholars on various – parish, country, European, or even global – levels. (For example, Mollat 1978; Geremek 1987; de Swaan 1988; Castel 1995; Gans 1995.) No summing up is intended here: I just pick some elements fitting my purpose.

With increasing social density and mobility the 'untouchable'[9] had become visible. In the growing cities they could become close neighbours. Their visibility may have been already uncomfortable for the 'established' whose sensibility had increased with the Enlightenment (Mollat 1978). In fact, the life of these endangered poor was much more exposed than that of the better-off in two senses. They were more exposed to all forms of physical sufferings, and to the public eye. The ills affecting them had become visible for instance through hungry street urchins, murdered 'illegitimate' infants (Chevalier 1958), home-less beggars or emaciated women. These sights affected the new sensibilities. The real trouble was, however, that the poor have become more dangerous than heretofore. They may have represented *direct personal* danger through the threat of robbing or committing crimes for subsistence. Or the danger may have been more indirect, when the poor were seen as a group representing or exuding physical and moral 'evils'.[10]

Because of all these facts, it became a must not only to take notice of the existence of these 'others', but also to do something in more organised ways than traditional charity did. When – with increasing density and geographic mobility – the poor had become 'strangers', traditional alms-giving became difficult because of the free-rider problem mentioned by de Swaan. (Others may profit from the appeasement obtained at my expense.) Also, when the

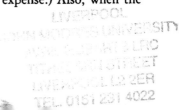

former hierarchical relationships of bondage or spontaneous submission were transformed into more horizontal connections, and the respect of (individual) human dignity has become an accepted value, the patriarchal forms of alms-giving had become – at least theoretically – more controversial.

The emergence of the working class resulted in new forms of misery and conflict as compared to the 'pre-industrial' poor. The workers' status was affected by new insecurities. The dangers of grave accidents, of job losses, of unprovided old age all increased. The family as the traditional helping agent was less available not only because of increased geographic distances, or smaller families, but also because the relatives of the urban workers were also without means. (In the towns one could not even fall back on subsistence agricultural production.) The problem was uncertainty in the immediate present as well as in the future. The dangerous character of working-class poverty was amply increased by the propensity and ability of workers to organise. Individualised solutions to these problems were unattainable to those concerned, and even the traditional organisations of mutual help failed to respond to the new needs essentially because of the scarcity of resources.

Increased competitiveness, growing individualism and the weakening of traditional moral authorities

The dilemmas related to competitiveness when it becomes morally approved selfishness, and is seen as the driving force of market success, had been discussed by many scholars since Kropotkin's book on 'Mutual Aid' (for example, Tawney 1964; Rotenberg 1977). The relationship between secularisation and modernisation has also often been on the agenda since Max Weber's work on the issue. From my perspective it would be important to find the connections between all three of the above trends. This task is not yet completed, thus only hypotheses can be formulated. The assumption is, by and large, that market-conform behaviours compel individual solutions, but many social problems such as those mentioned above are difficult or impossible to handle by indi-vidual means. The moral authority of religion, or any similar institution of traditional authority that could have harnessed market-conform egoism has waned away. Thus, new means had to be found to reconcile strengthening individualism with the increasing need of intervention in matters concerning the public.

The historically evolving answer had been, of course, the increasing role of the central authority, of the state to which we soon turn. But there are open questions which will be ignored hereafter. We do not know under what con-ditions, if any, may the state acquire morally compelling authority in handling the conflict between individualism and social troubles not manageable by individual means. We do not know, either, what may be the consequences of the weakening of moral imperatives if these conditions do not materialise, particularly under the conditions of globalisation.

Answers to the above challenges – the increasing role of the state

Increasing density, complexity, inequality and poverty within the frameworks of the unfolding market economy represented challenges to society. Obviously, social coexistence and the reproduction of societies was seldom, if ever 'unregulated', but the regulatory institutions and mechanisms underwent considerable change through time. To take only Europe, the power of the head of the household over the members, or the 'lord' over his 'subjects' was usually sufficient to regulate the coexistence of the relatively small and relatively isolated communities throughout the Middle Ages. In the localities – in villages, parishes, towns – instances of 'corporate power' had emerged. But as the chains of human interdependencies lengthened and multiplied, so occurred an upward shift in the power centres assuming regulatory roles.

In the Middle Ages there were relatively few problems requiring central regulation. I have gathered the impression that the first function which became centralised and had almost continuously remained through history at the top power level was coinage, implying the guarantee of the value of coins (*New British Encyclopaedia*, vol. 2: 333). Of course there always had been contenders (lords were often prone to coin their own money). However, the conflicts over the monopoly of coinage seem to have been relatively mild and usually transitory. It gives indeed food for thought how widely accepted had this state function become, and how seldom was it questioned even when the overall role of the state has been under heavy attack. It also shows an extraordinary trust in the state that (except in unusually turbulent times) everybody, anarchists included, use and accept valueless pieces of metal or scraps of paper at their nominal value if the state is assumed to guarantee the value.

How other matters have become gradually more 'public', more centralised depended on the outcome of the struggles between 'centralising and decentralising forces' (Elias 1982). The decentralising forces led for instance to the multiplication of autonomous states in Europe, while centralising tendencies within a given area, usually the emerging states appeared as a result of the fights of the parallel powers, that is the princes or kings, the lords, the church, the towns, or sometimes various oligarchies. These struggles ended with a – more often temporary than lasting – truce at different times. The open struggles between the church and the prince around the *right to promulgate binding laws* reached a turning point for instance at the Investiture Controversy. It is after the journey to Canossa that the Church (the Pope) has recognised the authority of the king in worldly matters (Badie 1987), albeit the contents and the boarders of the authority have continued to be debated practically up to our days.

The monopoly of using legitimate violence in case of internal and external conflicts (probably the most often mentioned and the best recognised state responsibility nowadays)[11] as well as that of *tax collection* was the stake of incessant struggles for centuries between the same actors. If we tend to define the state in our days just by the monopoly of violence and that of taxation, this may mean that their appropriation marks the demarcation line between the pre-modern and the modern state.

Literacy and *numeracy* had become increasingly important in these matters as well as in the spreading 'contractual culture'. Church monopoly in educational matters was slowly overcome because of overall social changes. But there was strong and lasting opposition against giving better education to the lower classes (for fear of losing cheap labour, for fear of new abilities to question the *status quo*, and so forth). Nevertheless, the operation of an increasingly complex economy, the spread of bureaucracy and the wish of strengthening the nation state required the transmission and the inculcation of common norms and codes. It followed from the nature of the need that basic education had to become public responsibility, and had to be publicly funded, at least in the case of the poor.

Public health and social housing follow a similar pattern. The need for them may be illustrated by the changes in urban public health arrangements. The lack of clean running water, of refuse collection and of sewage made it impossible to ward off contagion. Individual solutions for some of these amenities could have been financed by the rich, but this would not have helped, if the open gutter remained there. And their collective action was paralysed (as shown by de Swaan) by the free-rider problem. Thus, the responsibility was shifted this time, too, to the town, and ultimately to the state which was able to collect taxes and could build up the institutions of public hygiene. It has to be emphasised that this activity could be effective only if it encompassed whole communities.

The changing economy presented yet other problems. The self-regulating market, as it unfolded, seemed to take care some of the chaos, and this belief is still alive. However – as many historians have shown (from Polanyi on) – the smooth operation of the so-called self-regulating markets has always necessitated a considerable amount of outside (state) regulation and legislation. Indeed, each and every sub-field of economic life – from the protection of property and 'fair competition' to the regulation of traffic, or labour relations, or the quality control of goods for the protection of the consumers – has its own history of unfolding (state) regulation for the sake of the 'public good' (Hill 1976).

Industrialisation changed also the nature of pre-industrial poverty. Conditions prevailing in factories as well as the new risks of income loss connected with the workers' status has triggered waves of unrest and anxiety. The involvement of the state in handling the new risks and reducing the mounting unrest and anxiety was a necessity this time, too. It may have included strengthening control and repression, but also 'remedial' actions, including Factory Acts, labour market regulations and new forms of income support. All of them involved public action. The two early systems devised for handling the risks of the new conditions have become, or proved to be, inadequate: mutual help associations set up by the workers themselves did not work well because of the lack of sufficient funds (Hatzfeld 1971; de Swaan 1988; for Hungary, Petrák 1978); and commercial insurance which served quite well the better-off was unattainable for the majority either because of the lack of funds, or because of the failures of the insurance market (recently spelt out by Barr 1987; Burchardt 1997). The forms that state involvement has taken from the last third of the nineteenth century is a much-studied topic of social history both on the national and the international level (for instance Rimlinger 1974; Flora and Heidenheimer 1981; Baldwin 1990). It could take the form of social insurance 'invented' by Bismarck or of means-tested, and then (near) universal provisions, as was the case in Anglo-Saxon and Scandinavian countries. With the additional impetus of the first world war, and then of the World Crisis, the main risks – accidents, death and widowhood, sickness, maternity, unemployment – had been covered in most European countries at the eve of or soon after the second world war at least for workers.

Considering the nature of the early social functions of the state, it may be conjectured that the standards of the institutions and benefits thus created had to be relatively inferior. It is hard to discover strong social interests which would have militated for decent (and not minimal) levels of social assistance, or for high-standard public hospitals. Even without adequate documentation, social logic suggests that high-standard institutions serving only the poor or the workers had to be extremely scarce. And whenever we find them, it is almost certain that their existence will be due to the efforts of a strongly motivated and generous philanthropist, or to a particularly progressive civil movement.

Slowly, however, the above institutions have spread to the whole of society. The collectivisation of welfare or, in other words, the unfolding of national solidarities is really the story of the welfare state after the second world war (albeit in some countries, particularly in Scandinavia, the process started earlier). This latter period is not devoid of clashes of interests, of struggles and conflicts, either (Baldwin 1990). The motives for the later development may have been mixed. Solidarities forged during the war, the memories of collective sufferings or new progressive ideas may have played a role as well as the challenge of the eastern 'socialist' bloc, the interests of a growing state bureaucracy, or the self-interest of the middle classes who wanted to benefit also from their own taxes.

Countries of course differ as to the speed or scope of the developments and the standards achieved. However, about a decade after the second world war, 'collective, nation-wide and compulsory arrangements' had been developed over Western Europe 'to cope with inefficiencies and adversities' (de Swaan 1988: 2 and Conclusion), and also to promote such objectives as the reduction of social inequalities in physical and social life chances, or to enhance social justice (whatever this means) and the sense of citizenship. These arrangements helped to adjust people to the increasingly complex world, and restricted or corrected to some extent the market logic. In the modern welfare state, good-quality kindergartens, public hospitals and decent pensions ceased to be rarities. Good quality social insurance combined the market logic and individual self-interest (the 'value for money' requirement) and the moral imperative helping coexistence. Even social assistance had acquired – occasionally at least – forms compatible with human dignity. When their quality improved, the collective arrangements could become or could appear as less discriminatory, less enforced or less punitive. Hence, they could become more effective in their 'civilising functions'. With the help of all these institutions western societies had become somewhat better (at least according to my value scale). Poverty did not disappear, but its scope and depth were reduced. The poor had become less endangered, less dangerous, and suffered probably less. The gap between life chances was reduced in many walks of life, for instance the difference between the length of life allowed to the rich and to the poor, or to the children of rich and poor. Also out of the many anxieties and insecurities afflicting human existence some – those at least which could be reduced to a calculable status – could be alleviated.

However, this is not the end of the story. The legitimacy of state monopolies could not be 'eternalised'. Each of them has been questioned or attacked at turn by various social actors. Out of them, the market forces have become recently increasingly vigorous contenders in the provision and distribution of goods and services which had become collectivised. The controversies around the monopolies of nation-states are visibly growing in intensity with the process of globalisation. 'The dominant position of markets may be due to the fact that no supranational authority has the power to discipline transnational markets which increasingly threaten the sovereignty of nations. . . . With governments politically unable to rise above the national interest, the market wins' (Boyer and Drache 1996: 7). The parties involved now in these struggles include the nation-states, supranational agencies and the new international oligarchy.

It is a different matter to what extent all these processes took place in Central–Eastern Europe, and I propose to deal with this in a different paper. The main (preliminary) conclusions of this analysis may be briefly summed up for Central–Eastern Europe, and may not fully apply to Eastern Europe. The fissure between the West and the rest of Europe – and that between Central–Eastern and Eastern Europe – starting in the Middle Ages (Szücs 1983) impacted on the modernising and civilising processes up to the twentieth century. Despite deliberate and repeated efforts of 'adjustment', less has trickled down and went less deep. The collective and compulsory institutions of integration started to evolve relatively early for instance in Hungary, but the system expanded much more slowly. It was only under dictatorial state socialism that the compulsory and collective arrangements promoting 'modern civilisation', or creating conditions for its unfolding, attained to cover the whole of society.[12] The totalitarian systems, particularly at their early stages, certainly had momentous de-civilising features and impacts. None the less, the so-called 'premature' welfare state, and even the new ideology produced gains. I think the most positive outcome of 'socialist dictatorship' is the reduction of the civilisation gap both between east and west, and between the higher and lower echelons of society. Many civilising acquisitions spread through society, even if the very bottom may hardly have been touched. I believe that the chances of those countries to adjust to the requirements of political democracy and a market society, or to conform to the expectations of the European Union which they want to join, would be currently much worse without the 'premature' welfare arrangements.

Civilisation as a complex syndrome

The explicit and implicit, overt or covert civilising impacts of the school system, the health system and the social insurance schemes have been analysed by many. I want to focus here on some possible impacts of social security in the large sense. Social security in general, and social insurance in particular – even if compulsory – are instruments which give a sort of guarantee to be able to cope with future adversities or difficulties. These arrangements represent the compulsory institutionalisation of the ability of rational foresight (of deferring gratification if you wish), an ability which is socially very unequally diffused. This means that one is enabled to reckon with the future without too much particular individual effort. In this sense, the impact of these arrangements resembles that of the public monopoly of violence. Social security schemes reduce the necessity of being constantly on the alert for fear of (socially manageable) adversities in the same way that the monopoly of violence frees the citizen from the constant obligation of preparing individually for un-expected attacks.

Facing the future means of course more than saving (in one way or another) for old age or sickness. It involves the whole problem of social reproduction, particularly the preparation of the children for life, including their schooling. Of course, one never gains mastery over the future. However, when there are all-encompassing collective arrangements of social security, including those helping the children to prepare themselves for life, this increases one's autonomy over one's life-course. It may even motivate action. Let us assume that I may be confident that my child will be able to continue its studies in line with its interests and abilities, and that schooling will enable it to get ahead in life. Under these conditions it makes sense to encourage the child to work well at school. (Empirical findings for Hungary suggest that the availability of free schooling spread the habit, even among uneducated and badly off parents, to think about the future of their children as different and better than their own [Ferge 1969].)

A farther, and in my mind a socially and psychologically crucial, effect of social security is the reduction of the level of omnipresent anxieties, at least of those which may be socially manageable uncertainties. The social significance of anxiety and insecurity seems to attract ever more attention (Ferge 1996;

Marris 1996; Kraemer and Roberts, 1997). Psychologists may be correct in assuming that the feeling of security is crucial. In Freud's terms, *security is the absence of anxiety*. A child cannot rid itself of its more elemental anxieties and cannot develop properly if it lacks the mother, or at least a permanent, security-giving care-provider stepping in her place. We can feel anxious over the threats of nature; over the health or life of our loved ones (or of ourselves); over the stability of our relations with people; over risks of losing much of what we have; over the opportunity to secure our everyday bread by keeping our job; to be able to pay the next bill or the medication for our child or parents (Ferge 1996).

Some of those may be termed *essential anxieties* having to do with our biological, mortal nature, with our affections, or with our psychological dispositions. These anxieties seem to belong to the human condition itself, and cannot be 'abolished' without losing our humanness. Others may be seen as *existential* anxieties, stemming from social conditions. Both are, though, in Freud's terms, *real* anxieties, that is, not pathological or neurotic symptoms, and it is always painful to experience them. 'The kind of situation in which anxiety arises naturally largely depends on the degree of our knowledge, and on how powerful we consider ourselves in relation to the outside world.' Realistic anxiety is, however – Freud continues – neither rational nor expedient because 'it paralyses all action . . .'. It would be expedient, rather, 'to size up coolly one's own strengths in comparison with the magnitude of the threat, and then to decide whether to escape or defend ourselves, or perhaps an attack itself would provide more chance for everything to end well' (Freud 1986: 321, from Hungarian).

The human condition has always been fraught with sources of anxiety. Indeed, we know very little about how much the medieval man may have suffered from anxieties. Maybe a lot, if we recall superstitions and ghosts, demons and the various frightening representations of purgatory and hell (Le Goff 1988); maybe little. Perhaps in the absence of the means to create defences, the only way of a 'normal' existence was to ignore the incalculable dangers and uncertainties of the unknown. As a consequence, it may have become possible to accept without complaint and fear the acts of God, including natural calamities and man-made disasters, afflictions and death. And perhaps one could trust to get compensation in the next world.

More close to us, we know also next to nothing how much the poor suffered from the anxieties of sickness and old age before the appearance of the collective pension and health schemes. I suggest, though, that once the instruments of managing certain risks have emerged and become accessible, the former situation changes. We then become conscious of these risks as constituent elements of insecurity, even if this was not the case earlier. Again, there is a parallel with reliance on the police and legal redress instead of dealing individually with aggressive attacks. Once available, the instruments of risk management become important: if the access to these instruments is itself unsure, this causes anxiety and may become paralysing. This pattern also is part of the civilisation process – be it a blessing or a curse.

This conviction explains why I cannot share the negative assessment of many economists and politicians about social security when they affirm that social security has spoilt people. According to them, risk aversion has become a general trait that is a character failure. This defect should allegedly be corrected, and each individual should become responsible for his/her present and future.[13]

If we accept the historically barely contestable idea of a civilising process, then we should see it as a whole. We have to realise that it has affected both our superficial behaviours and our more deeply ingrained habits. Most of us living in complex modern (European?) societies have learned to use regularly soap and a towel. This has become our 'second nature' – at least as long as we have running water. It has also become our 'second nature' that (under normal circumstances) we keep as a matter of course the terms of a market contract, or that we seldom feel the urge to steal unattended goods in a supermarket. Meanwhile, we have also 'learned' through a long historical process to take it for granted that running water is normally available and affordable, as well as medical care or the school attendance of our children. We can often act more efficiently as autonomous individuals if our energies are freed from the fear of attacks or from elementary existential threats. I believe that these processes and the traits they produce cling together. The 'syndrome' of civilisation may be very different in societies with dissimilar conditions and histories. Also, it varies within a given society depending on the operation of the civilising process, on who was reached and how. But it seems to be a syndrome. I think therefore that it is a psychological and historical error to qualify some of the elements of the syndrome the 'inherent traits of a civilised person' and some others as defects of character.

And what if the state retrenches? – West and East

One could gather the impression from the previous arguments that the civilising process – at least in the West – was cumulative and followed a direct line. This is clearly not the case. Even though it is only a footnote in the manuscript of Elias written in the 1930s, he explicitly suggests what was presented as one of the mottoes, namely that:

> The armour of civilised conduct would crumble very rapidly if, through a change in society, the degree of insecurity that existed earlier were to break in upon us again, and if danger became as incalculable as it once was. Corresponding fears would burst the limits set to them today.
>
> (Elias 1939, I: 307)

It has already been suggested that the onset of a new decivilising process cannot be excluded on the level of (some) nation-states, or on the global level.

Civilisations have collapsed before. Although the idea of the 'end of civilisation' is put into inverted commas here, the dangers of 'decivilisation' still loom large and seem to affect first those lastly reached. However, they appear to impact also on those who reject both all moral authorities and the enforced authority of the state.

We have argued that out of the many historic processes of capitalist development, three had been particularly instrumental in propelling the growth of the welfare functions of the state. We have mentioned increasing density and longer chains of interdependence; the multiplication and the visibility of the dangerous and endangered poor; and the consequences of the simultaneous strengthening of selfish individualism and the decline of moral authorities. Apparently, none of these tendencies have subsided. The contrary would be more true.

Let us focus on the most compulsive problem, that of the poor. In the past one or two decades, new factors have contributed to the expansion of poverty. Among them we find growing unemployment, the destabilisation of jobs, declining earnings, increasing income and wealth inequalities.[14] These all may have contributed to the accentuation of such problems as homelessness, hopelessness, criminality and other forms of deviant behaviours. As a consequence, tendencies of social disintegration, marginalisation or exclusion, and sometimes the appearance of an 'underclass', have become parts of the social scene. The number of those who are useless either as producers or as consumers, who 'are a useless weight on the earth'[15] is increasing (Castel 1995).

Similar phenomena prompted the state 150 years ago to complete its policing functions with welfare functions. The state took action in the first place for the sake of the well-to-do and 'social peace'. Its action was also needed to shape a more 'civilised' labour force. The improvement of the conditions of the poor made them more fit as producers. Later on, they have become important also as consumers.

We currently witness the institutionalised weakening of the collective, all-encompassing and compulsory arrangements. There is a growing literature analysing the – real and alleged – reasons for trimming the welfare state (for example, Esping-Andersen 1996; George and Taylor-Gooby 1996). The first direct consequence of the cuts is the down-grading of the institutions: either their coverage may shrivel, or their standards may decrease, or both. Their attractiveness is weakening, together with the alleged readiness of people to pay taxes for deteriorating services. As the other chapters in this book show, data substantiate the contrary: in most European countries, East and West, people are willing to pay even more taxes for good or better collective services.

If the situation is similar to what it used to be 150 years ago, but the reaction is different, this must mean that the groups who felt themselves threatened and forced the state to obtain quiescence through improving the lot of the poor now feel less threatened. The reasons are diverse, and cannot be discussed here in detail. However, one element stands out, namely that the state is expected to change its profile. Its monopoly of violence is questioned in the name of the freedom of self-defence. This freedom is restricted, though, to the rich. For the others, the policing functions of the state have to be strengthened.[16] In fact, public safety remains important also for the better-off. Thus, they press the state to strengthen its regulatory and punitive role against those who endanger their bodily safety and property (Jordan 1996: 212–21). In all probability, the current revolt against redistribution does not really want to weaken the state. It just wants to change the balance between its oppressive and enabling functions. The state is meant less to serve the 'Safety of People' in general than that of those who have the most to lose and to fear.

We have argued that the process whereby the policing functions were completed and then partly replaced by welfare functions was instrumental in 'spreading civilisation' and making societies more liveable. If this is true, then the reversal of this process may trigger a process of decivilisation or anti-civilisation – even if the other processes, particularly increasing density and longer chains of interdependence among those who are insiders in the chains are not going backwards. The logic above suggests, though, that the process may not affect everybody – 'only' the 30 or 50 per cent who 'sunt pundus inutilae terrae', the dead weight.

The consequences of the waning away of elements of civilisation in some parts of society are easy to think through (logically, if not morally). If conditions change so as to make scarce the knife and fork, inside toilet, hot water, and then water itself (Huby 1995) as well as space for privacy, then habits tied to them have to change. All these changes, including the lowering of the level of shame[17] and the weakening of many other self-restraints set in with tragic rapidity in case of the homeless. But the non-poor may become involved, too. If the institutions of social security in general are weakening, the habits developed in relation to money, to time, to space, to self, and to others are all jeopardised (as shown for instance by the case of stolen electricity). More generally, the quality of society as a whole may be affected by these developments. This is particularly true if we accept the definition of social quality as recently proposed by a group of European scholars, who suggest that social quality rests on the degree of economic security, the level of social inclusion, of solidarity, and of autonomy or empowerment (Beck et al., 1997: 3). All of these bases are eroded with the 'decivilising process' described above.

The scenario is not rejoicing. And it may not be in line with what we like to think about 'European civilisation'.

Notes

1   I wish to thank the Institute of Human Studies in Vienna. Six months of visiting fellowship there enabled me to start the research, the first, yet tentative results of which are summed up in the present chapter. I have to thank also all those who made comments on former drafts: Shlomo Avineri, Herbert Gans, Don Kalb, Károly Kecskeméti, S.M. Miller, Pál Léderer, Frances Fox Piven, Agnes Simonyi,

Adrian Sinfield, Stefan Svallfors, Abram de Swaan, Peter Taylor-Gooby, and the doctoral students in Budapest. While most of their criticisms were justified, I ask to be excused if some of their comments had not been given due attention at this point.

2 While my starting point was the work of Elias, de Swaan and the Amsterdam School building on the work of Elias, I would agree with them if they disagreed with me because I do not follow exactly the original interpretations.

3 The very idea of civilisation as a process of imposing self-control goes back of course to Freud, as widely acknowledged by Elias and Swaan. The super-ego is not only an individual phenomenon – it is one of the connecting links to society. Freud explicitly says that *some* curtailment of individual freedom seems to be the price of civilisation: 'The liberty of the individual is not a benefit of culture. It was greatest before any culture, though indeed it had little value at that time, because the individual was hardly in a position to defend it. Liberty has undergone restrictions through the evolution of civilisation, and justice demands that these restrictions should apply to all' (1951: 59–60). It seems to me that it is just the 'necessary' or 'acceptable' degree of curtailment of individual freedom which lies at the heart of the current debates about the role of the state.

4 'Civilization becomes possible when a well-established agriculture and technology give rise to an economic surplus enabling the development of cities and a written culture' (*New Encyclopaedia Britannica*, vol. 23).

5 Or culture. I do not want to go into definitional problems, all the less, because there is a certain chaos even in the most 'scientific' literature. Encyclopedias, among others *The Columbia Encyclopedia* (1993), or *The New Encyclopaedia Britannica, Macropaidea* (1983) use these concepts (culture, civilization, modernisation) almost cross-definitionally. According to the *New Encyclopedia* for instance, with the advance of modernisation 'at any rate, the outcome will be a new world of civilization, heir to Western and non-Western *cultures* alike'. The different meaning of the concepts in different languages further complicates the issue as witnessed by the analysis of Elias on the French and German use of the term, or by the title of the seminal essay of Freud which is '*Das Unbehagen in der Kultur*' in German, and '*Civilization and its discontents*' in English.

6 The same 'rule' may not apply to groups or societies (nation-states) on various levels of civilisation if they get into conflict with each other. Less civilised, hence more violent, units may easily overpower the other party – at least on the short run.

7 The debates about the death penalty form an interesting case illustrating this point.

8 There is a new body of research centred on the decivilising processes which I cannot handle here in depth (Mennel 1990; Duclos 1993; Fletcher 1995, 1997).

9 The expression 'untouchable' is an appropriate metaphor here: it conveys the combination of social and physical distance.

10 de Swaan describes convincingly how and why cholera may be considered as the paradigm of urban interdependence (de Swaan 1988, Ch. 4.2).

11 It may well be true, though, that 'any state that failed to put considerable effort into war making was likely to disappear' (Tilly 1985: 184).

12 It is an ahistorical, albeit interesting question how this same process would have evolved if the Yalta decision about the partition of Europe had been different.

13 Interestingly enough, they never go as far as to propose that people build up their own defences against individual violent attacks. If this is spontaneously happening in case of the rich, this is just a sign that there is a syndrome: the weakening of some elements may have repercussions on others.

14 Martin and Schumann have calculated that in the coming years the rate of unemployment could increase from 9.7 per cent to 21 per cent in Germany, from 7.3 per cent to 18 per cent in Austria. Together with all the other changes on the

job-market, they project a 20:80 society, with 20 per cent in a good position, the others losing out (1996: 146–47).

15 The quotation is from an 'édit' of Charles IX from 1566, quoted in Castel (1995).

16 The increase of the prison population, particularly in the United States is well known. The rules of social assistance tend to become harsher, enforced 'workfare' is often replacing 'welfare'. The problem of minorities, migrants and refugees also often unleashes police violence.

17 Do we ever realise what does it mean for a formerly 'civilised' homeless in terms of physical suffering and a psychological demeaning experience to have no place to excrete?

References

Ariès, P. and Duby, G. (eds) (1987) *Histoire de la vie privée*, Paris: Seuil.

Badie, B. (1987) 'La pensée politique vers la fin du XVIe siècle: héritage antique et médiéval', in P. Ory (ed.) *Nouvelle histoire des idées politiques*, Paris: Pluriel.

Baldwin, P. (1990) *The politics of Social Solidarity. Class Bases of the European Welfare State 1875–1975*, Cambridge, New York: Cambridge University Press.

Barr, N. (1987) *The Economics of the Welfare State*, London: Weidenfeld and Nicholson.

Beck, W., van der Maesen, L. and Walker, A. (1997) *The Social Quality of Europe*, The Hague-London-Boston: Kluwer Law International.

Bourdieu, P. (1972) *Esquisse d'une théorie de la pratique*, Genève: Droz.

Bourdieu, P. and Wacquant, L. J. D. (1992) *An Invitation to Reflective Sociology*, Chicago: The University of Chicago Press.

Boyer, R. and Drache, D. (1996) *States Against Markets. The limits of globalization*, London and New York: Routledge.

Burchardt, Tania (1997) *What Price Security? Assessing private insurance for long-term care, income replacement during incapacity, and unemployment for mortgagors*. Suntory and Toyota International Centres for Economics and Related Disciplines. London School of Economics. WSP/129.

Castel, R. (1995) *Les métamorphoses de la question sociale. Une chronique du salariat*, Paris: Fayard.

Chevalier, L. (1958) *Classes laborieuses et classes dangereuses à Paris pendant la première moitié du XIX siècle*, Paris: Plon.

The Columbia Encyclopedia (1995), Fifth edition, Houghton Mifflin.

de Swaan, A. (1988) *In Care of the State: Health Care, Education and Welfare in Europe and the USA in the Modern Era*, New York: Polity Press/Oxford University Press (Page numbering is based on the multigraphied edition of Amsterdam University of 1987).

de Swaan, A. (1990) *The Management of Normality. Critical essays in Health and Welfare*, London and New York: Routledge.

Duclos, D. (1993) *De la civilité. Comment les sociétés apprivoisent la puissance*, Paris: Éditions de la découverte.

Elias, N., *The civilizing process*, vol. I. *The history of manners*, 1939 (1969, 1978); Vol. II. *State Formation and Civilisation* (1982), Oxford, New York: Blackwell.

Elias, N. and Scotson, J. L. (1994) *The Established and the Outsiders*, London, Thousand Oaks, New Delhi: Sage.

Esping-Andersen, G. (ed.) (1996) *Welfare States in Transition. National Adaptations in Global Economies*, London, Thousand Oaks, New Delhi: Sage.

Ferge, Zs. (1969) *Társadalmunk rétegeződése (Social stratification)*, Budapest, Közgazdasági és Jogi Könyvkiadó.

Ferge, Zs. (1996) Freedom and Security, *International Review of Comparative Public Policy*, 7: 19–41.

Fletcher, J. (1995) Towards a Theory of Decivilizing Processes. *Amsterdams sociologisch Tijdschrift*, 22(2) October: 283–97.

Fletcher, Jonathan (1997) *Violence and Civilization. An Introduction to the Work of Norbert Elias*, Cambridge: Polity Press.

Flora, P. and Heidenheimer, A. (eds) (1981)*The development of Welfare States in Europe and America*, London: Transaction Books.

Freud, S. (1951) *Civilisation and its Discontents*, London: Hogarth Press.

Freud, S. (1986). *Bevezetés a pszichoanalízisbe. (Introduction to psychoanalysis)*, Budapest: Gondolat.

Gans, Herbert J. (1995) *The War Against the Poor. The Underclass and Antipoverty Policy*, New York: Basic Books (A Division of HarperCollins Publishers).

George, V. and Taylor-Gooby, P. (1996) *European Welfare Policy. Squaring the Welfare Circle*, Houndmill and London: Macmillan Press Ltd.

Geremek, B. (1987) *La potence et la pitié. L'Europe et les pauvres du moyen age à nos jours*, Paris: Gallimard.

Handbuch der Europaischen Wirtschafts-und Sozialgeschichte, több kötet, Stuttgart: Klett-Cotta (several years of publication)

Hatzfeld, H. (1971) *Du paupérisme à la Sécurité Sociale*, Paris: Librairie Armand Colin.

Hill, Michael (1976) *The State, Administration and the Individual*, Glasgow: Fontana/Collins.

Huby, M. (1995) Water Poverty and Social Policy: A review of issues for research, *Journal of Social Policy*, April.

Jordan, B. (1996) *A Theory of Poverty and Social Exclusion*, Cambridge: Polity Press.

Kalb, D. (1997) *Expanding Class: Power and everyday politics in industrial communities, North Brabant illustrations, Ca. 1850–1950*, Durham and London: Duke University Press.

Kraemer, S. and Roberts, Jane (eds) (1997) *The Politics of Attachment. Towards a Secure Society*, London: Free Association of Books.

Kropotkin, Peter (first: 1902, 1955) *Mutual Aid: A Factor of Evolution*, Boston: Extending Horizons.

Le Goff, J. (1988) *The Medieval Imagination*, Chicago: The University of Chicago Press.

Martin, H. P. and Schumann, H. (1996) *Die Globalisierungsfalle. Der Angriff auf Demokratie und Wohlstand*, Rowohlt Verlag.

Marris, P. (1996) *The Politics of Uncertainty*, London and New York: Routledge.

Mennell, S. (1990) Decivilising Processes: Theoretical Significance and Some Lines of Research, *International Sociology*, 5(2): 205–23.

Mollat, M. (1978) *Les pauvres au Moyen Age*, Paris: Hachette.

(The) New Encyclopaedia Britannica.

Petrák K. (1978) *A szervezett munkásság küzdelme a korszerű társadalombiztosításért*, Budapest: Táncsics.

Rimlinger, G. V. (1974), *Welfare Policy, Industrialization in Europe, America and Russia*, New York: John Wiley.

Rotenberg, M. (1977): 'Alienating-individualism' and 'reciprocal individualism': a cross-cultural conceptualization. *Journal of Humanistic Psychology*, 17(3).

Soros, G. (1997) The Capitalist Threat, *Atlantic Monthly*, January.

Szûcs, Jenõ (1983) *Die drei historischen Regionen Europas*, Frankfurt: Verlag Neue Kritik.

Tawney, R. H. (1964) *Equality*, London: Unwin Books. (First edn. 1931.)

Tilly, C. (1985) 'War Making and State Making as Organized Crime', in P. Evans, D. Rueschenmeyer and T. Skocpol (eds) *Bringing the State Back In,* Cambridge: Cambridge University Press.

INDEX

abuse: attitudes to 17–8, 20, 24, 26–7; suspicions of 20, 36, 38, 41–2, 44, 47
Alber, J. 139, 145, 155–6
anxiety 228, 230–2
Australia 8–9, 137–8, 141–50, 152, 155, 161, 163–4, 166–7, 170–2, 174–6, 178–9, 181, 196

Baldwin, P. 34, 163, 183, 229
basic income 136, 144–6, 181–2
Bauman, Z. 135–6
Blomberg, H. 8, 43, 52, 56, 79, 101
Britain 6, 8–9, 106–12, 115, 119–20, 122–3, 126–7
budget deficit 35

Castles, F. 157, 164, 171
Center Party of Finland 63, 168
child care: *see* day care
citizen's income: *see* basic income
civil servants 88, 93–4, 96, 99
civilisation 10, 151, 219–25, 231, 233–5; *see also* civilising process
civilising process 10, 218–24, 233–5; *see also* civilisation
class(es) 5, 9, 11, 15, 40, 97, 118–20, 135–6, 138, 145–6, 151–2, 155–6, 163, 165–7, 198–9; differences in attitudes between 2, 10, 22, 24–8, 39, 42, 122–3, 127–8, 170–2, 176, 182–3, 208; *see also* middle class; working class
competitiveness 3, 5
conservative regime 138–9, 143, 147, 155; *see also* welfare state regimes
Converse, P. 90
Coughlin, R. 57, 114, 128, 165
cuts: in services 55, 57, 61, 64–6, 70–3,

75–9; in social assistance 76; resistance against 49, 79

day care 35–6, 61, 65, 71, 73, 76, 139
de Swaan, A. 219, 224–5, 228
decommodification 2, 9, 10, 141, 143
Denmark 7, 9, 13–14, 16, 18, 26, 28, 140, 224
directors 88, 93–4

earnings-related benefits: *see* income-related benefits
East(ern) Europe 3, 10–11, 190, 192, 219, 230
economic crisis 48, 53, 55–7, 62, 77
economic feasibility 17
Edlund, J. 8, 106
egalitarian(ism) 10, 106, 141, 143–4, 190–2, 196–9, 202–5, 208, 210–11, 213
Elias, N. 10, 218–20, 222–3, 227, 233
elite(s) 114, 183; in Finland 8, 11, 52–5, 57–64, 66, 70–3, 75–9, 87–9, 91–3, 95–7, 100–1; in Sweden 40–3, 47–8
entitlement rules 92, 94
Esping–Andersen, G. 7–8, 14, 35, 43, 49, 87, 94, 107–9, 115, 118–20, 135, 137–40, 143, 150, 155–6, 163–5, 234
etatist attitudes 192, 202, 204, 208, 211
executive officer 62–3, 66, 78

Ferge, Z. 10–1, 218, 231–2
financing: of services and benefits 36; of welfare policies 29, 36, 40–4, 47, 62, 109
Finland 8, 9, 11, 52–4, 61, 80, 87–8, 95, 140, 161, 163–4, 166, 169–72, 174–6, 179, 196

Printed in the United Kingdom
by Lightning Source UK Ltd.
127056UK00002B/76/A